# GOD & COUNTRY
## All Things Are Possible

**Jacqueline M. Arnold**

LUCIDBOOKS

Printed in the United States of America.

Due to the changing nature of online dynamics, websites, links, social media forums and references, no guarantee is made of the permanent reliability of these references. Always refer to the main website at www.sweetlifeusa.com for updates.

Photo credit:
Creative Services—Charles Plant, LLC for the photo of the author on the back cover
Sawyer Photography Bio Photo

First Printing: July 2016

ISBN 10: 1-63296-092-3
ISBN 13: 978-1-63296-092-4
eISBN 10: 1-63296-093-1
eISBN 13: 978-1-63296-093-1

Published by: LucidBooks, July, 2016

This book is dedicated to God and my country,
land of the free and home of the brave—
the United States of America.

# TABLE OF CONTENTS

Purpose ............................................................................... viii

Gratitude For America ................................................................ x

Acknowledgments .................................................................... xi

The Clarion Call .................................................................... xiv

Faith Or Fairytale? ................................................................ xvii

Introduction .......................................................................... 1

Chapter One: Surrendering It All ............................................... 15

Chapter Two: My Great Commission ........................................... 27

    America The Beautiful .................................................... 30

    America's Constitution .................................................... 31

    The Constitution ........................................................... 32

    The Bill Of Rights ......................................................... 34

Chapter Three: America's Constitution, More Than A Document .. 36

Chapter Four: We Are "One Nation Under God." ........................... 39

Chapter Five: A Move On Faith .................................................. 46

    God's Amazing Grace ..................................................... 51

Chapter Six: A Move By His Grace ............................................. 53

Chapter Seven: Inspired To Dream God-Sized Dreams ................... 68

# Table Of Contents

Chapter Eight: Absolute Faith..................................................... 78

Chapter Nine: Crossing The Jordan .................................... 96

Chapter Ten: The Adventure Begins ..................................... 99

Chapter Eleven: The Seven Year Journey .......................... 103

Chapter Twelve: God's Road Map ..................................... 118

Chapter Thirteen: Patriotic Reflections Of My Journey................. 129

Chapter Fourteen: Journey Home..................................... 133

Chapter Fifteen: A Car Wash Confirms My Travel Plans ............... 137

Chapter Sixteen: Wings To The West Coast........................ 144

Chapter Seventeen: Rerouted For A Patriotic Surprise................. 170

Chapter Eighteen: Standing For Christ Under Persecution .......... 182

Chapter Nineteen: A Home On The Horizon........................ 191

Chapter Twenty: My Jubilee Celebration .......................... 198

Chapter Twenty One: The Decade-Long Dream Interrupted ........ 228

Chapter Twenty Two: The Walls Of Jericho........................ 243

Chapter Twenty Three: The Jubilee Year Comes To An End ......... 253

Chapter Twenty Four: The Christmas Legacy .................... 259

Chapter Twenty Five: Cinderella's, America's Second Time
Around...................................................................... 262

Chapter Twenty Six: God Gets A Bigger Microphone For
His Message ............................................................ 269

Chapter Twenty Seven: Hundred Dollar Handshakes.................... 273

Chapter Twenty Eight: Aloha! Hawaii His Way ...................... 277

Chapter Twenty Nine: History Made, History In The Making ...... 294

Chapter Thirty: 30 Years Of Cleaning The Family Tree
—Deep Roots ................................................................. 298

Chapter Thirty One: Taco Tuesdays Bring May Blessings ............. 306

Chapter Thirty Two: Maine Miracles................................... 314

Chapter Thirty Three: Paul Revere's Ride, Jacqueline
Arnold's Jubilee ............................................................. 333

America's Call To Action ................................................. 333

Chapter Thirty Four: America's Call To Action! ...................... 336

The Lord's Prayer ......................................................... 339

Call To Salvation........................................................... 341

God's Expectations Are Simple......................................... 341

The Ten Commandments, His Decrees And Commands........ 341

Reconciled To God ........................................................ 345

America's Roots............................................................. 348

I Salute Our Veterans, Our Military And Their Sacrifices. ..... 350

History Dates To Remember............................................ 353

It's A Patriotic Movement ............................................... 354

Christian Leaders Are On The Move .................................. 356

Spirit Of America Days................................................... 358

America's Pledge ........................................................... 368

Flag Etiquette .............................................................. 370

The True Education Of Travel........................................... 371

Chapter Thirty Five: JerUSAlem—First To The Jews ................ 373

# Table Of Contents

America's Dates To Remember .......................... 380

   Presidential Legacy .......................... 383

   Which States Have You Been To? .......................... 389

   Can You Match The Capital To The State? .......................... 390

   National Parks Celebrate 100<sup>Th</sup> Anniversary .......................... 391

   National Parks Of The United States .......................... 393

Wisdom For Faith With Finances .......................... 396

   A Widow's Mite .......................... 396

   What's Holding You Back? .......................... 400

   The Sweet Life Story .......................... 404

   Let's Get Social .......................... 411

Next Adventures .......................... 412

Next Book Projects .......................... 413

Notes Page .......................... 414

My Legacy .......................... 415

Track Your Commitment Here .......................... 416

Time Is Running Out. The Time Is Now. .......................... 419

Call To Salvation .......................... 421

God Bless America And 1,000 Generations Of
Your Family Tree! .......................... 422

Jacqueline Arnold .......................... 423

Endnotes .......................... 424

# PURPOSE

This book is written for two major purposes:

To encourage every one of you to believe in your dreams, no matter how big they are, and trust God to deliver them, no matter what your life circumstances look like.

That was my dream—fifty states by fifty years—50 X 50. And, God delivered them.

> With man this is impossible; with God all things are possible.
>
> —Mark 10:27

He delivered them in spite of my life's storms and only $2.12 to my name.

I have a dream for America, and I believe God does, too.

While Evangelist Reinhardt Bonnke's prophetic mantra is, "America shall be saved," and I agree, I don't believe America is completely lost. America is hurting and broken.

America is wounded to the core of our soul and the core of our soil. And, while things look bleak—some say we're in our last days—God can do anything; He can show up with mercy and grace and heal our land and restore us to our former beauty, because

> "With man this is impossible, but, with God all things are possible"
>
> —Mark 10:27

# Purpose

This is the time for an American revolution: to wake up and stand up for our land and allow God to heal our hearts, our homes and our America.

Rediscover, reconnect, remember, travel across America, and reignite your spirit—so that we never lose the liberties, freedoms, and land we know and love from the dulling of our spirits, from our complacency, or from our quiet surrender. Let that be our legacy to the next generation and the world. Wake up, speak up, stand up for America.

And, in your self-discovery and re-discovery, may you reconnect with the Creator of it all. Isn't it time to reconnect, return, and remember the one who gave all for our beautiful land and the sweet life we enjoy every day? May my journey across America inspire you and ignite the Spirit of America from coast to coast.

And, believe God for the full restoration of America—because all things are possible.

> God's promise says, "If my people, who are called by my name, will humble themselves and pray and seek my face and turn from their wicked ways, then I will hear from heaven, and I will forgive their sin and will heal their land"
> —2 Chronicles 7:14.

# GRATITUDE FOR AMERICA

I am so grateful for being born in America, and especially so to have been raised in the heart of the South—there's no place I'd rather be, except when I am driving from coast to coast, enjoying His majesty; that's my happy place, too. My heart yearns for the Spirit of America to domino across our continent, for flags to unfurl from coast to coast, and for citizens of America to stand in reverence and awe of the God who created it all. In honoring Him, He might yet relent and bless America anew. Wake up America! Stand firm for your faith and our flag—for your family's sake, for the freedoms and blessings to flow, for the flags to wave, and for God to continue to bless our land. This is our call to action for patriotic and spiritual revival in America because, I believe, they go hand in hand. We bleed red, white, and blue because of His blessings. We are America strong because of the one true God and His continual favor and grace. Don't give up the fight! Rally—and rally boldly. It is time for an American revolution! Stand firm and watch the enemy retreat as the King of Kings is honored once again.

> God's promise says, "If my people, who are called by my name, will humble themselves and pray and seek my face and turn from their wicked ways, then I will hear from heaven, and I will forgive their sin and will heal their land"
> —2 Chronicles 7:14.

# ACKNOWLEDGMENTS

The list is long, very long, for this book to come to life. Many who contributed, didn't even know; it was their words of encouragement on a dark day, their offer to buy tea at Starbucks, not knowing I was on my last dime or my last thread of hope, an inquiry on my progress, a warm smile to keep me going, or a moment of time just to listen.

I especially want to thank my super prayer warrior Sandra Lynne Haner who offered me mighty prayer and covering wherever I traveled and believed in me and the vision the Lord had given me.

I thank One Life and Emerge small group for fierce and constant prayers for travel mercies, my writing, fresh revelation, and provision.

I thank Catherine and Jana and numerous other prayer warriors like Amy, Kari, James, Howard, Mary, Cindy, and many others who prayed. And, Rebecca for believing in my "Noah's Ark" calling for more than a decade. For Chris G., my fairy godmother.

Thank you Tricia for celebrating my 'graduation' in such a special way and for your wisdom and prayers.

I thank every angel who helped me move when things looked impossible.

I thank Joe, Jack, and John for having my back like family.

To Garry for being a special friend. God has extra blessings waiting for you.

I thank those who showed special hospitality during our summer adventure, especially Brandi. I'm thankful for all who opened the doors of your homes for me and my children, for keeping us safe.

Thank you, Bob, for offering us a new home.

I thank the bed and breakfast owners across America who offered me the King's Suite and the royal treatment.

I thank my friends at Pinewood Studios for loving me through this journey, for listening, for giving me a mic, and for being the multi-vitamin I needed every week.

Miguel, TerraGlobe, for faith, supernatural prayers and initial provisions. Melinda, we're on a similar journey of faith. Go, girl, go.

Thanks to Greg Bligh who shared his story and grew my faith with an unexpected seed. To Mark & Beautiful Earth Market for my own antique writing desk from the original surveyors of Wyoming territory, no less—making way to stake our claim for America from the very beginning.

For the churches that welcomed me with open arms and rich words of courage—Southside, Dogwood, Mount Paran, Destiny Church, New City Church, NCC Women's Group. To Trinity Church where I first asked for Absolute Faith. Thanks to Liesha Hall and her family who extended the invitation for me to attend one Sunday.

For those who gave me a buddy pass or two; thanks Emily. Thanks Sue & John. And, for 50th birthday dreams come true, brother Steve.

For opening up your family home, thanks Dr. Dave. It was a champagne celebration stay to remember for always.

Jackie Carpenter, for my seat at the table at The Christian View.

To Mrs. International, for my crown as Mrs. Virginia and the privilege to be counted in the Top Ten, Mrs. International, 2003,

# Acknowledgments

where my dreams, crown and platform prepared me for this journey and encouraged me to carry the torch for all these years to ignite the Spirit of America.

And, most importantly, thank you to each of my children for your patience and love, having to watch your momma on an unexplainable journey of crazy faith.

Especially to Kerrigan and Kellie who had to endure for so long, live the stretching of faith every day, leave your home and sacrifice much for this calling on my life. Hold on to every lesson. Always be bold for your faith, and remember that all things are possible.

To anyone else who feels they helped along the way, thank you. It did not go unnoticed. 2014–2016 held the greatest challenges of my life and to my faith. Thank you for every grace offered along the way to lighten my load. It was my cross to carry, the burdens and challenges of these two years. And I didn't expect anyone to fully understand, but to those who tried or offered a helping hand anyway, thank you.

Thank you for prayers and love, for projects that paid, for favors and blessings, for tea and lunches, for encouragement and hope, and for those few who sewed quiet seeds of love and provision; thank you from the deepest part of my heart. May it all have been worth it in the living out and writing of this book, and may it bring healing to our country and glory to our God.

—Jacqueline Arnold

# THE CLARION CALL

## AMERICA'S CLARION CALL

America is in trouble, my friends.

I urge you to take action to restore America before
the America we love is lost.

Take action to revive America before the God
who loves us sends his judgment.

This is *every* American's issue.
If you enjoy the freedom to wake up at your leisure,
walk out your door, and drive yourself to the place of
employment of your choosing; and if you enjoy stopping
for coffee or lunch at a small restaurant, your freedom
to worship in a church, or your freedom to choose how
to educate your children; or if you support the second
amendment and carry a gun or care to have a vote or
a voice; if you love these freedoms—any constitutional
freedoms, really—this is your chance.
This is America's chance.

It's a freedom thing! It's a family thing! It's a God thing!
Let the Spirit of America be your thing!
Take action America!
Together, we can ignite the Spirit of America!
No more grumbling, mumbling or stumbling—or
wondering where to begin.
Herein lies a plan to get started, in this moment.
Here is America's action plan.
May our land be richly rewarded, and
may God continue to bless America!

# The Clarion Call

## The Star Spangled Banner, Our Nation's Anthem

Written by Francis Scott Key in September 1814, while under fire by the British, "The Star Spangled Banner" tells the story of the tenacity and resilience of our country's flag, our nation, and the spirit of her people, America.

It became America's national anthem a century later in 1916. The lyrics, penned on the back of a letter, during a stormy night of fierce attack, still resonate with every American, transporting us to the moment of our country's first birth pains and reminding us of the cost of freedom. Stand and sing it now; be inspired.

### *The Star-Spangled Banner*

*O say can you see, by the dawn's early light,*
*What so proudly we hail'd at the twilight's last gleaming,*
*Whose broad stripes and bright stars through the perilous fight*
*O'er the ramparts we watch'd were so gallantly streaming?*
*And the rocket's red glare, the bombs bursting in air,*
*Gave proof through the night that our flag was still there,*
*O say does that star-spangled banner yet wave*
*O'er the land of the free and the home of the brave?*
*On the shore dimly seen through the mists of the deep*
*Where the foe's haughty host in dread silence reposes,*
*What is that which the breeze, o'er the towering steep,*
*As it fitfully blows, half conceals, half discloses?*
*Now it catches the gleam of the morning's first beam,*
*In full glory reflected now shines in the stream,*
*'Tis the star-spangled banner—O long may it wave*
*O'er the land of the free and the home of the brave!*
*And where is that band who so vauntingly swore,*

*That the havoc of war and the battle's confusion*
*A home and a Country should leave us no more?*
*Their blood has wash'd out their foul footstep's pollution.*
*No refuge could save the hireling and slave*
*From the terror of flight or the gloom of the grave,*
*And the star-spangled banner in triumph doth wave*
*O'er the land of the free and the home of the brave.*
*O thus be it ever when freemen shall stand*
*Between their lov'd home and the war's desolation!*
*Blest with vict'ry and peace may the heav'n rescued land*
*Praise the power that hath made and preserv'd us a nation!*
*Then conquer we must, when our cause it is just,*
*And this be our motto—"In God is our trust,"*
*And the star-spangled banner in triumph shall wave*
*O'er the land of the free and the home of the brave.*

The first verse of the National Anthem is typically sung at baseball games; however, unfamiliar to most Americans, the full version includes four verses. At the sound of the first note, bystanders should stand, place their hand on their heart, and pay honor to our country and her flag. For additional history, I suggest you view FlagRespect.com, by Pastor Dudley Rutherford.

# FAITH OR FAIRYTALE?

**Are all things really possible or is it just a fairytale?**

It began as a dream—50 X 50, fifty states by fifty years of age; it was my birthday wish

Then life happened, a life full of storms and obstacles and one loss after another, as well as a life of love and celebrations aplenty.

Then, came the calling of a faithful God and time to pursue a birthday wish.

In spite of life's circumstances but prompted by the Holy Spirit, I set out on a journey to see America, only to discover that all things truly are possible. I experienced a faithful God who led the way on a spiritual journey and helped me achieve my dreams in the process. I discovered a God without limits. I discovered a God who is faithful. I discovered a God who is love.

He has no favorites.

A world of possibility awaits you, if only you will turn to Him and trust Him.

Are you ready to create your very own sweet life and walk into the life God has waiting for you? Who knows if the dreams He is waiting to deliver are for His greater purpose, like this dream of mine to see America and His dream for me to ring the liberty bell along the way.

He has come to set the captives free! Through my journey, I've been freed to run into my Daddy's loving arms. Through my journey and this story, America may be freed. With eyes opened and hearts healed and ready to run back into His open arms. Our Father in heaven is waiting to receive each of us. Hang on to the coattails of the one who can. Don't look at how big your obstacles are; look, instead, at how big and faithful our God is! With man this is impossible, but with God, *all things are possible*!

# INTRODUCTION

I am "just a mom" by the grace of God.

I have five kids, three boys and two girls—a full house. After child number one, the doctor said I might not have any more. Six weeks later, child number two was on his way. Five. Yep, five—after the doctors said no more.

When the world says, "No," God says, "Yes!"

I am so grateful that God is a God of miracles. For that reason, I am "just a mom." I was just raising my kids, from softball to music lessons, from Boy Scouts to Girl Scouts, from cooking to laundry to bedtime stories; I was just doing my "mom thing," not expecting that God could use me in any life-changing, kingdom-impacting kind of way.

Have you ever thought that? What's your "just"?

Rejected and broken, achieved and accomplished, fallen and brokenhearted, battered by the storms of life, yet redeemed by the King, nothing but the blood of Jesus has saved me. That's my journey; that's my life—like this land—America.

Blessed, beautiful, prosperous, fallen, broken, wicked, cursed, and, yet, ripe for redemption, nothing but the blood of Jesus will save our land.

American soil, before it was even a drawn on the map was bought at a price, with the first drop of blood shed by Jesus Christ. Founded on Christian principles, with solid prescribing documents, Christian theology, and the promises of God, this country was meant for greatness. There was a covenant between our American forefathers and God. Our country and its future were dedicated to her Creator.

This land was blessed, having evolved into a superpower; however, corruption, greed, lust, lewdness and wickedness were heralded in, and the Bible, the pledge, and God were taken out.

> If my people, who are called by my name, will humble themselves and pray and seek my face and turn from their wicked ways, then I will hear from heaven, and I will forgive their sin and will heal their land.
>
> —2 Chronicles 7:14

The land—every inch of American soil—was bought at a price and paid for by the blood of the lamb, the Son of God, Jesus Christ.

> "For God so loved the world that he gave his one and only Son, that whoever believes in him shall not perish but have eternal life"
>
> —John 3:16

# Introduction

God is weeping in heaven for His children. God is weeping for America. He sent His only Son, and instead of placing our eyes on Him, we are consumed with things of this world, rejecting Him and His gift to us, forgetting our maker and His offer of eternal life.

God is a jealous God; His wrath is turned up as His beloved children have slowly turned from Christianity to Secularism, to New Ageism, and now are teetering close to Paganism.

> For from within, out of the heart of men, proceed the evil thoughts, fornications, thefts, murders, adulteries, deeds of coveting and wickedness, as well as deceit, sensuality, envy, slander, pride and foolishness." All these evil things proceed from within and defile the man.
>
> —Mark 7:22

Our actions, our news stories, and our newspapers are filled with stories based on the sins of our hearts, specifically enumerated right here in the book of Mark.

## First Commandment

He clearly gave us the Ten Commandments to follow so we wouldn't lose our way. And, the very first commandment is very clear: "I am the Lord your God, who brought you out of Egypt, out of the land of slavery. You shall have no other gods before me" (Exodus 20).

As is evident from the five o'clock news to the town events, we have forgotten our God; crime is up, stealing, theft, robbery, anger, rudeness, pride, ego, and selfishness have escalated as well. We had a sturdy list of rules to follow. And God calls us to follow *all* His decrees and commands.

We are not called to be perfect, but we must acknowledge that we have a long way to go back to the ways He has called us to. We must turn to Him and reconcile our hearts to Him. It is Him living and producing good fruit in us that helps us to walk according to His ways.

This is not legalism or perfectionism to seek to follow these commandments; this is a life journey that overflows from the abundance of your heart to honor and love God himself—and, the glorious abundance of Christ in you. It is Jesus living and producing fruit in and through you. He is the vine, and we are the branches.

> "Remain in me, as I also remain in you. No branch can bear fruit by itself; it must remain in the vine. Neither can you bear fruit unless you remain in me. I am the vine; you are the branches. If you remain in me and I in you, you will bear much fruit; apart from me you can do nothing"
> —John 15:4–5

Jesus is the grace in you to compel you to follow His commands.

For reflection, not to be misconstrued as "Rules for Religion," but only offered as a reflection to create a firm foundation, the following are the very commandments God sent:

- "You shall not make for yourself an image in the form of anything in heaven above or on the earth beneath or in the waters below. You shall not bow down to them or worship them; for I, the Lord your God, am a jealous God, punishing the children for the sin of the parents to the third and fourth generation of those who hate me, but showing love to a thousand generations of those who love me and keep my commandments."

- "You shall not misuse the name of the Lord your God, for the Lord will not hold anyone guiltless who misuses his name."

- "Remember the Sabbath day by keeping it holy. Six days you shall labor and do all your work, but the seventh day is a Sabbath to the Lord your God. On it you shall not do any work, neither you, nor your son or daughter, nor your male or female servant, nor your animals, nor any foreigner residing in your towns. For in six days the Lord made the heavens and the earth, the sea, and all that is in them, but he rested on the seventh day. Therefore the Lord blessed the Sabbath day and made it holy."

- "Honor your father and your mother, so that you may live long in the land the Lord your God is giving you."

- "You shall not murder."

- "You shall not commit adultery."

- "You shall not steal."

- "You shall not give false testimony against your neighbor."

- "You shall not covet your neighbor's house. You shall not covet your neighbor's wife, or his male or female servant, his ox or donkey, or anything that belongs to your neighbor."

Oh, how we have slipped into patterns of sin and normalized such behaviors. The next generation may even label us as old-fashioned for following them, but they are commands for even today; they are non-negotiable for us to receive the fullness of our blessing. Please, dear friends, we have all fallen, we stumble, but don't stay in your sin; seek a life of purity and one that honors your Father. There is no sin, absolutely no sin, that the blood of the lamb has not paid the price for. He took all of our sin upon the cross at Cavalry. But, we must run from our sin, give up our wicked ways, and turn to Him for reconciliation. If you have one shred of remorse or regret, any yearning to be free, confess your sins one to another and to the Father Himself. Repent and be healed, freed, and made new again!

There is abundant grace waiting for each one of us. This is the season of prodigal sons. Take this opportunity to be restored. Let America be restored!

His heart is surely torn over the sibling rivalry and hardened hearts, warring countries, and lying leaders. Brothers are turning against brother, wives against husbands, and society against babies. Unforgiveness, hate, anger, and judgment have darkened our hearts and divided our nation.

> "See to it that no bitter root grows up to cause trouble and defile many"
>
> —Hebrews 12:15

> "A new command I give you: Love one another. As I have loved you, so you must love one another. By this everyone will know that you are my disciples, if you love one another."
>
> —John 13:34–35

Love, honor, respect, forgiveness, peace, and kindness—where have they gone?

> "Let all bitterness and wrath and anger and clamor and slander be put away from you, along with all malice. Be kind to one another, tender-hearted, forgiving each other, just as God in Christ also has forgiven you"
>
> —Ephesians 4:32

> "'Lord, how often shall my brother sin against me and I forgive him? Up to seven times?' Jesus said to him, 'I do not say to you, up to seven times, but up to seventy times seven.'"
>
> —Matthew 18:22

He has prodded and prompted, prepared, and pursued us that we might return to his commands and decrees.

> "For you [we] have spent enough time in the past doing what pagans choose to do—living in debauchery, lust, drunkenness, orgies, carousing and detestable idolatry"
> —1 Peter 4:3

He has warned us, shocked us, cajoled us, and rocked us. Recall the stock market drops: 1929, 1973, 1980, 1987, 2001, and the largest drop in 2008.

And, if consistently clearing our lands and leveling our funds isn't enough, we got a wake-up call during the events of September 11th when terrorism hit our land and rocked our safety and jolted us out of our complacency. America came to attention, returned to her guard, and gathered her chicks in alignment, but it lasted only a short time; evidently, this was not a heart transformation. We must always remember.

And now, it appears, He has allowed us the consequences of our choices, giving us over to our depraved minds. There have been floods, hurricanes, earthquakes, and twisters, an increase of natural disasters and human havoc run amuck. We have invited the enemy to dinner, satisfied the cravings of our lustful hearts, and now we contend with terrorists, police under attack, children in the cooking pot, and Christians being persecuted. We side with corrupt politicians and engage in back-room, dirty politics with hidden agendas for financial gain (or vote for those who do) without recognizing our spiritual loss, the consequences of our choices, and the legacy we are passing on within our own family trees. We join in support of leaders who support the death of babies, yet, expect no blood on our hands. We have invited the Trojan horse inside the gates, within our borders, and, now, the borders have been compromised and safety as we once knew it, is lost as well.

We have cyber-stalking and skewed politicking, akin to George Orwell's pages of Big Brother. We have given the government the controlling authority over our freedom of speech, our 2<sup>nd</sup> amendment rights, and even our ability to train up our children the way they should go (think common core, world religion, and sex education). We have skewed our values, surrendered our principles, and fallen asleep in our God-given authority.

> "People will be lovers of themselves, lovers of money, boastful, proud, abusive, disobedient to their parents, ungrateful, unholy, without love, unforgiving, slanderous, without self-control, brutal, not lovers of the good, treacherous, rash, conceited, lovers of pleasure rather than lovers of God"
>
> —2 Timothy 3:2–5

We have shed the blood of millions of babies, and now from the blood-stained soil, the blood cries out, screaming out for vindication and justice. Hasn't enough American blood been shed? Total U.S. conflict-related deaths have been tallied at more than 1,354,664. The total deaths per war, according to data available on public records, is 116,516 (WWI), 405,399 (WWII), 36,516 (Korean War), 58,209 (Vietnam War), 294 (Gulf War), 2,229 (Afghanistan War), and 4,488 (Iraq War). Nearly *one and a half million* American lives lost; families have grieved, and the blood-stained soil is saturated by the sin of conflict, anger and unforgiveness.

> "Love one another as I have loved you" (John 13:34).
> "Do not let the sun set on your anger"
> —Ephesians 4:26

Why do our hearts struggle so to follow His commands? Why can we not learn from the history that is insistent to repeat itself?

The innocent cry out. Broken children from broken homes, who grow up without love and with wounded souls only repeat the cycle. Hurting people hurt people. Our heavenly Father grieves for His children. And our country is in a state of crisis.

But, thanks be to God, He is a merciful and loving God, yearning to gather His chicks.

> "If my people, who are called by my name, will humble themselves and pray and seek my face and turn from their wicked ways, then I will hear from heaven, and I will forgive their sin and will heal their land"
> —2 Chronicles 7:14

His wrath is bubbling up, and the birthing pains have begun. He is ready to draw the line in the sands of time. And, yet, He is a God of love and faithful to His word. He is a God of mercy. He offers abundant grace.

We are in a season of mercy with tremors of the earth and evangelical leaders crying out with altar calls and prophetic testimony of what's to come.

# Introduction

And, though He has given us over to our perverted ways and the consequences of our free will and poor choices—sexual immorality, adultery, murder and more—He is still waiting to receive us into His forgiving arms.

He has been calling up His army—you and me, the remnant of His people—who will encourage and teach, lead, love, and witness to one another; this remnant will intercede and pray for our nation of brothers. Our state of distress is no surprise to Him. He is in control. Though the world seems to be spinning out of control, it is certainly not. There is, after all, nothing new under the sun. But, oh, how He pursues us to return to His ways.

He will protect America. Many prophets and evangelists, including the likes of Reinhard Bonnke and myself, have heard God say, "America will be saved!"

He will offer us an opportunity for restoration, reconciliation, and redemption, but, first he wants us to come to Him with repentant hearts and changed ways. He wants our worship, our praise, and our hearts, and all this belongs to Him. He has strategically placed His people all over the continent, with visions, spiritual gifts, and heavenly callings to share His truth—truth that will penetrate the darkness and call His children to the light.

I experienced a vision of lighted luminaries around the entire border of the United States, as if the borders were marked by His eternal flame, and one by one, His children, all holding a lit candle, were gathering together to begin the prayer vigil. It took only one to lead the way, only one to begin the prayer of intercession, and soon many were gathered together to honor Him, the one true God. It was as if God was saying, "I am waiting patiently for you to come together in unity, in one accord, to ask for your

Father's blessing." And, eight months later, it was confirmed to me that a missionary, John (& Amanda) Vanderwalt of Israel Prayer Vision, had been praying around the border of America three years earlier, lighting flames of revival and praying for America in this same way. In his home in Israel he has a large map of America, surrounded with flames cut from paper and symbolically glued around the border of the United States. He has established the Gideon's Prayer Room to pray for America *from Israel.* The world over, God is telling His children to ignite the flames of revival and ignite the Spirit of America—*now.* He has awakened me many a night, saying "Urgent! The time is now, America. The time is *now.*"

People are crying out, "No more! Enough is enough." What has happened to America? Where is my America? I heard this from Oregon to Kansas to Minnesota, as I traveled 14 states in 18 days. Franklin Graham is finding this same spirit as thousands gather to join in prayer for Decision America and for a unified prayer to heaven. And California, a state many Americans identify as very diverse and liberal, enjoyed the largest number of supporters at these rallies, crying out for God and agreeing for America to return to God. America is taking a stand for her country and God.

God is simultaneously crying, "Where are my children? Where is my word? Where are my commandments? Where is my church? Where is my beloved?"

Many cry out for revival, revival, revival, revival.

"Wake up your church, God. Send your Holy Spirit and let the scales fall off your children's eyes. Awake the people. Restore America. God, please, bless America," we quietly cry out across

America from our prayer closets, our homes, small groups gathered in prayer, and our churches.

This stirring is all part of the Father's plans. We are beginning to cooperate with the heart of the one who made us. Are you ready to cooperate with heaven?

> "For I know the plans I have for you"
> —Jeremiah 29:11

Because He made us with His plans in mind.

This time, I heard a word. The prayers we have begun to offer are but a murmur, and the Father is waiting for His church to arise and shout to the heavens in one accord—a shout that will be heard around the world and awaken His people on every continent. For we are all God's children, all bought at a price, all sons of the King, and He is ready for His bride to come.

> "The Spirit and the bride say, 'Come!' And let the one who hears say, 'Come!' Let the one who is thirsty come; and let the one who wishes take the free gift of the water of life"
> —Revelation 22:17

We begin with repentant hearts. We begin with reconciliation to our Father. We respond with prayers, worshipping the one true God and letting go of things of this world. The Lord is coming back for His bride, the church, and His people. He is coming for a bride who is spotless and clean.

> "That He might present to Himself the church in all her glory, having no spot or wrinkle or any such thing; but that she would be holy and blameless"
>
> —Ephesians 5:27

It's time, America, for spiritual *and* patriotic revival. It's time for the awakening of America. This is America's call to action, and this is a story of my supernatural journey across America to beckon you to follow the lead of His spirit and to inspire you to remember the beauty of our country and the majesty of its maker.

So, what's your "just?" God is calling each of us at this time. My prayer is that you will read my story, be inspired to your own adventure, knowing my "just a mom" story, and discover an amazing God and an amazing America, sitting in your own backyard—just a prayer away, waiting to be romanced and reconciled and restored. Dare to believe that all things are possible and that God is a God of miracles and reconciliation and answered prayer—for you and for America.

This, my fellow Americans, is a call to arms; our beloved country is counting on you. This, my brothers and sisters, is a call from the heavens; our beloved Father is waiting on you. Wherever you are—"just" who you are—God is waiting and ready to receive you and use you. Are you?

# CHAPTER ONE

# SURRENDERING IT ALL

What would you give up for God? Would you give up your career, your financial security, your home, your family, or your stability? To achieve complete dependence on Him, would you surrender it all? What one thing would you hold back from the one who holds nothing back? Trust Him, the scripture says. When the chaos comes and when life doesn't make sense, trust Him—the one who is trustworthy.

But in our flesh, walking on water—turning our life completely over to Him—makes no sense, like in my walk of faith. Moving myself and my two children out of a perfectly good home with no home to move to, no resources, no job, no credit, no spouse, and no provider, because all this had been surrendered along the way was an act of surrender—trusting God with His promise of "trust me. Wait patiently." His whisper in my spirit was His promise, "I'll bring you to another house, just trust me."

One by one, I surrendered them all, all the things of this world, so important to my former self—trusting He had a plan and a purpose. The road was rocky, but He was faithful and showered me with amazing grace. First came a walk of intimacy like no other and then came the opening of my heavenly eyes—with just $2.12 and a Delta buddy pass, He brought me to 14 states in 18 days to fulfill two main purposes. To celebrate my Jubilee year, he brought me closer to my decade-old birthday wish to travel to 50 states by my 50th birthday, but more importantly He launched me on the Great Commission, to talk about His name to everyone I met and share His love for those thirsty to hear. He gave me testimony after testimony, miracle after miracle to share along the way. He was watering His people as I traveled America. Then, almost as a reward for walking on water with Him, He brought me from "homelessness" to the right-sized house for my family and His purpose. While it was easy to agree to His ask—after all, He's God and He can ask anything—the surrender didn't come without resistance.

> "And everyone who has left houses or brothers or sisters or father or mother or wife or children or fields for my sake will receive a hundred times as much and will inherit eternal life"
>
> —Matthew 19:29

## Walking Out the Walk of Faith

"I'm not moving!" my fourteen-year-old shouted as she slammed the door in typical teenage fashion. The pencil-scrawled note duct-taped to the door shook as the door reverberated from the impact. It was clear Kellie Camille was not on board for the move ahead.

Why should she be? She was no different from most teenagers in America today, with an expectation of a home, provided by a mom and a dad, a bedroom of her own to retreat to—a place to pin her posters of One Direction to the wall and crank up her favorite music. She was just a typical teenager, unsure of the change ahead.

It made no difference that her mom was doing her best to raise her and her 18-year-old brother, on our own since the divorce nearly five years earlier. It made no difference that every other part of her life was in proper order—siblings who loved her, a softball team who cheered her on, an A+ school, and peers she had been to school with since pre-school.

No. The thought of moving out of a perfectly good home to no home was not a concept she could accept. The landlord had demanded their property back, "so what?" The lease was going to expire and the landlords had a right in spite of the fact there were no other housing options in her school district, "so what?" No. This teenage girl liked her room; she liked doing homework on her bed and leaving heaping piles of laundry strewn about in the comfort of her own room. She wasn't about to give up her personal space without a good reason.

Where would they go? Where would her friends come and hang out? Where would all her stuff go? And, what of the couch? This was the couch that everyone complained about but secretly loved hanging out on after school, catching up with a snack mom had made while they were at school—like Rice Krispie treats and warm brownies, just out of the oven. Where would they gather now, where would they eat, and what would they eat?

What would become of all the family pictures on the wall, the holiday decorations, and the fishing gear? And the questions continued to mount. No, this girl wasn't going anywhere. It was way too complicated. Other people had houses, why not her? Why not us?

And, what about her brother? He was happy to be graduating high school in just a few short months. It wasn't his problem. He would be off at college soon enough. Why should he care what happened to the family china or what table everyone would gather around for Thanksgiving and Christmas dinners to come? He would be off at school and could easily pretend he didn't care.

But, he did; he stewed about it down deep and it showed in his short answers, his angry outbursts, and his cold shoulder. It showed by his absence from every family moment for the last month. It showed by his lack of connection and his early disappearance from the family.

The brokenness of my family was crushing to this mom whose family was the center of her world. Twenty-six years being a mom and now I had to stand firm, with my home broken, the walls of my house crumbling down around me, and my heart crushing. I had to stand firm because I knew, without a shadow of a doubt, God had called me to it.

> "The Lord is my light and my salvation—whom shall I fear? The Lord is the stronghold of my life—of whom shall I be afraid? When the wicked advance against me to devour me, it is my enemies and my foes who will stumble and fall. Though an army besiege me, my heart will not fear; though war break out against me, even then I will be confident"
>
> —Psalm 27:1–3

> "I will not fear though tens of thousands assail me on every side"
>
> —Psalm 3:6

There was doubt. There were wails. There were gallons of tears. But there was a steadfast confidence and trust in the Lord Almighty. My Lord and Savior had never once failed me, and I knew He was bringing me on a very special walk, if only I would first walk into the Jordan River and trust Him to dry it up and grant me victory.

Amidst the screams, the resistance, the doubt, and the fear, there was faith and forward movement. There had to be. God had confirmed it 100 times, 100 ways in the last three months. From provision of manna to healing miracles to repeated confirmations, God had provided many promptings and signs to assure me of this unique calling to surrender even my house to Him.

I was sitting at the corner table in the local Starbucks. In my spirit, I knew, but my flesh was still fighting it because it was such a big leap of faith, and I was desperately afraid of failing, not just for me, but for my children. I was praying and imploring God to confirm just one more time. Had I gotten it right? Was God calling me to move out of the very house He had brought me to just 15 months before?

We were living in another home then in the same town, just out of school district. That very morning I had driven the kids to their school, 20 minutes away, driven down an odd street, passed the golf course, and asked God if we couldn't move into a house in the school bus zone and, oh, by the way, the golf course would be nice.

Four hours later, after 15 months in our home, I was finally hanging the last of the pictures in my study, and the phone rang. The friend on the other end excitedly told us of a home we could rent on that very golf course where we now lived—the house God was calling us away from.

"Well, if God brought me to it, He can take it from me," I reasoned now that I was facing the decision to move from this same house.

I prayed one last time, admittedly, a little desperate, not really wanting to know the answer I wouldn't be able to walk away from. "Father, I trust you. Are you sure you want me to move out of my house? Completely? Now?" The scripture was clear. It was crystal clear:

> "and everyone who has left houses or brothers or sisters or father or mother or wife or children or fields for my sake will receive a hundred times as much and will inherit eternal life"
>
> —Matthew 19:21

My heart sank. It had to be done. God had been so faithful to me. I had to follow Him. I had no choice. It made no sense. I was a single mom with two kids. I had no money to make this move and nowhere to go. But I know my shepherd's voice, and I know what He was calling me to do. I knew, without a shadow of a doubt, He would take care of my children and me the same way He had taken care of us to date and brought us to our beautiful rental home on the golf course.

Over the course of months, He had prompted me and prepped

me; He had cajoled me and confirmed to me the direction I would go. As crazy as it sounds, it wasn't the world's way, but it was clear it was to be God's way.

If only I would move out of my perfectly good home, the home with the golf course views and the wildflower beds that I had grown to love and if only I would move out, on faith, with no resources, no plan, and no home to go to, God would sustain me and my children and bring me deeper still with Him. In the interim, He would bring me on an amazing Jubilee celebration and unwrap an amazing birthday box in honor of my 50th birthday, as well, where He would bring me across America, to 16 of the remaining states on my bucket list, so that I could receive my dream of seeing 50 states by 50 years, but more importantly, to walk into the Great Commission, spreading the message of spiritual and patriotic revival. But, more importantly, He was sending me so I could share the lessons of my journey, encouraging others to let go and let God, to seek Him and experience Him in new and profound ways and to be encouraged that in spite of the circumstances, He is faithful. He wants us to rediscover Him and the land that He has created for us and to return to Him with our whole hearts, forsaking the materialism of this world and the selfishness of our hearts. He wants us to trust Him for manna and not money from man.

Yes, it might have been a birthday cake wish when I blew out the candles a decade earlier, but it was definitely with a twist, unbeknownst to me, heavenly inspired. I felt God wanted me to canvas America, witnessing for Him and taking the spiritual temperature of His people to record it in this book that it might ignite His people. I had long wanted to buy an RV, skip out on traditional schedules, and venture across America, so the idea of exploring across the country, wasn't entirely new. He must have planted that thought in me early on in life because it burned in me, year after year. I could never get my family to buy into my dreams, so I had to wrestle with them, talk about them, and silently hang onto them for the right season.

While it seemed scary now, and not such a great idea considering the conditions—far from the right season, without money or a mate—I knew I had to trust Him. I prepared for the journey by emotionally letting go of my home, reading travel books of states I thought I might be traveling to—the 16 I had not yet been to of the 50—and attempting to frame it as an adventure, but, I so knew this was more than an adventure. This was a tremendous leap of spiritual faith and one that I would have to explain to my children and family and friends. And, one, I prayed, the world would not judge me for. This was not a selfish whim to fulfill a longtime dream, or an escape of reality from the burdens as a single mother; no, this was something I was compelled to consider from deep in my spirit. This was a calling I knew was on my life for a greater purpose.

Why this season, when my son was in his senior year? Had I misheard? God made me a mother, and He wanted me to care for my kids and provide for them and be responsible as their mother. Why now? Wasn't this premature? This was *far* from the right season. But, I have long learned, God-things happen in God's perfect timing, not mine. He blessed me to be a mother. He certainly knew my son was a senior and my daughter was struggling from anxiety from so much family turmoil, and this was just one more mountain to climb. He knew that, so I just recanted those things, but I knew I didn't have to figure them out because God had a bigger plan.

> "Trust in the LORD with all your heart and lean not on your own understanding"
>
> —Proverbs 3:5

Some things just don't make logical sense, but they make God sense.

So I recanted. If I would just trust Him, He would have a house waiting for us when I finished this mission—I knew this without a shadow of a doubt, because He is a good and gracious God, and He *promised* me. This was confirmed in my spirit and numerous times—no, multiple times, through prayer. And, so, without resources or the confidence of my family, I walked in the direction the Lord would have me go, knowing that my heavenly Father had a plan greater than I could imagine and that He was trustworthy. He was only waiting on me to trust Him first.

> "Trust in the LORD with all your heart and lean not on your own understanding"
>
> —Proverbs 3:5

## Mountains to Move

The boxes piled high in the garage, the emotions raged and rumbled like a twisty roller coaster, and I stood fast, reminding everyone to just trust our faithful God and honor Him in all He asked.

"Just keep moving forward, one box at a time."

I berated myself for foolish dreams. And I half-wished I could go back and just unwish it. This idea to travel to 50 states by the time I was 50 came about a dozen years prior. I love to travel. I was born with wanderlust in my blood, likely gleaned from all the hours of reading I did since I was a little girl.

When I turned 40, I thought, "Why not have a goal to strive for the next decade?" Setting my goal created a mindset that would ensure my dream would be reached when I turned 50. My brother Steve first started it with his 50 X 50 dream of a recreational boat, and it inspired me to do the same. I enjoyed having goals and setting milestones toward them. I had traveled to about 34 states at that earlier milestone birthday as part of my life's journey, without planning. So what were a few more states with ten years to go? I always set the bar high and reached my goals. Why not 50 states for my 50th birthday? It seemed like a simple birthday wish and an achievable goal.

I had done a lot of traveling in my life, but one thing that motivated me to the 50 X 50 of the United States was this burning question in me: "how could I, or anyone else, justify traveling the world if we don't even know our own backyard?" My heart is for America, and 50 X 50, which became my mantra, seemed like a perfectly reasonable goal and a great way to celebrate my 50th birthday. It was reasonable if all things in life were typical, if there weren't a decade of storms as there had been in my life prior to my 50th birthday, beginning most notably on my 40th birthday with a household move that led to great material loss from mold and mildew damage. So, with my 50th approaching, sometime around 48 or so, I decided to allow for all that life had brought my way and extended 50 X 50 to the end of my 50th birthday year, so in fact, I would be traveling and celebrating my jubilee achievement

24

the entire actual year. Technically, that is 50 X 51, perhaps, but it satisfied the 50 X 50 for me and acknowledged the decade of storms I had long been experiencing, adding the full year to offset some of the storms.

Little did I know that God had bigger plans than just a fun birthday adventure.

I had finally arrived a month prior to my 50ᵗʰ birthday, taking an assessment of my countdown of 16 states to go; I still had no finances, no job, no money saved, and now God was asking me to move out of my home, too? What kind of Jubilee was this to be? It's one thing if it was me—just me—but was He calling me to leave my home with my son and my daughter still under my wing, too? He had called me to be a mom, first. How was I to balance both and why now—my son had his senior year of high school to finish and his last summer before college to prepare? Surely, God knew all this. Surely, He wouldn't ask this of me—*now*.

But, as I studied His word and the lives of prophets and disciples in the Bible, it was clear; God's plan was rarely the easy way. The world showed up in fear and to mock. My landlord asked, "Where are you going to live? Are you and the kids going to live in your storage unit?" She was clear to say she didn't share our faith when I spoke with her months prior, so to her, the idea of breaching a contract and moving out was likely an inconvenience to her and certainly not practical or responsible in her eyes.

I greatly desired to stay in the house, get the traveling over with, come back to our home, and continue raising my family. The extensive trip no longer seemed like a reasonable goal, anyway. I truly wanted to abandon the plan once I realized the cost and the commitment involved. It was clear, through scripture meditations that God was asking me for blind faith, and that moving out and surrendering were key components to activate the blessing to come. I read where Joshua wasn't fully blessed until he first stepped into the Jordan River, full of water. I knew I was going to have to leap first before activating God's blessing and being able to fully understand what was being asked of me. I prayed God would be there to release His blessings and catch me.

When the world says "No!" God says "Yes!" And when it looks like there's absolutely no way, God makes a way. When things look impossible, I remember,

> "With man this is impossible, but not with God; all things are possible with God"
>
> —Mark 10:27

While doors were slamming, movers were coming, and emotions ran high, I clung to my faith, brushed back the streams of tears, and repeated, "I trust you, Jesus. I trust you, Jesus." And with lots of days, God-moments, and incredulous stories in between, God showed up to move us safely out of our home and to deliver a fantastic Jubilee celebration. For His word says,

> "If my people, who are called by my name, will humble themselves and pray and seek my face and turn from their wicked ways, then I will hear from heaven, and I will forgive their sin and will heal their land"
>
> —2 Chronicles 7:14

# CHAPTER TWO

# MY GREAT COMMISSION

God showed up to be true to His word. He launched me on the Great Commission across our beautiful country from Oregon to Utah, from Missouri to Wisconsin, from Georgia to the Dakotas—so that I could call His people to spiritual and patriotic revival and encourage them to pray and seek His face. And, so I could experience Him and discover an intimate walk of faith and relationship with Him. It's this adventure, my spiritual journey across America this summer, that I want to share with you.

When times get crazy in your life or seem impossible, when the days come that America changes or resources dry up or darkness hovers, I hope you remember some of my story of how all things are possible and how faithful God is when we stand on His promises and His word in steadfast expectancy. He always shows up, no matter how dark the day looks. I hope you will discover for yourself how far you can trust God, as I learned to do in this move, this journey, this transition of my home.

I discovered on my travels that people are thirsty for *more* of God across America. Citizens across the country are begging America to return to her founding precepts and God's commands. Americans are being bolder to speak about their Christian beliefs and what they expect of their America, and they are actively expressing their fears for our country. The mumblings of frustration are starting to resound. It is mostly unanimous; people are describing the state of our union as messy, chaotic, and definitely in crisis. And, time and again, I heard how folks just miss the America they once knew, the simple times, the America where God and country came together and everyone was civil and friendly and plain good neighbors. The message God had given me was received with open arms and hearts as I shared it from state to state. It is time for America to wake up and take action.

Over the course of this amazing journey with God, I got a first-hand look at America the beautiful and the patriotic and spiritual temperature of our country, and in turn, I experienced a walk of intimacy with the King of Kings and blew out the candles on a beautiful 50th birthday celebration.

The purpose of this journey wasn't just a trip that could easily be perceived as irresponsible if it were viewed from the world's eyes; it was to show the faithfulness of a Father who loves His people and who is yearning for them to remember Him with their whole hearts. This was truly a spiritual trip with heavenly prompting and provision. For those who turn to follow Him, He is patiently waiting and yearning to reward His wayward children.

God is a God of miracles. Nothing is too hard for Him—

whether providing manna, dreams, the seemingly impossible, new homes, birthday wishes, or crazy adventures. We must only open our hearts to Him and trust Him with the dreams of our hearts, our everything, even if it means leaving careers or homes or dreams behind. He can see the whole picture of our lives and He will always have a better way to journey.

After 64 days of travel adventure and homelessness—interesting, I was born in 1964—shuffling kids and homes and pillows, we settled into a new home, perfectly suited for the journey ahead. God is our Father; He is our provider, and He loves us. He is the only love worth fighting for, and He is faithful. It can be a difficult lesson—one our hearts already likely know but our flesh often fights to remember. This journey of faith, while scary, was extraordinary and demonstrates so clearly that when we trust God, He will never leave us or forsake us. And when we truly surrender to Him, He can really use us for His greater purpose, His glory. And that has always been my heart's greatest desire. I love my country—the red, white and blue—and I love my God; I want more than anything to please Him and glorify His name so that many can know Him, believe Him, trust Him, and love Him. It's my life's purpose to shine the light to Him, so many can discover the awesome God I know.

Journey with me across America to give the charge for America's call to action, to revive and ignite the Spirit of America, and to be the mouthpiece of our heavenly Father as He is calling each child back to His altar of grace. Sound the trumpets! Wake up America! The time is *now*.

God still wants to bless us, America, if only we will trust Him— with *everything*. *In God we trust—with everything*. Nothing is more valuable than the *free* gift of our Father's love and a first class buddy pass to our heavenly home. Let the charge begin!

"America the Beautiful" is one of the most patriotic songs for our country. The text was written by Katharine Lee Bates in 1892, during a trip to Pike's Peak in beautiful Colorado.


## AMERICA THE BEAUTIFUL

O beautiful for spacious skies,
For amber waves of grain,
For purple mountain majesties
Above the fruited plain!
America! America! God shed His grace on thee,
And crown thy good with brotherhood
From sea to shining sea!
O beautiful for pilgrim feet,
Whose stern impassion'd stress
A thoroughfare for freedom beat
Across the wilderness!
America! America! God mend thine ev'ry flaw,
Confirm thy soul in self-control,
Thy liberty in law!
O beautiful for heroes proved In liberating strife,
Who more than self their country loved,
And mercy more than life!
America! America! May God thy gold refine
Till all success be nobleness,
And ev'ry gain divine!

O Beautiful for patriot dream
That sees beyond the years
Thine alabaster cities gleam,
Undimmed by human tears!
America! America! God shed His grace on thee,
And crown thy good with brotherhood
From sea to shining sea!

## AMERICA'S CONSTITUTION

Our founding fathers were wise to think of our future. On September 17, 1787, delegates gathered to establish our national government and the laws that would establish our country's foundation. This document has survived centuries of life, war, turmoil, growth, and change. In this document, America's freedoms, rights, and truths are enumerated and outlined clearly for each American citizen.

This document is precious; it is not to be taken lightly. Read it. Comb through it. Let it resonate through you. Let freedom ring through every word as it becomes relevant to you and your life. Stand firm on these rights and declare each truth as you secure the blessings of liberty for your own life. Take ownership of every word and every amendment as your inalienable right as an American citizen.

Then, take action. Let nothing come between you and these precious freedoms that our founding fathers deemed appropriate to set forth for each of us and that our heavenly Father saw fit to inspire to them. They have been entrusted to each one of us that we may enjoy them, protect them, and pass them on as a legacy for future generations.

It is up to us to embrace these truths, relentlessly stand for them, and protect them. This is our first call to action. There comes a time you can no longer look the other way, and you must stand up and take action for something you believe in. We cannot keep being silent, "politically correct," or quietly complacent; we must not continue to pretend our country is not at risk. America is in the middle of an identity crisis, at the very least. There comes a time—and this is that time—to stand up as a nation and defend everything she stands for. Post your flags; take your stand.

This is that time, America. If the time is not now, then when is it? Lead the charge. Sound the alarms. Start the revolution in your home, in your neighborhood, in your town, in this season— for America. Ignite *The Spirit of America* from coast to coast, from sea to shining sea.

## THE CONSTITUTION

We the People of the United States, in Order to form a more perfect Union, establish Justice, insure domestic Tranquility, provide for the common defense, promote the general Welfare, and secure the Blessings of Liberty to ourselves and our Posterity, do ordain and establish this Constitution for the United States of America.

Our most profound legal document was signed to protect our rights, our homes, our freedoms, and our lives on American soil— for posterity; I love that. Our founding fathers thought of us as we now take the responsibility to take action to think of our children— for posterity. This Preamble to the Constitution is so much more than a reminder of middle school memorization and should be more than something we take for granted. This Preamble, our Constitution, and our Bill of Rights are our prescribing documents to guide us in the pursuit of life, liberty, and happiness every day in America. With a document that important to our well-being, we should be as familiar with it as we are the Ten Commandments, and we should talk of them, promote them, stand up for them when they are threatened.

More than 42 million immigrants live in our country. More than a half million immigrants become Naturalized American Citizens every year—more than 700,000 last year. They studied, they learn, and they thirst for the truths we take for granted, and they take the Naturalization Test to become American citizens. They beam with pride and burst out in tears because of the gift of opportunity America extends to them and their families (see www.uscis.gov for more information).

Sadly, most Americans have become passive toward these vital documents and the history they represent. Immigrants so diligently study our history, and yet Americans can't pass the citizenship test. We haven't thought about the details or bothered with the doctrine since grade school. I challenge you to wake up today and return to our roots. Read the Bill of Rights and the amendments; read them at your dinner tables, pass them around the family tree, and consider what they stand for and what it means to be an American where our freedoms are protected. Talk about what you and your family stand for. Remember to vote for leaders who agree with these doctrines or consider sending a candidate from your home to do so. Always vote. Always. Never throw away your right to vote—your country is depending on you. Let the truths and liberties of these important documents resound through your spirit and let them remind you of your patriotic heritage. Let them inspire you to accept your call to action.

And if you don't vote because you don't know who to vote for, go to the election office and ask who is on the ballot. Research who the candidates are and what they stand for. Pray on it, asking our Father in heaven to put who He wants in office and to guide your voting decision. It is good to vote. It is our American right to vote. Don't let fear hold you back from your right to cast your ballot. America is depending on you. So is God. Reflect on James 4:17 and do the right thing.

## THE BILL OF RIGHTS

These safeguard the essential liberties of every American. They are the first ten amendments of the U.S. Constitution:

1st   Amendment: Freedom of Religion, Speech and the Press

2nd   Amendment: The Right to Bear Arms

3rd   Amendment: The Housing of Soldiers

4th   Amendment: Protection from Unreasonable Searches and Seizures

5th   Amendment: Protection of Rights to Life, Liberty, and Property

6th   Amendment: Rights of Accused Persons in Criminal Cases

7th   Amendment: Rights in Civil Cases

8th   Amendment: Excessive Bail, Fines, and Punishments Forbidden

9th   Amendment: Other Rights Kept by the People

10th  Amendment: Undelegated Powers Kept by the States and the People

Read them for yourself at **www.constitutionalfacts.com**.

What a legacy for a country. They built a firm foundation on biblical principles and developed a Constitution with a Bill of Rights and Amendments that would provide sound guidance for over 200 years, for millions of Americans to enjoy life, liberty, and the pursuit of happiness. This is an incredible feat, something to be boldly proud of.

# CHAPTER THREE

# AMERICA'S CONSTITUTION, MORE THAN A DOCUMENT

I t might be a good time to reflect on the constitution of your very family. You see, this American revolution, in this day, is not only about America's Constitution, the document, but America's *constitution*—her character and that of the people whom she embodies. This might be a very good time to consider and declare your family's constitution.

Damaged relationships? Maybe now is the time for forgiveness and to be forgiven; communication and restoration are in order. Are you too busy to connect? Make time for scheduled quality time; make time for scheduled family meals. Are you away from the church and practicing of faith? It's time to invite heaven into your home by ousting media and chaos and overscheduled lives; perhaps it is time to reevaluate where you are, what you stand for, and where you want to be as a family. You have the controls—turn up the praise music, surf until you find more wholesome television like more Hallmark and less Hollywood. You need more of God's view on The Christian View (WATC-57, where you can catch me as a co-host, check local listings for air-time or call your station manager to request the programming be aired in your market, www. thechristianview.tv), and less of the world's view such as on the popular mainstream show, The View. Imbibe more History Channel and less reality TV. Engage in more one-on-one conversations and back to board games. Perhaps this is one place to start.

Every action you take is one step toward reclaiming the America we know and love. Restore families, and restore America. A house divided cannot stand and neither can a country. You are what you eat, watch, listen to, play, and absorb. A little yeast spoils the batch, so it may be best to eliminate what is corrupting our thoughts, hearts, and families and close those doors of opportunity. It's time to get healthy from the inside out, from the core of our souls to the hearts of our homes to the soil of our country. Strong families make a stronger America.

You might want to consider delegating a time to draw up a family agreement and write your own prescribing documents—much like the mission statement of Franklin Covey leadership teaching or the constitution of our country, but more like a document that defines your own family values, to be used as a guiding document in your daily comings and goings. Learn more about family declarations online at www.mydeclaration.org.

For an excellent example of a family constitution, download your very own Declaration of Independence and hang it in the foyer of your home as a reminder when you enter and leave your home. It's a good visual reminder of who you are and what values you hold dear, why you trade your time every day for the good of your family and, perhaps, even your country. Each citizen impacts our country daily with their job and performance, their actions, and their decisions or lack of them; reflect on yours that they may leave a legacy for your family and your country.

Another good document to frame at the doorway of your home is a copy of the Bible verse, Ephesians 6:10. It's the spiritual armor we have at our disposal to protect us as we face the mountains of the day. The Word says our battle is not with this world or the people of this world, but a spiritual battle that our Father in heaven has equipped us to overcome. We are victors because Jesus Christ died on the cross for us. Let us walk in that victory everyday. Let us fight the good fight without becoming weary for a better America because we are victors in the one who is already victorious.

With these clear reminders at the doorways of our homes, we will be less likely to become complacent or to have them taken right from under us, and we will have an arsenal of truth to defend our families, our homes, and our country. Embrace our country's truths and protect our freedoms—from the Constitution, to our spiritual countenance, let us renew America's Constitution as our unified highest priority and common core value.

> "As for me and my house, we will serve the Lord"
> —Joshua 4:15

The motto "one nation under God"—drawn from America's Constitution—will keep America strong when we stand up for it; your action, your dedication, your effort, your prayers, and your Christian walk will be a sacrifice pleasing to the Lord and God will bless America and hear the prayers of His children.

Why not begin with a fresh pledge to our flag and our God? *For God and country!*

# CHAPTER FOUR

# WE ARE "ONE NATION UNDER GOD."

**The Pledge of Allegiance of the United States of America.**

Did you know "The Pledge of Allegiance" was written to commemorate the 400th anniversary of Christopher Columbus' voyage to America? The phrase "under God" was added in 1954, during the Cold War, to clearly distinguish between the United States' Judeo-Christian beliefs and the Soviet Union's atheist beliefs.

Students have long been called to attention to recite "The Pledge of Allegiance" daily in public and private schools to begin the school day, until 1980s when the words "under God" and the pledge itself began to come under fire by atheists.

America was built upon Christian principles. Our first president, George Washington, saw fit to request a Bible for his swearing into office. America came into being as a nation as a result of fighting for her religious liberties. Why then would we, at any time, relinquish the freedoms of such principles, values, and allegiance or muddy the clarity of their terms? Why would we turn our backs on God who blessed our land and our nation with independence?

If citizens do not stand for their country, their flag, and her founding beliefs, how can they expect to enjoy the freedoms, liberties, and rights of the very country they live in? And, if we don't do it in peacetime, how much more difficult will it be in times of threat or war to muster support and courage to stand up for America and for God? The days ahead look dark; today is the day to prepare for the battle ahead.

How can one sleep in peace, knowing men have shed blood for this freedom and yet not stand in pledge and agreement to show honor and respect for this sacrifice? How can one accept the good from God, the blessings our country enjoys, and yet, not honor and acknowledge this good, fiercely holding on with the proper response of reverence and gratitude?

I will pledge allegiance to my flag and country because, to me, they represent an allegiance to my God who bestowed these wonderful gifts on me and who continues to bless me and my America every day. I often thank God with a grateful heart that I was born an American, especially in the South, with the gift of knowing Him and having a relationship with Him. How blessed am I! This is why I am often saying, "It's a Sweet Life™," because God has bestowed on us His highest blessing of life and freedom. It's a Sweet Life USA because I live in a beautiful, awesome, and amazing country; I have abundance and blessings and opportunity and freedoms that God has blessed me with. I jump to my feet at the opportunity to pledge allegiance to God and my country. I pray you still do, too.

## We Are "One Nation Under God."

"The Pledge of Allegiance"
Francis Bellamy
September, 1892

I pledge allegiance to the Flag
of the United States of America
and to the Republic
for which it stands,
one nation, under God,
indivisible, with liberty
and justice for all.

*I hope you were motivated to place your hand over your heart when you read that with fresh eyes.

I encourage you to take action by sharing the beauty of these words with your own families, to post a flag in your own yard, and to reflect on the important meaning of these words, including the price that is paid daily still for the privilege of these words and our freedoms. American soldiers are deployed on foreign lands still today; military families are impacted every day to ensure our nation will be free. Make your pledge; honor our country and their sacrifice. Determine to post the colors to show your appreciation and support. Display your American pride for all to see.

Stand united, America. Fight for the flag, America, and the Republic—one nation, under *God*, that we might enjoy the privileges and blessings that come with that. Decree it aloud and stand firm as Americans have done since 1892.

What legacy would we have to leave for the next generation if we simply let it slip from our hand? Take action by taking a stand, making the pledge, and keeping it alive in our schools and our communities. (Commit to support the *Spirit of America Days* 52 action step plan, listed later in this book. Share it on social media with friends and family.) Commit to being a leader in your community and share the pledge with your neighbors.

With people burning flags, calling for them to come down, and disrespecting them, we need to stand together and let it be known what the flag means to us and our families. More Americans might fly a flag at their homes and places of business if it were easy to install and clear how to honor the flag. Consider asking a Boy Scout troop to help you with this project in your neighborhood. Knock on doors and ask your neighbors to consider posting an American flag. Talk about the Spirit of America ideas at your home owner's association meetings, civic group, or town hall meetings. Watch the spirit catch fire in your town and inspire others across America too.

## Follow Flag Etiquette

I encourage you in many ways, make your flags visible. Fly your flags, yes. Wear your flags, yes. Display your flags, yes. Remember to please do so with reverence and in accordance with established flag etiquette and care. No one intentionally violates the flag etiquette code, so let's simply become aware and help others to, as well, so we can honor our flag with uniformity and respect.

## Did you know there is a Flag code to help us in honoring the flag?

## Pledge Etiquette

The pledge should be given while standing at attention facing the flag with the right hand placed over the heart. When not in uniform, men should remove their headdress with their right hand and place it at the left shoulder, the hand over the heart. In uniform, persons should remain silent, facing the flag, with salute extended. Veterans and members of the armed forces may salute whether in uniform or not. The hand comes over the heart as soon as the flag enters view and remains in potision until the flag is dismissed from view. Every America-loving citizen and resident should respect the American flag this way with their hand over their heart until the flag is retired or the last note sung. It's a responsible citizen who will boldly ask others to participate properly or model proper flag respect. Often, people feel awkward and just want a reassuring word of instruction or encouragement of the proper time of salute and dismissal.

It is always appropriate to stand, come to attention, and demonstrate still reverence, with the right hand over the heart, to show honor and respect for our American flag, as well as for our National Anthem. There are plenty of sources for flag etiquette, which might help clarify and educate you. Be sure to visit www. usflag.org to learn more.

Did you know The United State Flag Code establishes rules for displaying and caring for our national flag? The flag should never be used as apparel, bedding, or drapery, and it should not be embroidered on such articles as cushions or handkerchiefs and the like, or printed or otherwise impressed on paper napkins or boxes or anything that is designed for temporary use and discarded. The Flag code can be found in Chapter 1, Title 4 of the United States Code. Who knew? Take time to check it out.

Take a look around. Where do you see flags flying in your community? You can find one at city hall, the police department, and in schoolyards, and the biggest flags fly on sales lots at auto dealerships. I always love to see these large flags billowing in the wind. How about in your community? Take note of the number of houses that have flags displayed. Is this an area you can make a difference? Consider knocking on doors and encouraging your neighbors to come together to fly the American flag in unity for our nation.

While you are posting your flags, why not place a yellow ribbon on your mailbox to remember our military personnel who serve? An entire neighborhood emblazoned with yellow ribbons is a good daily reminder to pray for our soldiers fighting abroad every day and for our military families at home, waiting on their soldiers' safe return. The yellow ribbons and the American flags become our reminders of the sacrifices paid daily, what we stand for, and why we get on the hamster wheel of life every day. The flags and ribbons posted remind us of the veterans who gave their lives and those who served, only to return forgotten. The American flags and the yellow ribbons remind us that freedom isn't free and that we are all in this together, in unity. It fills our hearts with gratitude for what we do have; our American pride bubbles up and we immediately feel closer and more connected to our neighbors and our country. The flags and ribbons become our shield to the world and clearly convey who we are and what we stand for. It reminds us we are the United States of America, not one man out for himself. The flags and ribbons remind us that we have each other's backs, and the enemy will find an army of citizens who will bear arms and stand strong to defend their nation. The ribbons and flags remind us that there is strength in numbers, and God's sovereignty reigns and blesses our land.

We Are "One Nation Under God."

Journey with me on one amazing, supernatural adventure across America to reconnect with the land we call home and to discover a faithful God who provides amazing grace to those who dare to walk with Him. Buckle up; it's going to be a wild ride!

# CHAPTER FIVE

# A MOVE ON FAITH

Yes, it's true, while I was scraping for money to pay the movers and trying to pay the last of the utilities, not sure how I would meet the new demand of paying for storage units, I just kept moving forward in faith with the looming notion that I would be embarking on a spiritual journey of faith across America as soon as the house was cleared. I had but $2.12 to my name at the beginning of the week, and God kept confirming that once I packed up the house, my journey would begin.

It was unsettling, but I tried to remember all the times God had shown up with favor and finances; I remembered the time He brought me to my favorite beach and showered me with lunch and dinners—all impromptu gifts of strangers and the evident moving of the Holy Spirit. (See book 2, *eLph: A Love Worth Fighting For.*) I remembered that He was the same God today as yesterday. I recalled the victories and remembered His faithfulness of provision and promptings.

Still, fear crept in a wee bit. In my need to feel some security, I remember saying to God, "I'll go, and I know you can provide in supernatural ways, but please can I just have enough to pay for the buddy pass (a reduced rate airfare) and just one night's lodging? I know you will provide the rest along the way and it will all work out, but I'm going on faith and, in my flesh, I need a little encouragement for the journey.

And, then, just in case He needed to know exactly how much I anticipated needing, I added, "You know a trip like this is gonna cost—a lot!" and I paused to calculate the large number of the trip. I demurred and muttered much more humbly, "Well, just the first leg, just the first week of this journey is gonna cost a lot more than I even have the courage to say. I'm going to need *$1,500* for this first leg of the trip—five days, five states, and a lot of miles away."

There, I said it. It was a big number, but it was real. I felt a little guilty, rather greedy for putting a price tag on a spiritual journey of faith and then added, "Well, I can't help it, that's just how much things cost. $1,500. It's gonna cost *$1,500*." This time, I was more indignant. I couldn't believe I had the audacity to be so bold. I couldn't believe that I was really being prompted on this walk of faith at all, and here I was negotiating with God, the maker of the universe—my heavenly Daddy—on the actual cost of the trip. It all seemed so ludicrous, so very incongruous to the reality of my life in the moment. But, I know my Father in heaven's voice, and I knew He was prompting me to take this leap of faith for His purpose. It had burned in me too long, and I didn't even want to go anymore.

It wasn't me begging and pleading to go, rather I was trying to find a way out; I was ill-equipped, with no resources for such incredible timing.

I gingerly discussed it very vaguely with a few close friends whom I thought could understand it without judging me. One of my friends offered me a family and friend's Delta Airline buddy pass. My checking account still wasn't looking like it was prepared for a cross-country trip. In fact, I had about $2.12 to spend, but, I was set to travel *to the remaining 50 states, half way across America!*

"I don't think so!" my spirit kept yelling back at me. I can hardly explain, but I know it was what I was being prompted to do, and so I kept sifting the possibilities through my mind: potential travel spots, then even a few itineraries. And, as it turned out, God revealed He had a big purpose to this walk of faith. Knowing nothing is too hard for Him, it all unfolded as it was meant to happen because to God it didn't matter that I had limited resources—He's God, and He can do anything.

In spite of my finances and in spite of the fact that I had no home and none identified to move in to, God cajoled me to trust Him across North America. And this trip would cover 14 states in just 18 days—including to my greatest surprise and fear, due to the difficulty of traveling to it and its distance from home—Alaska.

Fourteen states, that's Missouri, Iowa, Minnesota, Wisconsin, Oregon, Alaska, Utah, Idaho Wyoming, Kansas, Nebraska, South Dakota, North Dakota, and Montana—14 in all, and not one state was easy to get to. Not one state would be fun to travel to alone. Not one state was approachable on $2.12 with no credit card as a back-up plan. Yet, all things are possible with Jesus Christ, especially for those who serve Him according to His will and believe in our heart and trust Him enough to walk in absolute faith, in spite of the size of the calling.

My journey is a testimony to that very walk of faith. My adventure with God was chock full of surprise and delight—He provided me opportunities to serve others, to testify in His name, to do book research on the spiritual and patriotic temperature of America, and to be treated like royalty by the King of Kings. I can't wait to finally share what I experienced with someone— with you.

This entire journey is for His glory, for all the doubting Thomases reading my story, and maybe for those trying to discern a God-sized calling in their life. We are called to trust Him in all things. He is faithful and trustworthy. He is worthy of all our trust and heart.

His word says we are not to rely on wealth, but on God (1 Timothy). I believe that verse is core to the Spirit-led journey I took across America. When the numbers didn't add up in my checking account, I was to dismiss the understanding of my flesh and trust Him deeply.

Now pack your bags, unpack what you know to be reasonable and logical when it comes to taking a long journey, and read what happens when I jump all in and trust Him with everything. I believe He is calling His people to trust Him in new and bigger ways in this season. I believe my story is to be a light to your path, a walk of faith that ignites your faith. I believe in doing so, you will be inspired to travel across America, to reconnect with your families, with America, with her majestic landscape, with your dreams, with your purpose, and with God Himself, the maker and giver of all of these amazing blessings.

I believe we are walking into a time when this kind of spiritual leading will be the norm and not the profound. So, buckle up for an adventure on His amazing grace. And read about the signs, wonders, and miracles I experienced on a spiritual journey of faith across America.

## GOD'S AMAZING GRACE

One of my favorite songs is Amazing Grace. The sweet sound of that very first note brings me to tears every time. It really resonated through me as I traveled across America and saw the majesty of the Lord's hand. The masterpiece He inspired for us to enjoy is breathtaking. I regret every minute I was blind in sin and am grateful for every moment of victory and grace. A trip across this country will inspire you to sing this song, I am sure, as it inspired me many a day, bringing a whole new meaning next time you hear it.

"Amazing Grace"
John Newton, 1779

Amazing grace! How sweet the sound
That saved a wretch like me!
I once was lost, but now am found;
Was blind, but now I see.

'Twas grace that taught my heart to fear,
And grace my fears relieved;
How precious did that grace appear
The hour I first believed.

Through many dangers, toils and snares,
I have already come;
'Tis grace hath brought me safe thus far,
And grace will lead me home.

The Lord has promised good to me,
His Word my hope secures;
He will my Shield and Portion be,
As long as life endures.

Yea, when this flesh and heart shall fail,
And mortal life shall cease,
I shall possess, within the veil,
A life of joy and peace.

The earth shall soon dissolve like snow,
The sun forbear to shine;
But God, who called me here below,
Will be forever mine.

When we've been there ten thousand years,
Bright shining as the sun,
We've no less days to sing God's praise
Than when we'd first begun.

# CHAPTER SIX

# A MOVE BY HIS GRACE

> "Truly I tell you," Jesus replied, "no one who has left home or brothers or sisters or mother or father or children or fields for me and the gospel will fail to receive a hundred times as much in this present age: homes, brothers, sisters, mothers, children and fields—along with persecutions—and in the age to come eternal life."
>
> —Mark 10:29

Jan 2014—May 2016. Two years of preparation, training, and persecution.

Pressure. What pressure? My fourth child was a senior in high school and ready to graduate, and all eyes were on me to celebrate this victory in a big way. In his eighteen and a half years of life he had made his sacraments at church, earned the

Gretzky award in recreational roller hockey, held two jobs through high school, and earned the rank of Eagle Scout in Boy Scouts of America. This was his time to be recognized. *But, what was I supposed to do now?* It didn't make a bit of sense; I had boxes coming in to be packed, my tasks outlined on a poster on the wall for the impending move, and zero extra dollars to spend on a celebration or a party, let alone emotional and physical strength for one more responsibility. But, it was his high school graduation, my last chance to honor him, love him, and celebrate him before he left the nest and headed off to college. He had earned a day of celebration for all the obstacles he had to overcome to stay on track for graduation. Where would the money come from for a graduation party?

What sane person hosts a graduation party at their house two days prior to a move? I don't know. But I never seem to take the easy route; I just try to do the right thing and pray God takes care of the details. This was no different. I planned an extensive barbecue menu with appetizers, desserts, and favors. I planned photo boards and table decorations. Together, my son and I made a guest list, but the burden of cost would fall all on me.

The numbers kept adding up. Where would so much money come from? God always takes care of the details, so I just kept planning, announcing, and preparing in between packing, churning out laundry, and praying for the day after the move to arrive quickly.

*Where will we go?* Many people asked where we would move to. I didn't know, but God did, I assured them. And, I thanked God silently for His provision and His plan; I reminded Him how much I was trusting and depending on Him.

And, then, I threw a question to my son: "What is your high school buddy and soon-to-be college roommate doing to celebrate graduation?" This question turned into a phone call to his teacher mom, only to reveal her end of school year tasks made it too difficult for her to plan any celebration for her son. This discovery made way for an obvious joint celebration for the boys and set up an opportunity for an increase of the necessary finances, with us equally sharing the projected expenses.

God always has a way of working it out, just in time, while all the while letting me plan and walk in nothing but faith, sometimes oscillating to doubt, but mostly trusting Him to come through and provide!

The other boy's mother, a busy teacher, was relieved there was someone to help create the event for her son and happily wrote a check for half the expenses. I reached out to his dad, who agreed to contribute the other half of the finances. My contribution would be the organizing, cooking, cleaning, and attending to all the details as party hostess. It was as if that was part of the plan all along, exactly how God had orchestrated it. This all came into place within a few day's time. I just love when God shows up because things always work out!

On graduation party day, packing efforts were suspended, and I went into full catering and cook mode, setting every party table up outside, shuffling borrowed tables and chairs from the church to the backyard, and creating a beautiful event for both boys that celebrated their lives and their accomplishments. God is so good. And I am so glad I said yes, in spite of the pending move. It is a sweet memory for us and was actually a relief in the middle of the move.

Then family arrived, and the final celebration came with the graduation ceremonies at the outdoor stadium, during which

I praised God for carrying me every step of the way. I released His mighty name across the entire stadium field. I'm sure He blessed every graduate there. In the midst of the storm, not knowing how I was going to pay to celebrate my son's accomplishments, here we were celebrating with family under God's beautiful blue sky. It was a beautiful evening and yet another accomplishment for my family, by the grace of God. It was truly through His amazing grace that I pulled this graduation celebration off.

Moments like this give us courage to keep forging ahead. After all, I still had one more child to house under my roof, love, and see graduate in a few years, and in the morning, reality would hit as the final stages of packing and moving would unfold.

There was a lot of work and a lot of unknown ahead. But God delivered a beautiful graduation celebration and a great, big confirmation of His faithfulness. I knew the future looked bleak from my vantage point, but I knew, without a doubt, He would be faithful and His amazing grace would get us through yet again.

God would show up with greater grace and mercy than I had yet experienced. He had a plan to love me through the pain and move me and all 2,600 square feet of belongings through the unknown. If you are in the middle of a huge storm, I promise you, no matter how impossible it looks, God can be the champion of your storm. God can be your provider, protector, counselor, and deliverer—you just have to ask, trust, believe with your whole heart, and let go. In letting go, I don't mean let go; I mean get going, but let Him lead and show up in His way. And, no matter what people and naysayers are chanting, no matter how bleak that journey looks, know deep, deep, deep in your soul that He is who He says He is, and He will come through for you.

There truly is no rest for the weary. The alarm clock was set early the day after graduation, and before I could pack, I had to clean up, clear up, and distribute all that remained from the graduation party. That meant tents had to be packed up and returned, trays cleaned, food dispersed, and a clean canvas created in my home to begin the next major project of moving. I had but hours to make it all happen.

To help things along, I found a neighbor having a graduation party across the street and hand-delivered the bouquet of graduation balloons and a table full of party supplies to be enjoyed at their party. The task was complete, and we both benefitted—I love the sharing of resources while clearing space. It's always nice to bless someone else, and my reward was the blank canvas I now had to work with.

With every step, I exhaled a deep breath and praised God for all that He had done and who He was. I kept my focus off the fear of the unknown and on the task at hand. How do you eat an elephant? You eat it one bite at a time. I wrote a very long list of all the tasks that had to be done through graduation and for the move and turned it into a milestone timeline on posters, which I taped to my kitchen wall to stay focused. Every time I accomplished a task, I marked off the task for victory. I took time right then to review everything I had accomplished and thanked God for every step forward.

In the meantime, I had to keep generating money in hopes of paying moving professionals for the heavy lifting. I identified items to purge and periodically would break to photograph them, post them on Craig's List or other social media, and go back to packing and sorting all the items to be moved. I had no idea where I was moving to or what I needed to keep or give away. I did have great experience as a former military spouse, having moved more than a dozen times in 20 years of service. I knew enough to get rid of as much as possible. See how God uses every experience for His good purpose? He was preparing me even then.

In spite of my time constraints and finances, I can only be who God calls me to be. And much of the items I sorted had to go to various charities in town, were repurposed to someone I knew was in need, or were donated in larger donation piles. This was very time consuming, but I knew it was the right thing to do. You can't out give God, and even in the midst of your own storms, thinking of others becomes better than an energy drink; it's very satisfying to help others.

Of course, there were the multiple garage sales in the final month and the sorting and pricing of items during the month of May. I continued to post major items on Craig's List and social media; however, in the heat of the moment, progress was my greater goal, and I would just load 10 baskets of items and mark them for donations, in spite of the cash value I know they would bring if I patiently listed them online. My higher priority went to the purging and being ready for moving day. God would take care of the cash or the replacing what I might need in the next home, and in so many ways, He did.

My military days of moving had also taught me to hold back the first 30 days (we labeled it "Hold Baggage"), because you never knew when your household goods would show up. So I made a 30-day pile. In this pile, I thought of all the things we might enjoy—swimming, hiking, beach time with friends. Yes, even in the lack, I knew that God did not intend to leave us on the side of the curb without, so I packed in anticipation of the good things I knew God would provide. Call me an optimist, but I know my God to be the giver of good things, and besides, I was a Girl Scout and a Boy Scout adult leader; "Be Prepared" was the only way I knew to operate.

Then came the big things, and this was harder. My first inclination was to just get rid of it all, start giving away my furniture and just move on, but the practical side of me wanted to remind me that refurnishing an entire house can be costly (I learned that the hard way, you can read about it in *The Military Family: A Casualty of War*). I didn't exactly have a savings account for this transition. So I did my best to identify the basics of a household and imagined myself moving to my favorite cabin in the mountains and asked, "What would I really need?" It helped a lot.

I tagged everything with a sticky note "Keep" or "Give" or "Store" or "Hold" and started my tagging process in the far corner of the house with the stack of magazines. Magazines were an easy purge, but who was I kidding? I now had 5 days left to move an entire 2,400 square foot home and a garage loaded with possessions and all I had disposed of were about ten *Southern Living* and *Leisure and Travel* magazines. The mountain looked too large for me to climb alone.

My 14-year-old daughter showed up in full force with lots of encouragement and cooperation. She started in her room, packing things up, marking them, and using neon-colored duct tape when we ran out of packing tape. The support was great, but boy were we exhausted and disheartened by the first day's end.

The next day, the movers were scheduled to come for the first phase of the move, to get the larger items, including the beds. It was overwhelming, hardly anything had been boxed up to make a dent in what was to be moved, and I was feeling like a failure in the face of my big task. I made a dash to the local grocery produce department to get more boxes and text a friend from prayer group for support. Thankfully, she came with another girl to help. My yoke got lighter when they arrived; plus they prayed with me right away—what love!

It wasn't just the physical or logistical part of the move; I was juggling the flow of finances too. I stopped in at the moving company and asked for grace to hold the check for a week after the move to buy time for an anticipated check. It was the check that would have paid my rent, but without a house, I wouldn't have rent. So now I would have some moving dollars for the moving company.

With any overage cost, I would have to gamble with the flux again, waiting for the next deposit to provide for today's needs and address next week's needs at that time. I was amazed when the movers agreed, but then again, A Better Way Ministry moving company is a Christ-centered business, and this is how God shows up to be our provider when things look impossible. He moves hearts, shifts the atmosphere, and sends unexpected favors to meet our needs; He always has *a better way* than circumstances may lead us to believe. I made sure I had enough cash to tip the workers after a hard day's work, so they could be well fed and rewarded immediately.

The movers came, and with them went our beds—the move was real, as real as the fact that within a few short days, we would be without a home and no idea where God was calling us or moving us. I ignored the fact that I had no savings, no employment, and no cash in my checking account. God was on the throne and His word said that He is my provider. I was trusting Him on that.

My daughter and I responded by making a huge palette on the floor out of blankets and coats for us to sleep on the next few days. My two sweet friends packed my kitchen, taped boxes, and prayed in encouragement, sharing stories of their own life's trials along the day. And after his long day of work, my friend's husband came to help meticulously clean and vacuum the entire upstairs so I could continue packing and clear "quarters" and keep my "quarters" (my security deposit). These were generous hearts sharing the love of Christ.

Victory! In two days, with a few extra hands, half the house had been emptied.

But there was no time to relish in the celebration. I had reserved the moving truck from the storage unit complex for free and was limited to only one hour on the third day of my move. I had managed to fill the front room full of boxes by bringing the packed boxes down from the upstairs level. By consolidating all the boxes, it cleared the entire upstairs, making the space available for cleaning and consolidating the boxes in one area for easy pack out to the truck.

My daughter and I were helpless with this man-sized task. My prayer friend, Sandra Lynne, assessed the situation and sent a text to several lifelines, and within minutes we had the help of one generous friend from the local coffee shop. When he showed up, I realized he was an acquaintance of mine, but he volunteered as the servant of Christ, not knowing who would be blessed other than a single Christian woman in need. Dave, a former Army soldier, is a good man.

Still the task was beyond reasonable. The entire room was full of boxes stacked to the ceiling. The truck had to be picked up, loaded, driven to the new storage unit, unpacked, and returned to the pickup location five miles away within one hour.

Let me tell you how I know God is a God of the impossible: because I have experienced Him. While we all started loading, shifting, and moving the boxes, my two prayer friends began their praying, and just as we walked out the door with the last box, ready to rush out the door, my friend, Kathryn insisted, "Wait, let's pray." And, standing by the front door frame, with arms loaded, we prayed and agreed that God was a God of the impossible and could even elongate time.

Still, we hurriedly made our way to the storage unit, unloaded the boxes into the unit, closed the truck, and raced, without speeding, over to the original location to return the truck. To all of our amazement, especially the staff at the Cube Smart storage unit, we completed the task in just under an hour! God had indeed elongated time and gave us strength for yet another victory in this daunting move! It was events like this that kept pulling me along to victory.

Day three of the move, the landlords were getting anxious and came to inspect the house and the progress of the move. They were less than pleased, in spite of our best efforts and the extra good cleaning, that the kitchen was only mid-way finished and the garage was still full to the brim. With firm words, they let me know I needed to be cleared of the house at our agreed upon date. I could use the garage for five extra days was a generous offer they came up with on their own, seeing that it was filled to the brim and not possible to move within 48 hours. But I would have no extension on the interior of the house, regardless of the obstacles and enormity of the task. They insisted that we had better get busy to meet the looming move-out date and hour.

With that, we worked through the night, but still had much to do come morning. I stood overlooking my garage full of belongings, including the baskets still left from the last garage sale, which I had already mentally designated for charity. I prayed out loud and claimed God's help. I prayed Psalm 91:4. I shouted to all the debris and boxes stacked in my garage how I knew I could trust God for help and how I was relying on Him and how the mountain was too big for me, but not for my God. And, then, I wept. "God, nothing is impossible for you, but this is impossible for me. You. Have. Got. To. Do. Something." I pleaded for His help from the depths of my soul.

That night, in spite of my move and the pending tasks, in spite of aching from sleeping on blankets on the floor, in spite of my unknown future, I cleaned myself up and went to a monthly church meeting where I volunteered as the recording secretary. For two hours, I joined in prayer and praise and supported the work of the Terra Globe International Ministries group with about 20 other Christians sold-out to God.

At the end of the meeting, we invited a roundtable of discussion, and I shared a brief synopsis that I was in the midst of moving. I shared my dilemma of being out of funds, unable to hire more movers, believing I was going on a God-sized mission to write a book, but not being clear on every detail. I shared how my landlords had given me five more days, but I knew I needed to be done sooner than later to leave a good impression as a Christian family and to free up my initial deposit fee, and to be free from this burden and oppression. It was only a few genuine minutes.

At the end of the meeting, they took up a love offering for the ministry, something only recently started for the growth of Terra Globe Ministries. I was touched when the pastor announced it was to support me with my move and my mission ahead. It was very humbling to have that gift of love and encouragement offered. About $350 was collected. It was a huge inspiration and seed of encouragement. It was the seed of what God would bring my way to begin His journey.

The next day, I sat in my garage and cried while I made packing progress through every tear. I also broke out in praise and worship when I was swept away or had cleared a box. At the end of a day of packing, clearing, and sorting, my landlords made another visit to clear and inspect the interior of the house, which was now, finally, empty.

After two years of living in this heaven-sent home, having faced financial giants and tribulation, it was time to leave, but instead of a fond farewell and a "job well done," there was turmoil. Just two days earlier, the landlord said I could have use of the garage, but now on this checkout day, they indicated that it did not include *access* to the space unless they were present. This would limit me on when I could access it to work in it and would prevent me from preparing it before helpers came to finish the move out; in addition, I would have the added burden of their presence during this time. It seemed degrading and humiliating.

With my kids hovering in the garage as they waited for me to talk with the landlords inside, looking confused, knowing there was an awkward confrontation on the other side of the door, I was sent on my way, not through the front door, but, escorted out through the interior garage door and locked out of the home I once knew, banished to exit through the box-filled remnants of my household goods still stacked and waiting to be packed away.

The kids and I quickly exited through the open garage door and convened in the driveway so I could explain how we would not be going back in and that we had the week to clear the garage of our remaining belongings. There were tears of shame and pain that streamed across our faces. It was a harsh ending to a confusing time. I hand-delivered my rent promptly 22 of the 24 months. I remained an occupant and paid late fees the two other months. I took care of the interior and was respectful and grateful for every bit of maintenance and repair, offering iced water and lemonade with their every visit. But there was no time for tears now, there was still moving to do.

The children and I parted, with my son heading to a friend's house and my daughter and I to a different friend's house. Here I would thank God for a place of refuge and implore Him for answers for the future. Where would we live? What plans did He have for us? And, why did my family have to be separated during this transition?

The next morning, I dug into the belongings in the garage with fervor, knowing I had no other choice. Sheer will would have to be my strength. I posted the items available for charity. I texted my church friend asking for help.

To my surprise, God already had a plan in place. Men I had never met, but friends of friends present, some I met once at the meeting the night before, and spouses of my two girlfriends, came trickling in, and we got to work.

In the midst of this hard work and my humiliation of cleaning out the garage with strangers present and pressing hard under the time constraints, the landlord was showing the house for sale, feeling it was also to monitor my progress. It was humiliating and made the task all the harder.

I knew I had to hold my head up high. We had to show them Christ and what He could do. What I couldn't have accomplished in a week, they accomplished in a day. Folks came to pick up the charity donations. These men of God came to offer their brawn and their time, and with me sorting, packing, and directing the task, God sent an army of servants to empty my garage in just one day—broom swept.

I was moved to tears. Even the 10 bags of overflow garbage was toted away by one spouse and his truck and taken to the dump. Only God. Only God can move a 2,400 square foot house with no money, little talent and time, and a handful of folks with open hearts. Only God can do the impossible, and only the impossible can be accomplished when we partner with God and trust Him to deliver.

Now during the course of the move, lots of testimony and God-stories were exchanged, and at the end of the day, not only time, but tithe was offered as well. God had moved their spirits to share financial support, as well, to encourage the journey ahead. I was another third closer to that big number I needed to accomplish this goal.

The following and last day of this move, I stopped to go to church, to thank God for His faithfulness and ask Him for guidance and strength for the uncertain days ahead. After church, a friend asked how he could help. I said there was only one last load of donations left and he offered his truck and his help following church.

Coincidentally, I did not know my oldest son was coming to

town to work his weekend job, and he showed up just as we arrived at the house for the donations. It was a two-man job, due to the weight of some items. God had perfectly orchestrated even that—helping hands—at just the right time. The landlord came to inspect and was shocked at the empty garage.

"How did you do that?"

I smiled and said, "That's what happens when God shows up and sends His church to help." How satisfying that was to relish in.

Before the sun had set, God had moved a spirit who offered a check. This angel simply said, "I felt God told me to give this to you."

And with that, within five days of facing mountains, tremors, moving, and the impossible, God had cleared my house, moved it to four different storage units and provided exactly $1,500 for the first leg of His journey.

# CHAPTER SEVEN

# INSPIRED TO DREAM
# GOD-SIZED DREAMS

Before we pack our bags and hit the road, you might ask, why in the midst of all this turmoil would a trip be a part of God's plans? And what would make you think you were meant to do that now?

I didn't arrive at this overnight.

For more than a decade, almost two, I held on to a dream to travel to 50 states by the time I was 50; it was just a goal. I love travel. I love adventure. It sounded like fun.

Life was full of storms and hardships and financial turmoil, so the closer it got to my 50th, the less important the goal seemed to be to me. I have had the blessing of doing a lot of traveling in my lifetime—34 states and over 30 countries, so letting go of this goal was not that difficult. I have enjoyed a lot of travel and didn't feel like I was losing out. In fact, with all the burden of the last decade—from accepting 25,000 pounds of household goods, dripping wet and soon laden with mold and mildew on my 40th birthday, to now, there had been so many storms, I didn't really have the energy or tenacity or mindset to truly want to reach the goal anymore. I much preferred to put my MBA to use, find a job, start earning, saving, and investing and reinventing my future.

But, God had other plans. The 50 X 50 trip was no longer for me. It was obvious, after spending a year writing six other books for Him, that it was for Him, all along. The adventure was for me, but the story was for Him. He needed my eyes and my surrendered will and my engagement to write a book that would inspire and wake America up and remind readers about America the beautiful and His amazing grace. He needed me to go on this journey more than I needed to meet a goal to see 50 United States.

This trip wasn't for the selfish satisfaction of my flesh, though, by grace, it was the satisfaction of the greatest desires of my heart. No, it was so clear to me along the journey, God's message was for me to tell His children:

> Command those who are rich in this present world not to be arrogant nor to put their hope in wealth, which is so uncertain, but to put their hope in God, who richly provides us with everything for our enjoyment. Command them to do good, to be rich in good deeds, and to be generous and willing to share. In this way they will lay up treasure for themselves as a firm foundation for the coming age, so that they may take hold of the life that is truly life.
>
> —1 Timothy 6:17–19

His desire was for me to write down every experience on a scroll and share what I had experienced, so that others could come along the spiritual road of faith and hear the mighty voice of their Father, too. He yearns for His bride. He wants intimacy, and that takes trust and pursuit and faith and stepping away from the trappings of this world. Though, when I did, I was given an adventure and opportunity to enjoy the things of this world as I passed through.

This fragrant invitation had been wafting through my life since an early age, in preparation for this big trip across America, in God's timing and season. In fact, after the Twin Towers came down in September 2001, God stirred in me a patriotic passion and a spark to ignite the Spirit of America through a national observance of a patriotic season. I first outlined it in December 2001 and sent it to the office of the President of the United States of America the following year. There was a cordial letter of acknowledgement with the gold seal and all from the White House, but I knew it was destined for more. I felt it was only a temporary, "No." I knew that I was meant to lead this charge, to ignite the Spirit of America across the nation, and America was meant to return to its patriotic spirit. She just needed a leader to ignite the flame, and I was willing to do my part to lead the charge as the scribe and town crier.

In 2002, I turned my message into a solid platform of patriotism and volunteerism and earned the local title of Mrs. Newport News International. For a year I volunteered for many civic organizations and public and private schools, encouraged others to volunteer, and collected over 3,500 of their volunteer hours, as well. I competed in and won Mrs. Virginia International, which afforded me the ear of the Governor and helped me earn access to Congressional Representatives, eventually garnering their endorsements. I was successful on all accounts, including six signatures and another letter of acknowledgment, gold seal and all from the White House.

By the fall of 2003, I had earned the state title and was competing in Mrs. International, competing against women from all over the world. I persistently prayed the Prayer of Jabez that I might have my Father's blessing and favor, according to His will for this door to open:

Jabez cried out to the God of Israel, "Oh, that you would bless me and enlarge my territory! Let your hand be with me, and keep me from harm so that I will be free from pain."

And God granted his request.

And God brought me Isaiah 54 time and time again:

> "Enlarge the place of your tent, stretch your tent curtains wide, do not hold back; lengthen your cords, strengthen your stakes"
>
> —Isaiah 54:2

I knew that this would mean big things, but did not expect the battle that would ensue as a result of that prayer. Just as they were calling out the top ten, I had a behind- the-contestant-row-view and felt I heard, "I have this for you, but not like this." I was called out to place in the top ten, but not the Queen's court. I did not take home the crown or the runner up banners; God had another plan that would lead to victory for Him. He had a journey ahead that could not be construed as my own effort or luck or favor, but a victory possible only by His might, power, and strength. And, at the finish line, bystanders could only be left to exclaim, "But, God!"

Perhaps not in the very difficult moments, but I am most grateful God brought me through the journey this way, to keep me humble and grateful, not walking in pride, but grace, so that at the moment of victory, all glory and honor will be given to Him who is deserving of all honor and praise, not me. I am just the scribe, the recorder of His books, the mouthpiece for His messages, and a vessel for His purpose. I love pageantry and crowns for the glitz and glamour and the scholarship dollars, not the accolades. I am grateful the crowns I have earned have opened doors and prepared the way for this message. I'm glad through the fire, all glory shines to Him, and doors now open without a crown.

Little did I know it would take 10 years to realize the answer to those prayers of Jabez, and I would journey one thousand steps pursuing God as my reward and not a crown. Little did I know the journey I would go on or how far God wanted to enlarge my territory, or what the cost of this walk would be! I would soon trade my pageant heels for rain boots and my crown of rhinestones for puddles of tears but receive, instead, a radiance that comes only from Christ and an unexplainable joy.

It was evident in April 2013 when I passed by a golf course one morning after dropping the kids off to school and headed back to our home, which was out of the school district, that the place of my tent was still expanding, and God had a vision for that. Having dropped my kids off at school after our 20-minute commute, as I turned my head in the direction of the 17th green on the local golf course, I asked God to move us to a house there—it was, after all, in the school district. I did immediately admonish myself for asking for such a lavish extra, simplifying the morning transportation was all I was really pleading help with. And, yet, within a few short hours, that very prayer was answered. It was a surreal thing to have my prayer asked and answered so visibly and quickly. He was on the move and up to something, and the time had come for His answer to those prayers of mine from years earlier, as well; this was just the beginning. Spring 2013, a full ten years after I started praying the prayer of Jabez, I would begin to see my prayers answered. Answers have been unfolding since, as I now approach the end of my Jubilee, or 50th year. It is no coincidence to me, this unique summer of 2015, is what God was leading me to all along.

You might remember how through multiple deaths of immediate family members, wars and deployments, extended unemployment, financial hardships, and eventually, divorce, that God has been working out the details of this part of my journey for nearly two decades. That's not unusual, for Jeremiah, Moses, and the Jewish people, exile and desert for decades were quite typical. Modern day folks are just like them, continually living and "writing more books" of the Bible; they simply aren't added to the Good Book in print anymore. While two decades—that's 20 years—seems like a lifetime to family and friends and the person walking the walk, it's very typical of a spiritual walk with God. In fact, I am certain my life has been a fragile balance of victory and defeat, chaos and calm, loss and joy for as long as I can remember. I would have hoped my walk would have been different, easier, but I received no such blessing.

The Word says there is joy in suffering and that faith brings perseverance.

> And not only this, but we also exult in our tribulations, knowing that tribulation brings about perseverance; and perseverance, proven character; and proven character, hope; and hope does not disappoint, because the love of God has been poured out within our hearts through the Holy Spirit who was given to us.
>
> —Romans 5:3

It is hard medicine that one challenge simply leads to another, but it's true; and there are blessings for this.

So even after moving a lifetime of belongings and my children and I to this lovely four bedroom home in the month of May, positioned on the 17th hole of the local golf course and within bus service to their schools, it would be exactly two years later in the month of May that He would snatch it right back and the landlord would demand the property for the purpose of selling it in this seller's market.

Was this the Promise land, this little patch of heaven on the golf course with the wildflowers and the sunroom? Or, was I going back in to Exile as it seemed to be?

"It's His house. He has that right. It's their house. They have their right," I reasoned through the change on the horizon.

He brought us to the house supernaturally. He can ask us to trust Him and move on into another supernatural walk. All things are His. And that truth, while sometimes challenging, is easy to accept and walk out under the covering of His wings in a walk of crazy faith.

It was unnerving because I was walking a tightrope of financial trust, and that would make this leap of faith an even bigger mountain to climb. I believe I had followed His calling to abandon corporate America and my MBA dreams, to walk in faith and trust a year and a half earlier when I left my position as a National Sales Director to start writing books on my life's storms and testimony and depend on His leading and provision for *everything*.

The notice to move would bring a huge financial impact and would make qualifying for a new house nearly impossible— but God, He was my ace in the hole. When all things looked impossible, I remembered, all things are possible with God. God was aware; it was all part of His plan that I might walk it out, lean in to Him, and share with others how things might look without dependable income or food or provision or even a future plan, but trusting only in God as the only resource I would need. I believe it's a testimony for the next generation and for a future point in time when America's resources and security might be threatened. This walk of faith in finances and housing I share might be the strength needed to help someone else walk through the fire and trust God for their daily bread in the very real sense. I pray this isn't America's future. But, trust me, miracles and manna are very real and true today. I have many stories to share to illustrate my experiences and this truth.

> Remember how the Lord led you all the way in the wilderness these forty years, to humble and test you in order to know what was in your heart, whether or not you would keep His commands He humbled you, causing you to hunger and then feeding you with manna, to teach you that man does not live on bread alone but on every word that comes from the mouth of the Lord.
>
> —Deuteronomy 8:2–3

We know, with confidence that He loves us. He sent His only Son as a sacrifice for our sins, for mine, while I was yet a sinner. Only someone who loves me could do that. All I have is His and all He asks is okay with me. He will and has provided the manna for me in the wilderness before. We are not to lean on our own understanding, but to do as He leads and trust that He sees the bigger picture and knows the better plans for our future. It's like that with God; He deserves our absolute trust. And, besides, His way is always better; it always works out better, anyway—every time.

I began to look in the rearview mirror and ponder the sequences and timing of things. I began to see a pattern with May. I even pulled out old leases and contracts to verify the dates.

May 2011, my divorce is final.

May 2013, I moved into the house that God had seemingly arranged on the golf course—my little patch of heaven.

May 2015, God had us move out of a perfectly good house, let go of everything, and follow Him on a faith walk across America.

There's something about this two year interval and the May mark that seems intentional.

In fact, God seems to bring me to Leviticus and atonement repeatedly, so I am inclined to think of this faith walk, the act of surrendering my home, as an offering. Though, yes, I know Jesus Christ on the cross was the final offering, the lamb that was slain to cover and atone for all sacrifices, I just feel this was a sacrificial offering in some sense. And I was brought to Acts 28:29–31 repeatedly, which brought a sense of confirmation to my own two year pattern.

> "For two whole years Paul stayed there in his own rented house and welcomed all who came to see him. He taught with boldness and without hindrance!"
>
> —Acts 28:29–31

Maybe the two year intervals were coincidental, but it seemed to resonate with me that God was pointing me to something intentional when I would read Acts.

Maybe it was simply a walk of faith and love. I may never solve the puzzle. The reason is not as important as my "Yes!"

> "Love the Lord Your God with all your heart and all your soul and with all your strength"
>
> —Luke 10:27

# CHAPTER EIGHT

# ABSOLUTE FAITH

> These commandments that I give you today are to be on your hearts. Impress them on your children. Talk about them when you sit at home and when you walk along the road, when you lie down and when you get up. Tie them as symbols on your hands and bind them on your foreheads. Write them on the doorframes on your houses and on your gates.
>
> —Deuteronomy 6:5–9

This move would give us plenty to talk about 'round our dinner table, for sure. And, I was often on my soapbox for Christ to my five kids—just ask them!

I think our creator was serious when He gave these words. And, yet, it seems we have discounted their importance and diluted their meaning; I think we have forgotten. I think the journey ahead will remind me, and I will have much to bring back and share and, yes, impress upon my own children. This journey is for me, for my children, for you, and for your children. This journey is for America. This journey is to remind America about Deuteronomy 6:5–9 and inspire families to connect to God again. How diligent have we been in following these God-given words? It's time to wake up, America. If you have been remiss—return and take the journey with me. It is evident, there is room for great improvement or I would think this generation wouldn't be so lost and wandering. Many speak with disdain about our country and are worried for future generations. It is time to take action. We can't just talk the talk. I am compelled to walk this way in faith and water my children with words from the Good Book often and to encourage others back onto the path God has uniquely chosen for us.

When did we fail as parents, as a nation? Many say it was in the early 60s when daily Bible reading was taken out the classroom. Personally, I think it was the free thinking of the 60s that lead to the open doors and the cracking of our solid foundation and eventually to the breakdown of our families. Nonetheless, we can't go back; we do the best we can where we are today, but we can return to His altar of grace, repent, and reconcile from where we are and begin again, fresh and new.

I love this scripture. When we return to God, He will return to us. He wants to always be on our minds. He is a jealous God. Perhaps Deuteronomy 6 is the best gift of wisdom we could pass on to our children so they can begin their lives in the right direction and their new families can begin in truth and wisdom with these instructions and create a solid foundation. Perhaps returning to our roots and the core beliefs God has set out for us is the beginning of healing and restoration for us all. I believe when we teach the next generation God's truth and return to Him, America will be restored. It begins with stepping into our full authority as parents, cleaning up our own lives, getting back on track, connecting as families, uniting as neighborhoods, coming together as communities, and reconnecting with America and the blessings we have; remembering, reconnecting, recommitting, repenting, reconciling, refreshing and returning to the values and commands we know to be true and right—life God's way. It's a Sweet Life, USA™; let us walk into the gift with reverence and gratitude lest it be taken from us.

My heart overflows, and if it means taking a leap of faith across America and shamelessly, transparently sharing what I have learned, I'm in. In fact, I'm all in, for God and country.

Joshua had the same calling. It wasn't until he walked into the bed of the Jordan River that the Lord dried it up and made a way. So I am guessing it will be the same for me. Once I move out of the house and show up in faith in the middle of the river bed, with rushing waters around my ankles, clinging to the hands of my children, God will show up to prove faithful and lead the way. I am confident of this. I love Him with all my heart, so I'm willing to take the leap.

God was good to prepare me so I didn't just have to leap after a fleeting thought. He began to prepare me one year earlier when I had a shaking and a shift in my life. I asked Him to show me absolute faith, but He was already preparing me to ask for that very special gift.

In *Eat, Love, Praise Him!* books three and four in the series, you can read more about my "ask and answer" to absolute faith.

But, suffice it to say, I unknowingly asked for this journey. Yep, be careful what you pray—God answers. Having been a guest at Trinity Church in Sharpsburg, GA, I heard the pastor, Mark Anthony, share an amazing testimony of boldness how he boldly approached a non-Christian warlord in India, and in awe, I simply said, "Wow, God! I want that. I want absolute faith."

Little did I know what I was asking for. But, I'm sure God was prompting me for that precise prayer so that He could bring me along this journey of faith and show me a walk of absolute faith, one that He had planned a long time ago.

He prepared me back in September 2012 when I was still knocking on doors trying to find a corporate job and doing life the American way. An hour prior to hearing from the CEO of a major hospital system, where I was up for a position as Director of Public Relations, I felt God telling me and confirming in scripture that I wasn't going to get the job, that, again, He had something else for me. Tears came, but so did acceptance. It had been a long year, scrapping through my family's financial need, sending out résumés, and praying for a position. But, no, God had something else in mind. So, I prayed for a reprieve of some kind so I could do it God's way.

He sent me my first marketing client who needed help writing a blog. That very day, I became a marketing consultant for Source Point Coaching. CEO Jack Perry wrote a large check within five minutes of meeting me. I knew it was God confirming my direction and that He had another plan and would take care of me; it was the first time in my job search I didn't have to sell myself or convince the interviewer I was skilled and competent. Jack showed up ready to hire me on the spot.

I left that meeting at Starbucks, amazed at the power of God and when I exited the door, I heard in my spirit, "Do you want to do it your way or are you ready to do it my way?"

"Your way, God, I'm all in, your way!" I exclaimed silently.

So, over the course of the next year, I served Jack's business needs for growth and supported his marketing and public relation needs. In my free time, I paralleled some of the efforts to begin developing my own brand and business efforts. It had its challenging moments, but we were a good team. And I am grateful to him for trusting me to help support him in his business goals. He was a lifeline for my family for the entire year, through the provision as well.

This was a living example of my Sweet Life philosophy—support small business and entrepreneurs because you are not making a corporation fat, you are helping a small business owner send their kids to ballet classes, softball seasons, college, and providing for their family in meaningful ways. That year of work was very meaningful.

God had His hand in the journey of Jack and Jackie all along. With every up and down, we were both closer to the moment of separation and promotion. Then after exactly one year, God said it was time, time for me to write the book He had pressed on me since 2008, and time for Jack to launch into his own realm as a national speaker. (www.sourcepointcoaching.com).

I searched online for help. I started book one and worked on it for six months, but the progress was slow and in the wrong direction, and I knew I would need a little professional help to get it done this go round. I found Ann McIndoo of *So You Want to Write a Book* and, with little thought, signed up right away for her program and her California retreat. Her program has great value, but came with a nice price tag.

The very next day, Jack called to say he had connected with a national publicist and would be launching without me; it was time to move on. I panicked. Now? Never mind we had agreed to this one-year target, I had just said yes to a $5,000 writer's retreat and now I would be without any additional income.

God was waiting, waiting for me to turn to Him in protest. His response was, "I know; go anyway."

"Go, anyway?" I was incredulous. I hope He saw a shortcut I couldn't see. Due to several events and lots of favor (you can read about in more detail in *Eat, Love, Praise Him* book two), I went to Costa Mesa, California and against all odds, spit out not one, but two books into first draft manuscripts. And, with my heartache and my surrender, God fulfilled a childhood dream of mine and made me an author—for His purpose.

The incredible part is that I had not applied for a job in over a year, not since the hospital job one year earlier. But, God had lined one up for me as National Director of Sales for a Christian Jewelry company (www.ctbling.com). It was quite the whirlwind, from author to corporate dreams coming true. Was this Cinderella's happily ever after ending? It certainly had all the trappings of a fairytale: dreams come true, a dream trip down the coast of California, and a choice position. It was a dream until a grenade was tossed into my heart and Cinderella was left standing by herself on the dance floor, 12 minutes before midnight with a broken heart and broken dreams.

Later, doing trauma recovery transcription for a documentary, I realized Cinderella had experienced over 50 traumas in her life, and this was the straw that broke the camel's back. It would take a trust walk with God on a journey of faith to recover from this one. (Read more in the *Eat, Love, Praise Him* series and in *Courage for Cinderella*.)

Yes, after a 38 month long romance, I was jilted, without warning on the dance floor New Year's Eve, 12 minutes before midnight—just like Cinderella. I was left in tatters with a shattered heart.

Two and a half months into the new job, the 64-hour work weeks, if you counted the four hour a day commutes, and a broken heart led me to walk away from the position I had long awaited, my dream position. But God knew. The money earned in that short time was exactly the amount I needed to pay off the writer's retreat. God had provided.

And, my parting words when my not-so-Prince Charming asked, "What will you do for a living, to pay your bills"?

"He has never once let me down all these years—amazing grace. I'll live on His amazing grace!" I firmly stated with tears rolling down my cheeks. I was so certain and so emphatic because God had set it up for there to be no other way and no other option, but Him.

I knew in my spirit it was going to be a trust walk, but in my flesh I thought surely I'd have to offer my help, so I earned my real estate license in the first three months following that heartbreaking day. Every day God was showing me, "No!" Then I took on a marketing client who went haywire and sucked 120 hours out of our 12-hour client agreement, leaving me without time or provision for the summer, and God was firmly saying, "No! No real estate, no marketing, no job, and no income." It was no sense to try and figure it out, until my June rent was due and the teacher was about to teach me what absolute faith looked like.

"Where will that rent come from, Lord? I have tried everything. Now, it's only you who can fix this." Sitting on the couch with my June rent now due and in the grace period, imploring God for help, He reminds me to look at my divorce decree. My alimony was for a three-year period, which had just ended with May, the month prior. "No," I thought, "that ended." I had not looked at my decree in at least a year, but God pressed my spirit, so I retrieved it and indeed, right there in black and white, it was to go through the month of June. I gulped courage and sent a text to inform my former spouse and *without any hesitation at all*, he *immediately* deposited the money, and I was quick to pay the rent with it, just like that. Now, that's a Holy Spirit moment. I was amazed, relieved, and perplexed as I marveled at that experience. What a close call! I knew God had done that. I had not looked at my decree in over a year.

That was round one. Things always happen in threes—Father, Son and Holy Spirit. All of June, there was no fruit; I had no labor and no fruit. It was time for July's rent. What would I do? Write the check. God prompted me to write the rent check, but, without any income, how would I fund it? I wrote the check out on July 1st, but played the waiting game through the afternoon of July 7th, my grace period, and was in the last hours of having to deliver it for payment. I was frantically imploring God for a solution. I went through a bunch of names in my mind in case I could think of one who might have concern for my situation. God stopped me. That name. He highlighted it saying, "Reach out now." I did.

This person was headed out for the day, but stopped *in their tracks—right in their driveway*—to write me a check to cover my rent; it was a large amount. I was astonished. How obedient and generous and surrendered that person was. I was sick with pride and fear—it was humiliating to have to ask for help. I begged for future mercy and release, but God had said, "No, do not do anything else. Witness in my name. Write the books. Trust me."

I was ever grateful someone would be so surrendered to God as to write that check for such a very large amount. I was ever grateful and indebted to God for His prompt reply. My home, our source of safety and refuge, was at stake.

And so it went, until August, the third month, and God made it clear it was time for me to walk away from my home and trust Him deeper still. It was time to make the call; it was time to pay the August rent, and I couldn't write the check. I didn't search for work or find work; He had every door closed, so how could I?

I began to share with one or two very close friends that God was telling me not to work and to move out of my house. They thought I had for sure lost it from the struggles of life and that I needed antidepressants or a man, but I knew otherwise.

I felt it clearly. So I began to witness in His name to my kids, to everyone I met at Starbucks, and to my landlords, who didn't appreciate my Good News or my lack of rent funds, but generously listened to me speak. I made no effort to resolve the issue of rent through work efforts, but I prayed, asked for prayer, and considered possible solutions every day as I diligently thinned my belongings and prepared my house. Instead, I chose to respond to my call for His Great Commission by packing and surrendering to His will. It was a stressful month of missed calls, messages, late notices, and finally, coming home to an eviction notice taped to my front door. At the last moment, the last week of August and three painful landlord meetings later, against my request not to, family intervened and paid my rent. My daughter had taped a sign on her door that read, "I'm Not Moving." My high school son was slamming doors and more than angry with me. And I stood firm that God was calling me to do this. In the flesh, it made no sense. In my spirit it resounded with His truth. It was heartbreaking.

When the August rent was paid, I didn't know what to think; my path didn't look as clear anymore. I was nervous as a cat. One day, August 29, 2014, to be exact, I remember fleeing God. I had no money in my account, and it was obvious that money could not come my way during this teaching period of grace because every ask, effort, and résumé sent returned a no. I asked God, anyway, for a small amount of confirmation, but big enough that it would be recognizable to confirm His calling for me to walk away.

"God, if this is you, let not $1, not $10, but $100 come my way today. It won't be enough to pay any bill on my table right now, but just enough to hear your confirmation." I knew that would be satisfying to me. I would know then that I was meant to move and travel with Him, even when it made no sense.

I went about my day. A friend had recently introduced me to a friend, Gregory Guenter Bennett Bligh, who had written a book, *Midlife Crisis on the Road*. And, I had, no coincidence, agreed to meet him well in advance on this same day before I knew of my journey with rent. We met at Starbucks and talked about books, being authors, and how to make it into a business to fund our deeper yearnings of wanderlust. He shared his travel experiences. How interesting it was to me that he lived my dream, sort of, to go off the grid to travel half of America for six months with his wife. It had been a soul-satisfying journey for them. He was very nice. We had the University of Georgia in common and shared fun conversation about the travels he enjoyed with his wife on this trip as well. It was a reprieve in the confusion of my journey.

But, as soon as we said goodbye, I headed home in doubt and grief and tears, pulling myself through the day of chores. In spite of his story of enjoying adventures, I couldn't see the possibility of my road trip. After all, he had a corporate payout of thousands of dollars fall into his lap, and I had next month's unpaid rent looking at me.

At the day's end, I plopped on the couch with his thick 1,070-page book on my belly, and I flipped it in my hands and put it down. There I laid out to God my sadness, my weakness, my despair, my uncertainty, but also the trust I had in Him. And then I flipped open the book again to read for a short break from piles of papers staring back at me, and tucked in the inside of that book, I discovered a crisp $100 bill. I burst into tears. How could he have known? God hears me. God sees me. God knows my need. God is faithful. I was wrecked. God had confirmed my move and my trip with my $100 prayer.

I sent the author an email, but he never replied. He was like an angel who didn't want to be recognized. That day, he was God's angel, a messenger of hope for me to follow God's prodding. I knew then, the trip across America would come to pass for me, even when it didn't look like it. 50 states by 50 years, extended to include the whole 50th year, due to life's storms (but 50 X 51 didn't sound as cool).

I had boxes to pack, an uncertain move ahead, two kids still under my roof, very limited income, and I had only been to 34 states, which meant there were 16 still to go. How on earth would I get to 50 states? How on earth would I cover 16 states in one year, let alone with no income, when it has taken me two decades to cover 34 states? I couldn't even fathom it. But, I still made a list of the states to explore the possibility. I did list all the states I had been to. I did look on the map and ponder how I might tackle the states should an opportunity present itself. Until the wee hours of the night, I dreamed what could be if I dared to dream that it would be. And, with that, I felt at least I had this dream of possibility to get me through.

September was quick to come, and while I was waiting to hear God's direction for the house and income, I began with the yard sales and frantically giving away stuff and downsizing, uncertain where God was taking us, but knowing for certain He would. He wanted me to get rid of stuff, all the materialism that had held me in bondage. The rent was now due again, and I had no clue how to respond. Things that were selling were also paying utility bills and living expenses.

It was ludicrous that I had an active real estate license, two master's degrees, and a myriad of marketable skills and God was telling me to not get a job, not even an hourly job or a side job—nothing; just depend on Him. And I walked in that obedience.

I called the movers again, had boxes delivered by friends, and had friends and my prayer group praying for me. I looked for a house to rent, and there were none on the market in this busy moving season. When there was one, it was quickly rented before I could make an offer. It was as if everything was slipping through my fingers and God was saying, "I know. Trust me."

The movers were in the truck on the way, and the last house had just been rented under me. My son started asking if we could just stay in the house until he made his Eagle Scout, which was only two months away, and finished his senior year at school, just eight months more. I began begging God for mercy. When the movers called me *from the moving truck en route to my house* and I had no understanding of where we would go or how I could make it happen, I called it off. I told them to turn around; I wasn't ready. I was nearly hyperventilating and stretched for answers; I wasn't ready.

I repented; I had lost courage and begged God for mercy to allow me until the end of the school year. I had heard God, and I trusted Him, but not enough to go this far without one clue what was on the other side. I would have to get a job and still do what God would be calling me to do, but I couldn't let my family down like that. And, none of this crazy stuff made sense. And, I was a mother; I had to be responsible for them.

Was I hearing God clearly? Was I losing my grip? It had to be God. Because my rent was now a week late and my landlord was calling for a decision. I placed an ad to sell our golf cart and it sold immediately for exactly the amount due for rent and my late fee, and I was able to pay just three days late. We live in a community with 100 miles of golf cart path. Everyone drives a golf cart. We use our golf cart every day. It was a hard choice to put it up for sale, but rent was so much more important. It was another humbling step to be without the golf cart for the remaining eight months in our house on the golf course.

After two months in a row with late fees and an hour of proselytizing, would my landlords even let me continue to stay in the house through my lease period of eight more months? It was only two payments, and I had paid the late fees. So after much discussion and very uncomfortable discussions, they agreed.

But they clearly stated that there would not be one extra day of extension—not even for senior graduation celebrations. The contract would not be extended beyond its end date. With all that commotion and creativity and grace, I had bought an eight-month extension.

Everyone breathed easier except for me. Yes, the rent was paid. Yes, we could stay. But I still was in a house I had no income to support, and God had been clear that I was not to work except on writing books and witnessing for Him. Depression set in for a few weeks, and I thought I'd lost the battle until God began showing me His plan with a new direction. Thank you for grace, for mercy, for compassion, and for redemption.

Within a week, I was given the opportunity to be a guest on a television show called "It's Up to You," with Jackie Marsh Brown. I naturally thought that would generate exposure for the books I had written and put me back in the income-generating mode, God's way. I felt release was around the corner.

Lean not on your own understanding, but God's because our plan is never His plan. There was indeed great exposure, and it was a great show. I was a natural, they said. And, the favor? That one show led me to be on television, promoting my books on Atlanta Live, another show in South Carolina, which also aired in Arkansas, as another bonus, and over and over again throughout the year. There was a lot of favor. But, zero book sales and zero paying television assignments—zero. I was still a student under God's tutelage, earning my PhD, for sure. There was no worldly financial relief anywhere.

I wanted to follow God with all my heart, and I wanted to do it His way, but there was no way I was going to accept all that chaos to churn up again in October, the month of both my son's 18th birthday and my 50th birthday. It was going to be my 50th birthday. So, in review, I moved into my home on my 40th birthday to mold and mildew and experienced a disastrous military retirement move (*The Military Family: A Casualty of War*), and now I was going to be forced out of my home on my 50th birthday? Would this be the end of a decade of storms and stench and household goods and bondage and chaos? When would relief and release ever come my way?

I determined there would be no more life celebrations stolen. No!

I went on a warrior's path of prayer through my home, calling God on every promise, reminding Him of His covenant to His children, and demanding no less for blessings for 1,000 generations and for Him to undo this mess of my life. I was looking to put down roots. I was looking for my faithful God to show up and take over. In doing, so I surrendered everything I could think of, repented, forgave, let go, and loudly let God know He could have it all.

I literally opened my back door and my front door and called every evil spirit out and invited God in and told Him to take any item in my house that He wanted, anything that was not of Him.

Recall that in September, I started downsizing, posting pictures of things for sale on Craigslist and community boards, on grocery store bulletin boards, and the like.

Within five minutes of my outcry, I got an email from a man a few hours north who wanted to buy my prized possession—my 10th anniversary wedding present that I treasured still—my ebony black, high gloss baby grand Yamaha piano. Every child had stood by that piano for pictures, for milestones, and for celebrations; I cherished it. Without missing a beat, I said yes, in spite of the fact they were offering nearly *half of its value*. Because of the timing of my warrior prayer, I knew this was God's answer and He evidently wanted me to let go of every possession I owned. It was His. So, I let it go.

I did take pictures, including the serial numbers, and even my kids were astonished I was letting it go. My younger kids were the ones to say, "Don't worry, mom, maybe we can buy it back for you for a Mother's Day or something."

It's just a possession. God is greater. It brought great joy to me over the years, and my children recognized its value. It had represented so much through the transition of my divorce and moving twice after. It represented victory in spite of storms that I got to hold on to it, but now it served a higher purpose. I thanked God for letting me hold onto it for so long. I know someone else would give it the voice it deserved.

With that cash sale, I was able to pay my rent for three months and provide a very small, but thoughtful, Christmas to my children. God was good at just the moment I needed. He had a plan to teach me, to hold me, to help me, and to provide for me. I just had to trust Him in new and unusual ways to become completely surrendered.

Come the first of the year, I thought I'd try my hand at real estate again—just to test God, I suppose. That, and there were still five more months ahead to pay rent and cover moving expenses. But, God clearly said "No!" again. When, after two months and 40 hours of showing one client houses with no avail, I backed into a retaining wall in the dark of night while showing the very last available choice in the inventory, costing $2,000 worth of damage to my nearly new car. I had to drive around with the damage for two months before God revealed to me an extended warranty policy I had purchased that covered the repair.

A lot of lessons and a great deal of patience and humility were learned during this season of faith and trust. And, for the next five months, I learned to trust God in deeper ways. I could not pursue work, but in a time of imminent need, I would meet someone, and a small, but laborious project would fall into my lap. I wasn't proud so I typed, I cleaned, I professionally organized, and I sold everything I owned that I didn't currently need. In every project, God opened my eyes to new lessons—showing me a history of weaknesses in my own life and areas I had to clean up. It was a stripping away and a cleaning out. He was cleaning out my closets, so to speak, and in between, I was physically cleaning out my closets and my garage and my house, and sometimes others, and preparing for the next part of this journey, which was still very unclear, but with a knowing I couldn't define.

These projects were rare and few and far between. God kept showing me the verse,

> "You were sold for nothing, and without money you will be redeemed"
>
> —Isaiah 52:3

It was obvious; He didn't want me to have the comfort of the green stuff our society is so caught up in pursuing and trusting in. The more I prayed for it, the bigger my demands became. So regardless of the amount of the income, I was chasing the mountain of need. Money in my hand would be like sand. It wasn't about my desire to work and produce, it was my spirit knowing that God was closing the door on money-making opportunities and telling me, "No! Don't trust the world; trust me."

It was definitely a new way of operating—in my flesh, but through the Spirit. It wasn't an easy walk, and many days, I was left in a puddle of tears asking God to show me why, heal me, deliver me, and clean my family tree, only soon to find peace in my prayers and beg for forgiveness of my unbelief. God's way is never the easy way, but it's always the better way and for His greater purpose. So what that I was caught up in this story and my children had to hear "No!" often, or that I had to take a job or two and balance school and sports, or give up sports to take on a job to help with their own demands. I was walking a faith walk and leaving a legacy far greater than the material things we were chasing for temporary satisfaction. It wasn't always easy to keep everyone's temperament even and understanding through the long journey, but overall, the kids and I had lots of valuable conversations, and I'd say they are each pretty well grounded—college graduates or students, leaders, volunteers, holding one or two jobs, saving, and giving. Thanks, God, for that life lesson for us all.

# CHAPTER NINE

# CROSSING THE JORDAN

In March, my mother lost her husband, and I flew home to help her get on her feet. They were married six years; the happiest she had ever been, she said. It was true love and joy for her. After a week of my extended stay, I had to get back to juggle more bills and income for my own household. In spite of my storms, there was always time to serve, love, help others, and encourage them in their storm, especially my mother. The Bible says honor your mother and your father. This was our season to give back.

This one was the tipping point, I suppose. It had been a long year of stress and the unknown, of God's unexplainable faithfulness and my unexplainable situation. I began to put on weight rapidly and was generally starting to weaken. In April I went down for the count—three weeks fighting something that I couldn't bounce back from, and to my disappointment, I didn't lose an ounce. Who does not lose weight after three weeks of crackers and soup? It was a struggle to get out of bed and after a week or so of recovery, still difficult to find my energy again. It swallowed up my time of preparation for the move and graduation, and May hit me like a ton of bricks. The sickness was just another way God wanted me to be totally dependent on Him, I suppose. I was grateful for my health after that episode and knew even more how dependent on Him I am. I am sure it served to punctuate that there was no question that the provision and the move had to come about from Him—not by my strength or wisdom, but from His might and power and Spirit, according to His word.

I put up posters in the dining room, outlining the many tasks that had to be done to successfully finish the school year, graduate my senior, prepare, pack, and move in time, as agreed. All the while, I was posting things for sale online, identifying what I could sell, shuffling things to charity drop-off sites and just flying by the seat of my pants to make everything function properly.

I gingerly shared with a good friend and my children that I thought it was time for my RV trip across America—the one the kids refused to go on when they were young, but the one I always wanted to go on. My friend was all for it, knowing, too, the Lord was calling me. My kids laughed half-heartedly, not wanting to encourage me any more with that crazy thought. They could only see our life from the inside, without means, selling everything to stay afloat; they could only see the impossible the world had posed.

But, God had shown me and told me these things were possible (Mark 9:23). And, I chose to believe Him.

So the journey began. Obedience brings blessing is what I have read in the Word. In the midst of my storm, in the middle of packing and the pending move out hour, I stopped to meet an obligation to take minutes at a prayer meeting of an International minister Miguel Escobar of Terra Globe Ministries. God is good and blessed that offering of service and time. Near the end of the meeting, Pastor Miguel asked me to share a few minutes of my story. I first talked about the supernatural walk God had me on and the pressing to travel across America and write this book. Then, he tossed a small wicker basket on the table and stated very matter-of-factly, "We take up a love offering, this, for our Sister Jacqueline. We encourage her on her journey."

It was the first time I had ever received a love offering and encouragement for my journey. How blessed I was, but it was more than just the few hundred dollars collected, a seed that would bring a good harvest to get me moving as God's witness; it was the seed to confirm to me that God is my provider and He would be my provider for this journey when it seemed there was no way. That gesture would give me strength in the days ahead when I would face other moments of financial need.

I'm so glad that I took a break from the pressing need of my packing to serve and meet someone else's pressing need. I'm so grateful God didn't let me miss that blessing. And, grateful to those who said yes to His ask, to toss a $20 bill or a blessing of some kind in the basket on my behalf. That first seed would give me the courage to keep asking God for His provision every step of this crazy journey.

And, with our things packed up and stored away in four different storage units, at two different facilities, and a good night's sleep, I knew it was time to walk into the Jordan River and pray the Lord would show up, in spite of what it looked like in my flesh.

# CHAPTER TEN
# THE ADVENTURE BEGINS

June 1st, I frantically searched the internet and the Delta app on my phone for flights to Minnesota, and nothing looked good; they were all overbooked and oversold. The flights were overloaded, and to boot, they routed through a busy airport leaving greater risk for not getting on a connecting flight. My daughter's anxiety was rising, and though she supported what I was doing and kind of, sort of, understood what was happening, she wasn't completely on board to be without her momma on top of having no home of our own for her entire summer break, no less.

The pressure was mounting as I searched for answers and a reasonable plan for the days ahead. I knew, with a small degree of certainty, I had a loose plan in place. I knew she would be safe and happy at her friend's house and on the one or two excursions already planned for her to enjoy with friends. I knew my son would soon be on his way to the beach with a friend's family and would return with the hospitality of another friend's guest room to lay his head. While it looked like chaos, I knew there was a plan of sorts in place, and like every summer before, it would work out with the help of friends and summer excursions, with summer sleepovers and days spent occupied with friends; this was nothing extraordinary, I assured myself best I could.

In the flesh, it did look like chaos, but in the spirit, I knew it was a sound plan—God had prepared the way and worked out our five star accommodations ahead of time. While tenuous, like a teeter totter once balanced, it brings great fun. If just one event didn't go as planned, it could topple the other, but it could play out just as I kept repeating it in my head—with me in Minnesota and trusting God for every blessing, and another typical summer for our family. That settled, I allowed myself to get back to the logistics of planning.

With so many roadblocks, I stopped searching for two or eventually, even one seat on the flight. Non-revenue travel in the summer was like playing Russian roulette, and I couldn't afford to get stuck in any airports or stalled in the ground covered; summer was only here for a short time, and I had one chance to carry out this calling in the allotted days of summer. So, what were my options? I looked at a Rand McNally Pocket Road Atlas, what would soon become my constant companion, and determined St. Louis, Missouri would be a good mid-point drive and a possible airport connection to pick up a flight for the longer half of the trip to Minnesota. Minnesota was the furthest northern point of the trip. If only I had been able to make it there a previous summer. Now, I had to shoot for it come car or plane.

With every change, my daughter's countenance did as well, and her certainty of going to her friend's for a week while I was away waffled. Her emotions became as unsteady as my flight plan, and I realized then that this was the opening I had been wanting all along—an opportunity for her to come with me, at least part of it, to enjoy the travel, to see that her momma would be safe, to see what it looked like when you lead a Holy Spirit life. God waited until the very last minute—His perfect time—so that Kellie would come to terms with the opportunity on her own, not forced.

From the beginning, she was steadfast and adamant, "I'm not going! I don't want to be stuffed in a car for 1,000 miles. I don't care what you are doing, but I'm not being called to do that." And, the closer it got, "I don't want to go to my friend's for a whole week. I don't want you to leave me. I want to go to Mall of America; just get me there and not all the rest of the long road trip." I laughed. This was a package deal, honey, and I was so not the captain of this trip!

With that nearly resolved, I researched a rental car from Peachtree City to the St. Louis Airport, and due to the drop-off fee, which was crazy expensive, I knew I was driving my own car. I was grateful for the Nissan Altima I had purchased just one year earlier, by God's grace and prompting, and the fact that it got up to 38 mpg on the highway. I guess God knew I would be putting a lot of mileage on my car; it would make for an economical ride, at least. I loved driving, and I loved my ride, which was a good thing because I was going to have plenty of both.

I still tentatively hoped to drive to the St. Louis Airport and leave my vehicle for the week in extended parking and fly to Minnesota, but as it would turn out, that was not meant to be. Kellie and I would experience the entire week together—all five days and 2,500 miles, by car—my car—and watch God show up with incredible presence.

What a loss it would have been had I pushed my own agenda, flown to Minnesota and left Kellie in Georgia. She would have missed out on so much fun and so many blessings. God had a much better plan all along and plenty of blessings for both mother and daughter on this incredible journey. This is exactly why I encourage families to make the commitment to travel America, to reconnect, to engage, to spend valuable time together bonding, exploring and enjoying the amazing, abundant blessings God has given us. That's exactly why I say, "It's a Sweet Life, USA." We are one blessed country.

We could be living in a dry desert—instead, we are blessed with a diverse landscape. With one brush of the Master's hand, we have beaches, mountains, prairies, and coastlines to enjoy. We have a beautiful America to explore and discover and take delight in. We are entrusted to honor it and enjoy it and give thanks for it.

Get going, solo or with family or friends. Make memories. Discover America; appreciate it and fall in love with it all over again.

This land is your land, this land is my land
From California to the New York Island
From the Redwood Forest to the Gulf Stream waters
This land was made for you and me.

A popular and familiar folk song written by Woody Guthrie.

# CHAPTER ELEVEN

# THE SEVEN YEAR JOURNEY

• MISSOURI • IOWA • MINNESOTA • WISCONSIN

Off on an adventure, unsure of our route, but knowing that God was in control and at the helm would make for an exciting road trip for sure. My daughter was uncertain, but I could read her reluctant satisfaction that she had come along to see what a walk of faith and this journey was all about. She could see it now with her own eyes.

We headed to Chattanooga, an easy two and a half hour's drive. I am certain I poured out my witness the first hour and a half, explaining my walk, what we might encounter on our journey, and how God might use it. My daughter was full and not at all thirsty for more, I might add. When the eye rolling became intense, I was interrupted by a phone call from a sweet friend who had a litany of "why" questions for me and asked me how could I be doing this and not looking for work. I don't blame her. It appeared that I was running away from life, but I knew in my spirit, I was being led and running into the life my heavenly Father had for me.

I patiently answered her questions for about a half hour and then politely cut the interrogation off. Jesus knew the truth of my convictions, and I was compelled to follow Him, regardless of what others might wonder or assume. We had, with good timing, arrived at our destination. The first stop: fun, designed especially for my daughter. I had wanted to take the kids to Ruby Falls and Rock City many times before, but never could get the finances and the free time to line up between school, sports, and activities with friends.

I determined before leaving town that this trip would include fun and refreshment for Kellie and me after the burden of the move, as well as patriotic and spiritual research for this next book, and then I would make room for whatever else I felt I was being led to in the moment. I wanted to be a good steward of the time and money God had afforded us and also make it so much more meaningful than touching toes in every state. I wanted to experience, explore, enjoy, connect, refresh, and remember. I wanted to make memories with Kellie and reward her for her part in this journey. I wanted it to be as meaningful as possible to me, this gift God was placing before me.

It seems Ruby Falls was part of the plan in God's will too because it was there I would receive confirmation of the next leg of my journey and, at the same time, discover the best barbecue restaurant in the South. Oh, He knows how I love to eat good food, and the South certainly knows how to deliver. Don't worry, I'll share more ahead.

Ruby Falls was an amazing underground journey, where we

were guided on a group tour, up close and personal with geological wonders of rocks and minerals in a cavernous maze, leading to the most amazing reward of an underground waterfall. God always leads me to a surprise encounter, and waterfalls are one of my favorites.

As we were enjoying the walk and the wonders of the rocks and their formations, I was also praying, thanking God for this experience and for reprieve. In spite of all the turmoil and disruption, there was this one little period of time and unique experience where Kellie could just be a kid and have the pleasure of a summer vacation and special time with just her and me, unfettered and unbothered by life and bills and struggles. God blesses us so, and I was grateful.

My thoughts did intermittently trail off as I wondered what our travel schedule would really look like and what answer I would give when Kellie asked what destination was next. Where were we really going? I knew enough to break the states into the achievable travel goals, a few at a time. I knew that this leg would include Missouri, Iowa, Minnesota, and Wisconsin—four of the 16 states I had left to travel to in order to make my "50 X 50" goal—they were a drivable swoop from north to east to south. And then, once at the tip of the North American continent, I would have to make the trek back south through Illinois, Kentucky, and Tennessee in order to get back home. Though I had been to these states before, and even lived in Tennessee twice, we still had to drive through them to get back to Peachtree City.

As I was drifting off in thought, the sound of the tour guide's voice brought me back. How long had I been lost in thought, again? She was spitting out a ton of interesting facts, and I found myself wishing we lived closer so my daughter could be saturated with all this science and information on a regular basis.

As I stood in line within the group, I turned to the left and then the right, smiling and acknowledging the guests on either side of me, and never meeting a stranger, I jumped right into a chatty conversation as we made our way to the next information point. I think I commented on the sweatshirt one of the guests was wearing. When I felt the warmth and knew they were receptive to conversation, I asked where each was from—Peachtree City to my left and Portland, Oregon to my right. After my experience at the car wash in town yesterday, this just confirmed that the next leg of my journey would take me from Peachtree City to Portland, Oregon. With that said and done, I smiled with God and relaxed into the present moment, finally able to fully enjoy the rest of the tour with my daughter. God was the tour guide of this trip, and He would use indicators that made sense to me to guide me along.

The waterfall was mesmerizing. It was a 145-foot drop of rushing, almost magical, water. God's creations are soul stirring. It's breathtaking and surprising and delightful and makes me want to drink in so much more of our American landscape.

The entire experience was incredible: the rushing sound, the pure surprise of it all these hundreds of feet below the earth's surface, and the sheer surprise that Kellie and I were standing there after our monumental move and future uncertainty. It was such a God-moment for me. Why do we fear anything in this world when we know without a shadow of a doubt there is a God and He loves us and cares for us and showers favor on us, and, best of all, that He is in control even when it seems our life is out of control? When we see with our eyes the incredible majesty of His creation—even in the secret places—how can we doubt still? A person's soul is changed on a journey across America, and for us, our journey was just beginning.

On the return trip out of the cave, Kellie was quick to the front of the line to be the line leader, under the tour guide's wing. It was satisfying to see her soak everything up like a sponge. Meanwhile, I did my best to be an investigative reporter without being disruptive. With every pause and moment of observation, I found a way to ask questions. This resulted in the tour guide sharing information that only a local could know. She told me of a Christian group of sisters and offered insight for a great barbecue restaurant, which I knew would be our next stop. It pays to stand at the front of the line and make small talk with the tour guide.

Following the tour, we enjoyed a massive gift shop, where I didn't dare to spend money on a souvenir or more "stuff," but where we panned for gold in a running stream and enjoyed an ice cream on the patio. We browsed over the rows and rows of collectibles and curios. Ruby Falls was a worthwhile stop and a beautiful start to this trip and, with the ice cream to punctuate it, a sweet experience for mother and daughter. God is good to us, even in the midst of life's storms, and this kickoff let me know there would be more sweet experiences ahead.

Next stop: barbecue for dinner.

We were a little leery. You never know what you are going to find in a back road barbecue restaurant, especially one that was built of wood with a simple screen porch door. The gravel parking lot crunched under my car tires, and Kellie and I both looked at each other as if silently asking, "Should we risk it?" I was hungry and besides, the Ruby Fall's guide told me it was not to be missed, so we rolled our eyes, laughed at our predicament, and ventured into The Hickory Pitt Bar B Que in Ringgold, TN. We were the only guests—not very reassuring, but it was a little early for dinner; we must have just been the first guests, so we took a chance and, boy, how we were rewarded.

Let me tell you, be careful before judging a book by its cover or a BBQ joint by its screen door and empty parking lot. Oh. My. Goodness. It was good! Pulled pork sandwich and barbecue brisket plates with fried okra, beans and fixings were more than delightful. The piquant sweetness of the brown sugar sauce and the tender, smoky meat led me to know we had made the right stop.

With full tummies and satisfied spirits, we drove in the direction of St. Louis, Missouri, spewing gravel rock from under our tires as we pulled away. We drove through this small town, a hint of Americana past and turned left in front of the office of the hometown weekly paper, *The Gazette*. Having started as a journalist for the *Gulf Shores Islander* weekly paper in Gulf Shores, AL, the sight of this fading piece of history put a Cheshire grin on my face. It was getting late, and I was apprehensive about heading to an unknown city such as St. Louis, but God had protected me on many trips before, so I reassured myself with Psalm 91:4 and the promise of His covering.

Eventually, the chatter came to a simmer, and my daughter fell asleep in the passenger seat next to me. I missed her company as I maneuvered the ever-curving, mountainous roads. But, I am never really alone. While I drive, I play country or spiritual music low in the background and seize the opportunity to carry a never-ending prayer conversation with Jesus. Jesus is my traveling companion;

it is so much better than traveling solo. I am sure I thanked Him and fleeced Him 100 times in that conversation. I was so grateful for what was behind me, from the move to the storage units to the provision and the barbecue dinner, and I was fleecing Him in so many ways to make sure my car was headed in the right direction—His direction.

I had no idea where we were staying this very first stop, so I simply put Downtown St. Louis into the GPS. At the dinner stop, I was intermittently checking the Delta flights and seat capacity for stand-by passengers to Minneapolis International and looking for possible hotels and pricing that fit my tight budget in St. Louis. I had to check mileage to the airport and costs and lots of details to make a good decision—thank goodness for Google!

With overbooked flights to both Minneapolis, MN and the nearest airport in Wisconsin, I was at a decision crossroads. Would I make the very, very, long drive to Minnesota, just to get to The Mall of America, which just happened to be on my state list? Was it really that important? I reminded myself of the goal—50 X 50. How likely was it that I had intentions to be on the flight to Minnesota seven years earlier when I started on the spiritual journey of faith, starting with my Christ Renews His Parish (CRHP) retreat weekend at my church? And here I was starting again, only working on the ending of this journey—with Minnesota, Mall of America as my first destination. God has a way of tying all the ends together.

Mall of America was Kellie's one reward for being my traveling companion for this many miles. No, turning around was not an option. Turn around or plunge ahead? I told God I was "all in" a long time ago, so it appeared then I would be driving the entire

2,500 mile trip and, with that, Kellie would be with me every mile. Time to plunge ahead!

I researched rental cars quickly, not wanting to run my new Altima into the ground, but, again, the drop-off fee made it unreasonable on my modest travel budget. It was clear at this juncture, still, the two of us, mother and daughter, would be making this spiritual journey together on the open road.

For a moment, I began to teeter. Maybe I was being too goal-focused, too determined to "just do it." Maybe I should turn back. It sure was a shorter distance to drive back to Peachtree City than to push ahead to Minnesota. Was that even drive-able? What an unfathomable distance. Who drives that? "Are you sure, God? Is this you or me?" Oh, the torment of our flesh when God is trying to teach us to operate out of our spirit.

Kellie must have sensed my angst and the quick snap of the dragon tail turns because she started stretching and opened her eyes enough to check on me. She was my little guardian, always checking in on me.

I smiled at her cat stretch and gave her a moment to become aware, but then I was quick to get her reassurance.

"Kellie, I'm starting to feel as if we should go back and give up," I actually said this out loud, semi-defeated, unsure of my judgment in all that was happening.

"I feel I should go home and get a job." She looked at me, with a glint of hope in her eye that clearly told me she deeply hoped I knew what I was doing. And, then, as quick as I said it, I recanted. "No. If God wanted me to have a job, He could get me a job." And, just like that, it was resolved and settled, and I had peace in my spirit. In doing so, Kellie saw my resolve to follow God; any hopes she had of us turning around and her waking up in her own bed again were gone. And, not a minute later, my cell phone rang.

"Hello. This is Mr. Jones from the XYZ Staffing Services Human Resources Department, is this Jacqueline Arnold?"

"Yes, it is," I replied with a quizzical slant in my voice, a creeping smile and a side glance to my daughter that indicated something God-size crazy was happening.

"Did you apply for the Executive Director position of the (XYZ) Chamber of Commerce?"

Flabbergasted, I gushed, "Yes, I did." Quickly searching my memory, mentally sorting files of tasks I had performed and papers I had emailed, I recalled I had submitted my résumé for this position at least *eight* months earlier. "But, do you mean the Executive Director position of the Chamber of Commerce that I applied for last fall?"

"Yes, that's the one," The HR representative stated back. "The position was held up and we haven't filled it yet. I've been looking at your résumé and your experiences, and we would very much like to interview you for this position. Can you be available June 20th for an interview?"

My heart raced, calendar pages flipped through my mind. June 20th? I wasn't even sure what today was, what state I would be in, how I would find a copy of my résumé, or appropriate interview attire. So many questions flooded my mind as I tried to prepare a response. "Yes, of course, June 20th would be perfect," I replied calm as a cucumber. "How do you feel about Skype for an interview?" According to my loose plan, I would be somewhere about South Dakota about then, too far to get back to South Georgia for a one hour interview. "I just did a Spark Hire interview online and never went onsite for an interview." He was very hesitant and we penciled it in, but I knew he wasn't especially keen on the idea, and I would have to vet out my trip more thoroughly and see how I could possibly get through this adventure and be back in town on that precise date, all the while ever aware of the financial limitations to achieve this. We finished the conversation, and I squealed with both delight and sheer amazement. Kellie was laughing and smiling and rolling her eyes all at the same time.

"Did you just hear that?" I couldn't emphasize the God-timing enough. I had just said, "If God wanted to give me a job, He would," and right then the phone rings with a job interview from not just any position, but an Executive Director position I had applied for almost nine months ago. Yes, indeed, if God wanted me to get a job, He could arrange it, and He didn't need me to do it! I was astounded by my Father's love and power, and I was so thrilled to have my youngest daughter as a witness to that.

"But, you know, I probably won't get that job, Kellie," reality was settling back in, "God has already confirmed to me I won't be getting a job; I'm to do this trip and write this book. But, the point is, He could if it was His will, and look how He showed us exactly that. He is so faithful; we never have to doubt."

At 14 years of age, she had just witnessed firsthand God's faithfulness and divine connection in a powerful way that words alone would never have conveyed. That was definitely one for the books. This trip was an adventure and so much more, and we were barely out of the South.

Throughout the trip, I could see how God set it up perfectly for her to experience my journey, to experience America, and to be the beacon of light for the next generation. And, this was just one example for her to bear witness. God is a God of perfect planning. He is a master of details. I could not have asked for a greater gift from all the hard work and fear of moving. But I did receive this gift of adventure and travel in double portion, not just for myself, but for my daughter, a representative of both my children—my family—and the next generation. *God is so good.*

We hummed along in silence and soft music for a good distance before I recalled we still didn't have a definite destination or accommodations for the night, and it was nearly dusk. With her assistance, we started Googling Kayak.com and Marriott.com and looking for a hotel at a good price. I landed on a Marriott, one of my preferred brands, and she dialed the 1-800 number and handed me the phone. The operator was so nice, his joy spilled over the phone. I explained my need for accommodations, my uncertainty of the best location. Soon it became clear the reservationist was another heavenly appointment.

Our conversation turned to our current locations. He was in Orlando, which gave me a moment to brag about my two children who attend college in Orlando, and soon we both became unusually chatty. He just returned from a spiritual retreat in Orlando, so I began witnessing about my journey and the books I write. He continued to share and witness, and it was, without a doubt, obvious to Kellie and me how big our God is and how small our world is. No matter where we are, God is in control of it all.

Throughout the entire conversation, it was obvious God brought us together through a 1-800 number in order to encourage, share, and connect us on our journeys. I did, eventually, manage to get a confirmed reservation for an overnight accommodation and a few other blessings from that call, and Kellie, the tweenager, soaked it all up with thirsty wonder. It was one more of God's confirming winks.

I put the address of the hotel in the GPS, and she fell deep asleep this time, satisfied her mother had a plan and no longer needed her assistance. I crossed the state line from Tennessee into Missouri. "Yeah, a new state! One down, 15 to go," I cheered the victory alone, as Kellie slept. Maybe it was possible. It didn't seem reasonable, but I remember, with God *all* things are possible, and I try not to reason through it, just diligently drive ahead, using my GPS, my loose travel plan and the lead of the Holy Spirit in my gut, determined to follow Him for as long and as far as I can.

I came back from my prayer, night-time driving trance and glanced down at the GPS, only to realize it has gone off the satellite and I am now driving in a new state, new territory, in the dark of night, off grid. I gulp. Well, I'll have to do it the old-fashioned way, with road signs and driving intuition; surely, it will snap back into action by the time I reach downtown, a major area. I was wrong. That was a bold move, to keep driving without good directions or a clear idea of my destination. I saw billboards and directional signs and took a chance at an exit toward downtown and what I hoped would be the location of our hotel. Driving through an urban area, past plenty of apartments, dark city parks, where the side streets narrowed and the traffic thinned and those walking the street looked a little questionable, I began to doubt my trusty GPS and intuition and called out to God for courage and covering. I made a turn down a busier street, only to come to a stoplight in the dark of night. A dark purple Charger, with super tricked-out wheels and lights and such pulled up next to me, revved its motor and approached with every obvious intent to look into my car, over at my daughter and I. The bright streetlights caused my daughter to wake up, blink, stretch, and ask where we were. I smiled and tried to appear calm so as not to startle her. "Honey, I'm not really sure, the GPS is out and I am a bit uncertain, but just act normal. And whatever you do, don't make eye contact with the driver next to us."

We made it through the light only to pass a fenced, abandoned lot and to get stopped again at the next light. She had finished stretching like a cat and sat at full attention, laughing at our circumstances, which was helpful to relieve the anxiety. At the corner gas station to the left, an unusual assortment of late night guests were walking about and conferring with one another; another car backfired from a dirty muffler. I prayed hard, slightly murmured to the red light to turn and make way for me. And, when it did, I made a quick U-turn to retrace our steps and at least get back on the interstate. As I did this, a green sign that welcomed us to the city limit came into sight. It was the town that made news headlines for rioting and racial tensions just last summer. And my teenage daughter and I had found our way to the very center of that very town at 1:30 a.m., on the very first leg of our journey. What in the world was I thinking? "Good Lord, help me out of this and keep me from moments like this again." It was good history lesson, I suppose, a good lesson on navigation and a knowing that I had nothing to fear, in spite of the wrong turn, as God had His eye on us. My heart was sad for this town, and I prayed. I was sad that I even felt like this anywhere in America. But, true enough, I likely wouldn't have felt at ease in any town in the middle of the night, lost and without a helpmate to redirect me. Yet another reason I yearn for the Spirit of America, that we can return to a day of safe travels anywhere and a day when peace is restored everywhere in America.

As I made reentry on the interstate and regained my focus, the GPS engaged and showed me I had only missed our hotel by one exit. We were now about 20 miles from our destination, retracing our path on the interstate, but in the opposite direction. The hotel was across from the airport and was a convention-size Renaissance hotel. It was beautiful and a welcome sight for two weary travelers.

The price was right, the décor was decadent, the beds were fluffy and lush, and we both felt like princesses in the palace. Wow. God has a way of pulling me through and treating me like royalty! I didn't feel very royal schlepping a ton of luggage and trying to pack and repack it so we had just the right attire for the direction of our trip; I repacked it for ease in and out of hotels throughout the week.

The next morning I was still Googling and taking notes and tentatively coming up with a plan. I didn't want to miss anything, and yet, I was anxious to get to our Minnesota destination because it seemed so far away and because the goal seemed to get there, tag base and head south. I was still pretty unclear on what I was doing, but I knew in my spirit so strongly that I was to get through all the rest of the states to complete my 50 X 50 trip, and God would guide me through.

How many times had I talked about this trip, supposing I would be in an RV with all my children in tow exploring America? I had delayed the departure and now, in spite of low funding, was going to make it. But instead of a family-packed RV, I upgraded to hotels and only one child in tow; too bad the other kids missed out on this great adventure. I tried to entice them, but sometimes you can't get teenagers to budge—just watch the movie *RV!* That's great for a laugh. I was still going, just an adjustment to the original vision. This trip, I was going on angel's wings and the leading of the Spirit—by car, by plane, and by foot.

# CHAPTER TWELVE

# GOD'S ROAD MAP

After a sumptuous, restful sleep, we packed up without sleeping in and called for a bellman. It was a God appointment, really. We spoke and witnessed non-stop all the way to the beautiful lobby where I was feeling like a celebrity by his amazement at my story and the tour of this golden palace of a hotel. It turns out he was a pastor in his off-time and loved my God-calling story to travel across America for patriotic and spiritual revival. I was full before I even had breakfast and settled in to my car.

Anxious to make our destination or not, I wasn't going to leave without taking in a few of the important sites of St. Louis, Mo. Our first stop was across the bridge and to a walkable, artsy section in the Central West End. We spotted a French bistro, Crepes: etc., that looked inviting due to its sidewalk seating and foot traffic for entertainment. What an excellent choice! With a Swiss omelet in a folded crepe for me and crepes Benedict in a hot iron skillet for Kellie, it was hard to not be completely satisfied under the warm sun. To find crepes was a sheer delight for us as they are a particular favorite of mine.

A chalkboard inside posted a favorite quote and was perfect for my focus on life that I explain in *Eat, Love, Praise Him*!

> "Nothing would be more tiresome than eating and drinking if God had not made them a pleasure as well as a necessity."
>
> —Voltaire

And, oh, how I delight in good food.

If we are going to eat, anyway, we may take stride to partake in exceptional food—food that surprises our eyes and delights our palate, food that is soul satisfying and nourishing to our body. After all, God gave us a bountiful harvest to enjoy, the fruit of our soil and the reward of our land. A few extra moments and an intentional choice to eat well and eat healthy, makes life all the more delightful and satisfying.

Eat well, love one another and the sweet life you have been blessed with, and praise Him in all things from eating to traveling to working to life!

Crepes—not talking low calorie, but healthy—are good for the palate, mind, spirit, and body. These crepes and this eating experience fulfilled that for me. God is good, and I find crepes are too. I was practically singing after that morning experience as we headed downtown to drive by the landmark sights of this town.

Not up for a great deal of sightseeing, but not wanting to miss out, we did a drive by tour of St. Louis. We took photos of the popular Busch Stadium, home of the St. Louis Cardinals, the capitol building, and of course, the popular Gateway arches. They were undergoing renovation, and a visit across the arches would have entailed parking at a distance, making quite a trek, skirting past scaffolding, and was more than we were up for. Yep, the arches looked great from the comfort of our car. Since they are 630 feet tall, we were able to snap a few pictures from the car. The gateway to the west, it was thrilling to know I was finally experiencing that trek I had long dreamed of.

I even managed a picture of the Edward Jones Dome at America's Center to send to a friend who is a local representative for Edward Jones in Peachtree City, a multi-purpose dome, maybe not a major site, but it kept me connected to home, even without one, to my friends back "in the bubble."

Overall, it was an exciting start to our adventure and a royal experience, but St. Louis didn't really leave a profound impression on me, what with the excessive traffic, construction, and lots of concrete buildings. I am sure if I had come for just a game or a weekend of fun, it would have opened up to reveal a great time, but as I was anxious to be on my way and head north; I was underwhelmed by the traffic and construction of this popular city. It did seem concentrically located and walkable and, again, would probably offer great weekend fun on a return trip; we were simply ready to drive on and make headway to our primary destination: Bloomington, MN.

So east we headed, looking for Highway 80 to Iowa, but I think we managed to turn on to the back road, Highway 34. Iowa—what would be my purpose or destination there? Nothing monumental seemed to stand out. I never really dreamed of going to Iowa—New York, California, Colorado, but not Iowa. All I could think of were flat views and cornfields. I couldn't just drive through, though. For the state to count as one of the fifty, I had to have a destination, enjoy food, a purpose, a taste of and flair for said state and have a conversation or two with the locals. Airport touchdowns didn't count in my book. My journey had to cover a bit of eat, love and praise Him kind of experiences—food, the sweet life, and connecting with His presence.

Iowa was going to challenge that model, or so I thought. While, yes, there were unending cornfields and miles of desolate highway roads that I hope never to cover by car again, Iowa provided a few experiences, a definite patriotic vibe, and surprising sweet food.

I am certain Kellie and I took a wrong turn to a back highway, and surely, there was an alternate route from Missouri through Iowa to Minnesota, our destination, that might have been more direct because our road seemed unending, but we didn't find it. Instead, we had the pleasure of miles upon miles of two-lane country highway, with very little opposing traffic—that part was good, at least.

I kept a close eye on my gas gauge and squirmed in my seat from the boredom. Where would we refuel? Very sparingly, we would find a Philips 66 type old-fashioned gas station, and when we found a more modern food and gas store, it was in the nick of time for a restroom break. Miles upon miles of witnessing to Kellie turned to silence, then to stupid jokes and boredom, and then silliness set in the further we got. There was a good hour of agonizing endurance broken up by a few stop signs—yes, on the highways, leading to a different meandering route and more miles of farmland. A random hay roll, spray painted red, white, and blue, with a soldier scarecrow wearing camouflage-stuffed pants, always brought a smile to my spirit and confidence that across America we truly are united, even when the news reports don't seem to convey that.

It was these moments that I paused to pray for our farmers and their hard work and endurance. It was in these moments I thanked God for America, the heartland, and His bountiful harvest. It was in Iowa I felt close to the heartbeat of America, where everyday people worked the land so we could be well fed. There's a certain amount of pride in that. I blessed them as I passed. I blessed the work of their hands. And, I was blessed in return.

The roads were monotonous, and we were pressed to drive on, even at the expense of passing the one tourist attraction along the route, was it the Lewis and Clark Interpretive Center or something about literature? I only recall that I wished I had stopped; I know it would have been informative and interesting, but making headway north was much more satisfying at the moment. Sorry, Iowa, I am sure it is a great contribution to history and satisfying to tourists, but I just couldn't do it this go-round.

Kellie helped me search bed and breakfasts on the internet when the GPS would communicate with the satellite, which was very sporadic. We called a few, but found only one with vacancy. We plugged it into the GPS, grateful for an evening destination.

It was still quite a distance before we turned onto the major highway headed north, passing through Iowa City and Cedar Rapids. Our anticipation soon turned to skepticism when we turned off the highway near Cedar Rapids and weaved in and out of neighborhoods, rounded the bends of a very dense and worn-down apartment complex, and turned onto the grounds, just beyond the wire fencing. Not a good feeling. Kellie immediately begins claiming there is no way she was staying there, even if "it's priced just right and past supper time and they had a confirmed vacancy." I determine that the GPS is wrong again and make a sweeping U-turn, only to catch the two-story stucco building at the bottom of the hill, looking too much like an inn out of an Alfred Hitchcock movie. We begin laughing our heads off, speculating on the rooms and experience we might have had and high-tailed it out of there. I'm sure it was lovely. I'm sure it was historic. We were both sure it was not for us.

We headed past Marion (my Dad's middle name!) and landed in Blackhawk County (the aircraft my former spouse used to fly for the Army). I took that as a sign we were meant to be here to unwind part of my past.

So what that it was 6:30 at night and we had no reservations? God always had a place for us to lay our head. We just had to keep driving, knowing that something would soon feel right and prevail. Kellie kept searching towns ahead, managing the map book, Google, and unfamiliar destinations on the map. I directed her just past a smaller town, Cedar Falls, assuming there might be greater availability with less tourist interest, and the gander paid off. We landed a hotel for about $100 that was quite satisfactory and far less eerie feeling. They directed us to a restaurant area downtown with a college feel.

We walked up and down the sidewalk, enjoying the shops and considered all the restaurant choices. They were a little pricey, but it was too late to find another option. We were drawn to a newer one that had just opened. We were careful about our selections and had a surprisingly good experience—food, service and folks. It was a long day of driving, we had missed the one landmark on the map, and had not experienced anything eventful in Iowa, but we left with a satisfaction that the heartland of America was part of us, part of the hard-working, big-hearted America that we hoped to find and experience. State number 36, done (June 5, 2015). June 5 was my mother and father's wedding anniversary—odd how the coincidences keep lining up.

We were up early and headed to Bloomington, Minnesota, state number 37 and our target destination of Mall of America. This little excursion was only delayed by seven years. I envisioned floors and floors of stores, an ice-skating rink and roller coaster center stage. As the largest mall in America, touting 520 shops, it smelled of hours and hours of shopping satisfaction.

We got an early start, not wanting to waste one minute of opportunity. The mall was extremely approachable, the parking garage easily accessible, and the red, white, and blue logo design especially thrilling. I expected to be overwhelmed. When shopping at Atlantic Station or even Lenox Mall in Atlanta, GA, traffic could be a bear and discourage a day of shopping, so for this to be America's largest mall, I was pleasantly surprised.

Kellie and I had a typical, fun-loving mother/daughter day of shopping in this fabulous establishment. My first find was America and I was quick to snap a photo of the store sign. We wandered, half-dazed, and passed things like Bubble tea, which caught our attention because our little town is known as "the bubble" and my company motto is "It's a Sweet Life in the Bubble." I immediately thought how our "little bubblers" would drink up bubble tea, but we kept moving. Kellie brought me into a little surf shop and scooped up a pair of beach flip-flops on sale for a few bucks. I stopped and took a photo at a store or two (my favorite was a store that had the logo *What's Your Dream?* printed on a window of aerobic wear). Well, obviously, here I was standing in this dream of a mall, and in spite of not having a home, a husband or a job, I was *living* my dream at Mall of America, Bloomington, MN; that was state number 37, checked off and enjoyed.

After shopping, we explored The Hard Rock Café, and I picked up a rhinestone-studded tee to remind me of this adventure and a man's tee for my son, Kerrigan. He might still be angry, but I knew, eventually, he would come around, and I wanted to let him know I had been thinking of him and missed him.

I was so tickled to hear Kellie inquire about a military discount and further thrilled when they offered 15%; it made my tee purchase seem less indulgent. A nice conversation honoring the military and their sacrifice ensued between my daughter and the tattoo-emblazoned clerk with the perky personality and the warm charm. It was very satisfying and the defining experience when I realized Minnesotans could give Southerners a run for their money in the hospitality and friendliness department. I was happy to see the patriotic spirit so warm and flourishing so far north. I came to learn it's called "Minnesota nice." And, boy they are so nice; it warmed me from the bottom of my toes.

Kellie indulged her inner child with a run through the Nickelodeon expressway and even enjoyed a ride on one of the amusement rides in the middle of this amazing shopping mall. We wrapped up our day and enjoyed a corner table, nearly in the mall walkway and had the most delicious French fries with Parmesan cheese and truffle oil, Mediterranean pizza, and a healthy salad. It was a fun, urban mall meal and was a perfect finish to our day.

With the sun ready to set, it was time to cross the border and head to Wisconsin.

The sun was setting as we crossed in to Wisconsin, my 38th state. The Bed and Breakfast we hoped to stay at in Winona was full for the night, so we stopped at a chain hotel in Eau Claire. The next day we headed right for Wisconsin Dells and took a duck tour on the Wisconsin River to see the picturesque glacier-carved sandstone formations. It was a beautiful day, with the sun gleaming off the water and a bunch of nice folks onboard the duck watercraft. It was surreal to think that Kellie and I were even here, enjoying this event. As I posted about the ducks on social media, so many people commented that they had been to see the Dells; I was surprised at the volume of responses. It seemed remote to me, but a regular favorite of several families. We laughed, we grinned, and we enjoyed the spray of the water as the amphibious craft entered the lake. It was satisfying, and all I could think is "God is good." What a blessing. I picked up a rubber ducky key chain to remind me of how amazing He is and how many adventures He has taken me on.

We jumped on the shuttle that took us from the center of town to the duck boat ramp and launch pad and headed back to the parking lot in this little German replica town. The town was festive and charming and very inviting. It was so much fun and uplifting to our spirits to take it all in. We posed by silly 3-D statues like an Oscar Mayer hot dog, draped in an American flag cape and an ice cream cone. I especially loved the one of Elvis. We ventured into a gourmet Mac-n-cheese restaurant where they served Mac-n-cheese in creative ways in sizzling personal-size iron skillets. Macs on Broadway was beyond amazing comfort food and the portion was abundant and spilling out over the skillet. I was soon savoring every steaming bite and brewing up how to open one up near home. What a fun idea.

As I headed east, I had my heart set on a bed and breakfast in Sturgeon Bay or the Green Bay area, but their policy was that overnight stays were limited to adults. With my 14 year-old in tow, I used it as a deciding factor to skip the coast of Wisconsin, knowing that I would be back to this state to explore some more in the future, and headed south. I was truly hoping to make Milwaukee and check out the Harley Davidson Museum before closing, but we were cutting it too close and didn't make it. Instead, we waved from our car on the highway as we drove by the large building, visible from the highway, promising to be back soon. Wisconsin was a fun, diverse state, and I was so happy to have passed through and stopped for a night. Already, I couldn't wait for a return trip and plotted all the locations and landmarks I would visit on my return trip.

This early departure made time for us to meander south on the back road. What a beautiful experience of farms, waving to Amish farmers who first waved to us, passersby, majestic landscapes, and a stop at the popular Carr's Valley Cheese store. I almost missed it, the small store on the right hand side of the curvy farm road, but I caught the sign just in time and nearly skipped into their empty parking lot. I was skeptical. I grabbed some coins and bought a cold, old-fashioned root beer canned soda from a vending machine. Once inside, my heart was delighted by the quaint storefront and the view of the cheese factory. The showroom was closing in about five minutes, but the store clerk was absolutely delightful and eager to help us. We had great samples of creamy cheese and bleu cheese and watched a promotional video on the cheese-making process. It was delightful and educational. I took a look through the mercantile while Kellie and the clerk, who offered samples, talked cheese and a variety of samples. I saw a display of cookbooks from a local author and, as a self-published author, felt obliged to support her project. The title, *Remembering When*, discussed a myriad of depression-era foods and included the author's childhood memories of days gone by. This was a heart-grabber I knew my mother was sure to enjoy, and the patriotic flag cover was the deal cincher for me. I scooped that up along with a few goodies like crackers, two cheese samples, and caramel Cow Tales, for Kellie and I to enjoy in the car.

I shared my testimony and my witness, and the lady behind the counter was just as supportive as she could be, encouraging me with every word. What a delight that such a small enterprise could feed and satisfy so many customers across America, an American enterprise born out of a dream and plenty of hard work. It resonated to my core that this is the type of America I knew existed still today, the kind of America I know that maintains values and hospitality and hard work, all of which America was built on. I happily paid my tab and wished her well.

We snacked in the car as we headed toward Fort Atkinson, decided upon simply because Atkinson was my maiden name. All these little whispers, which caused me to pause, reflect, pray over my family tree, forgive and thank my ancestors, were whispers I could not overlook.

# CHAPTER THIRTEEN

# PATRIOTIC REFLECTIONS OF MY JOURNEY

His whispers were promises I knew I could count on and that He was reminding me of His promise to bless my family tree anew for 1,000 generations. "You shall not worship (other gods), or serve them; for I, the LORD your God, am a jealous God, visiting the iniquity of the fathers on the children, on the third and the fourth generations of those who hate Me, but showing loving kindness to thousands, to those who love Me and keep My commandments" (Exodus 20:6).

It is His promise to bless one thousand generations, and I wanted every blessing for the obedience of following Him on this crazy journey of faith. Although, He is reward enough, and this journey in itself was gift enough of His love for me. Kellie and I were just along for the ride; I didn't want to miss one blessing for my family tree and all of America.

We were blessed to talk to so many people and share my passion for patriotic and spiritual revival—to share how God was calling me to leave my house and my possessions on this journey of faith across America to test the patriotic and spiritual temperature and to encourage others to turn to Him. I shared about the Sweet Life and my message to do what's in your circle of influence when life gets out of control. I explained that maybe you can't find a job or you go through an unexpected life transition or—the possibilities are endless—but holding on to the coattails of Jesus, you can trust that everything will be okay. You begin where you are, with what you have, with what you know, with what you can do, no matter how small the step. Small steps can look like my idea to sell little $5 car magnets with a simple message of: It's a Sweet Life. I sell these around town, and often that's my only source of income for the day or the week.

People were genuinely intrigued by my walk of faith, God's faithfulness, how big a God He is, how far I had come, and how passionate and patriotic I was in my expression of my personal testimony. They applauded me and encouraged me and reinforced how happy they were I was taking this bold step. To be clear, it wasn't me; I was only doing what the one who created me had called me to do. I was the vessel, the scribe, the willing servant, and all glory is to Him. I'm thrilled He is allowing me to play the leading role in managing this message and this project.

"America needs this," they would say. "Keep going; I don't know what it's going to take for people to wake up, but they need to hear it."

Yes, I would agree, America is in a mess, but God is still on the throne, and His grace is sufficient if only we would wake up and acknowledge Him. They loved the message and my mission. It was very encouraging and kept me going.

God just threw in the tourist stops and the fun events for Kellie and me to be encouraged, maybe as redemption for our tears and sorrow before and through the move, but I am certain it was to express the depth of His love for us.

> "Those who sow with tears will reap with songs of joy"
> —Psalm 126:5

I know that there is no amount of searching in books or on the internet that I could have done that would have allowed me the same insight into our country, her landscape or her countenance. For example, when we encountered the beautiful American flag billowing in the wind, catching our eye as we drove was unimaginable. Pursuing its lead, we encountered a quaint, small town with a Wall of Honor for all the veterans of their community, sponsored by the American Legion. It is my heart's desire for every town across America to erect such a memorial. We need to honor our veterans and our current soldiers. We need a visual way to honor them and also to remind us daily of the sacrifices made for our country. We must never forget; we must always remember. America needs to stand strong with such displays; flags need to be billowing in the wind in every small town across America.

My research across America revealed so much about the true temperature and peoples' true love and concern for America. It warmed my heart every time I encountered memorials and monuments like this. I was doubly thrilled when I saw American flags on display along the entire downtown main road or on lampposts of the primary business and shopping district. America should rally for this display of our flag year round. The trip was undeniably essential to conveying my passion and sharing America's desire to ignite the Spirit of America again because I experienced it first hand, the same way I encourage every family in America to. Go explore. Go see for yourself. Reconnect with America, get to know your neighbors, and get to see what our God has provided for us. We have been given a beautiful, amazing landscape and home to dwell in. It's almost a sign of ingratitude when we take it for granted and don't embrace it or explore it. I challenge you to challenge our next generation to make travel across America a priority. I hope my journey across America inspires you.

It will change you from the inside out. It will ignite your love for America and for Him again as you realize the magnitude of it. It will spur you to care again, to show up again, to wake up, to unite and not judge, to love and not just tolerate, to dispel the fear, and have your eyes opened wide to God's amazing grace.

# CHAPTER FOURTEEN

# JOURNEY HOME

Our last stop out of Wisconsin was for cheese curds. Ooey, gooey, stringy, chewy, piping hot, salty, crunchy Culver's cheese bites were a perfect reminder of Wisconsin. When in Wisconsin, take my advice, be a cheese head and stop at Culver's and order the curds. We enjoyed Culver's in Kenosha, Wisconsin, and it left a lingering memory before we headed through the more familiar states ahead toward home.

As I was driving, I was mentally adding up the cost of the trip, reviewing our stops, considering the sites I had seen and soon realized, the money had been mostly spent and I was cutting it close, I was sure. According to my math, it was time to scurry home. But, I we had just crossed over to Illinois—a state I had been to with my older daughter for Miss Teen International when we went for a mother/daughter trip in 2003. It didn't really count this go-round other than as a cut-through to get home and a reflection of the special memory.

I was a little concerned about the potential cost of a hotel for the night against our remaining funds, until I remembered our good family friends from Florida had moved just outside of the city of Chicago to the suburbs. What a great opportunity to visit them, catch up, and at the same time, spare the cost of a hotel. I felt a little timid about the call as I had not talked to them in quite some time, but when I reached out, they were so gracious and excited to host us, I knew God had nudged me in that direction and made a way for us to stay. Trust me, traveling can help you rekindle old friendships and strengthen family bonds with distant relatives. I have many times called teachers, childhood friends, college sorority sisters, and family friends only to have the doors of hospitality swing wide open; each of us delighted in the human connection and the rekindling of friendships and family. Travel connects us.

It was a bit out of the way, but the reward made it worth it. They were sweet and fun, greeting us in the dark driveway, waving us in as if we were very special guests. The family of three gathered in the living room and shared in every bit of conversation, catching up on family events and travels. It was so nice to have such hospitable hosts and a captive audience. How fun to connect with family friends so far from home, on this long, unexpected excursion. America is really much smaller than we realize. Think about the friends you know and take a look at a map; I bet they polka dot the map and would have a bed to offer you too. And, if not, I am sure they would offer a hot mug of good cheer and warm conversations for your time.

When they showed us to the basement guest room, there was a photo of my brother with our hosts on the shelf to greet me, and it was like I was home with family, though I was multiple states away. The family was really closer friends with my brother, but had adopted each of us, having drawn close to our family while living in the same community back home in my original home state of Florida. It was just a warm, feel-good night. We were so grateful for the lodging and full from the friendship. It was a great night's sleep. God was so cool to plan that bonus for us. He is so amazing; trust Him. He takes care of the sparrows, and He will take care of you, too.

In the morning, we headed out just in time for Annie, the daughter, to head out to school and our hosts to get to work. Kellie and I made our way through Ohio, Kentucky, Tennessee, and back to our sweet state of Georgia by evening.

Five days. 2,500 miles. We were road weary, but satisfied. We were ready to be back in our "bubble," but our beds were still waiting in storage units for a place to call home. For tonight, a friend's guest room would be our accommodations. A hot shower, a comfy pillow, and sleep to refresh our bones and my soul would be a satisfying end to a full and complex week. I drifted to sleep praising God for His provision, His grace, His sovereignty, and His protection. I rested under the covering of His wings yet again and, thanked Him for the adventures ahead and His promise to be faithful to provide a house for the kids and I in time for a new school year, come fall. I whispered goodnight to my son before I drifted off, sad we were temporarily sleeping under separate roofs.

The next morning, I awoke at a normal morning hour. A day in town without our home would seem to spin one out of control or off course, but I decided I would treat it like any other day, starting at Starbucks for tea and running a bunch of errands. Life, after all, still has demands with or without a home. I picked up the shoes from the repair shop I had dropped off before heading out of town, dry cleaning from the cleaners (using my coupon mailed to my former address), and checked in at the storage unit, just to make sure all the household items were safe in storage without disaster.

I remember sitting in the parking lot, tired of the string of errands, intermittently content and yet, questioning my sanity thinking, "God is this you?" I know I just drove from Georgia to Minnesota, and that was crazy. I could hardly comprehend that I had done that. It was surreal enough not having a house, but taking a trip of that magnitude, with barely any resources or plans was baffling even to me, and I was freely participating.

I started the week with $2.12, and I was finishing the week with just about the same, but much fuller, much more tired, and having experienced four new states of my beautiful, patriotic country. That's bizarre enough in itself, not to mention, *what was I going to do for the next dollar?* I can't just keep pretending I'm on some road trip with monopoly money and no credit card. Forget even that, what I have already done out of sheer, blind faith. I am now at 39 states and yet I have 11 to go, thinking of the adventures that lie ahead, I was incredulous and beside myself. Does God really intend for me to get to the remaining 11—still now? How is this even possible?

*All things are possible with Christ.* I hang on to the verse and as many of His promises I can think of. I felt so clearly in my Spirit-leading up to and during the journey and even now; I would hang on to the vision fifty states by fifty years.

And, I reminded myself of that feeling in my spirit, "If you trust me to leave your house and follow me across America, I will provide another house; just trust me."

## CHAPTER FIFTEEN

# A CAR WASH CONFIRMS
# MY TRAVEL PLANS

I know there's a high probability of Hawaii on the horizon, but first Oregon.

It's always a puzzle how things happen in such perfect timing. I was sitting in my car, all by myself, having driven from the storage unit to the front of the building, parked in front of the office, and preparing to go inside and pay my monthly storage fee. I was feeling overwhelmed by the high cost of having four separate storage units while we waited for our house. I was pondering finances and my future and my next steps, and a swirl of questions formed in my head. I felt doubt and fear staring me in the face, ready to jump right in and taunt me. At that very moment, as I was pondering this very question of both possibility and impossibility, sitting in my scorching hot car with the windows all rolled up, about to hop out of the car to walk into the office, I received a text message that confirmed to me and made sense to me, that Hawaii was definitely on my horizon. My projected fiftieth state was Hawaii, and the opportunity to go there told me that 50 x 50 was not a dream, it was becoming His promise; He was insistent, and I believed that amidst the uncertainty of my circumstances, I would follow him all the way to even Hawaii.

My international minister friend, Miguel Escobar, sent me a beautiful photo by text. It was a vivid, color photo of a beautiful island with beautiful flowers, an ocean, and a volcano; but, where was it?

"Where are you?" I asked by text, knowing he travels often and marveling at his incredible timing.

"I saw this at Truett's Luau Grill in Fayetteville, GA; it's a picture on the wall," was his text reply.

He wasn't aware that traveling to Hawaii was on my bucket list, nor that I was meant to go to all fifty states, yet, he had sent a beautiful photo of Hawaii at the exact moment I was asking God for confirmation of my next steps and His travel plans for me. That simply couldn't be a coincidence. I burst out in incredulous laughter and thanked him for the beautiful picture, captured spontaneously and sent to me. It brought me great joy the rest of the day.

My quick text response was: "I'm going to Hawaii for sure and your picture just confirmed it! Yes, maybe we will go to Hawaii to preach and evangelize together one day. But, I know God has a plan to bring me there very soon."

With that, I went inside to pay my storage unit fees and not worry about the size of the check that had to be written and the limit of my known income stream. God was my provider. He was leading me on this Spirit-led journey, and I was going to have to trust Him—completely. I was so grateful for His leading and confirmation to keep me going.

As I returned to my car, another friend called me to meet up at the Peachtree City Farmer's Market, a favorite Saturday spot. I loved supporting the local vendors and small business owners, plus, I was once a vendor there—the only woman certified by the Department of Agriculture to sell Georgia Wild Shrimp at the Farmer's Market. It was a smelly, yet satisfying, job. I was happy to work from the bounty of the sea and make so many people happy with fresh caught fish and shrimp. I had traded in my crown for rain boots so I could tromp through the fish houses and visit the docks of the coastal towns, gathering the bounty of the sea to resell. It was a season of my life, a season of training, I'm sure, to demonstrate I was willing to do anything and be humble to boot; it likely prepared me for this very journey.

My friend and I met up for an hour or so and walked around enjoying the market and the day—just like any other day, as if I had a home in town. I was picking over the vendor's offerings as if shopping for that night's supper. I did enjoy something to eat, and we sat at a picnic table to soak in the sun. Farmer's markets are very rewarding; support them weekly when you can. Farmers work hard for our harvest and our health. We owe it to then to support them with our business.

My next errand was to get my car washed after all the miles I put on it. I usually go through the Brushless Car Wash on Crosstown Drive, since they also offer me shelf space to sell my car magnets, but today I found myself on the other side of town and saw a group of youngsters with a car wash sign. I remember the days of high school car washes, raising money for band and chorus and class projects and was quick to turn in to support them. I moved to the sidewalk to avoid the suds and the silly sprays of water between the volunteers and struck up a conversation with the young adult on the sidewalk closest to my car.

I was talking about the Sweet Life magnets on my car and sharing the message of my ministry and my heart and he was quick to tell me this was his family, working earnestly to clean my car. They were a large, home-schooled family who came out to support their sister as she was raising money for a mission trip to Ireland. I knew immediately that God had sent me to this car wash that I had no original intention of going to.

He called his sister over, and I prophesied some encouraging words to her. It was obvious she was full from receiving them. Her mother joined her side as I prayed and we chatted non-stop while the brothers washed my car. I talked about how I had just returned from my journey and thought I might be continuing the adventure this week, yet the destination was not currently clear to me; I intended to fly to the furthest point west I had not yet been to in order to cover a few more states.

The mother stopped me and called one of the sons over and relayed my story. He said, "Well, I just got back from Portland, Oregon." Portland. I remembered the visitor in the Ruby Falls cave next to me being from Portland, Oregon, suspecting it was my next leg, so I perked up. The boy said he flew in to Portland, Oregon, rented a car to Bend, and played golf at Brasada Canyons Golf Resort. As soon as he said golf, I knew God was nudging me there with confirmation. With a freshly washed car and a connection to a Spirit-filled family with a mission of their own, I knew I had the starting point of the next leg of my journey.

My car was refreshed, I was refreshed, and it was time for the first annual community picnic. I couldn't go empty handed, and I had to remind myself, I was low on cash. I stopped into a small Asian specialty market and the dollar store located next door and assembled an eye-catching treat to contribute. A sand pail, a festive pinwheel, and a few dozen fortune cookies made a sweet summer gesture. I added my Sweet Life magnet and felt it was a complete package with a personal touch for my hometown, even if I didn't have a home here currently.

The picnic was hosted by a company that had great success with a slogan similar to mine using social media to mediate community conversations. We exchanged car magnets, I congratulated the event team on their success, and I went about shaking hands of my neighbors. It was my Sweet Life, *Spirit of America Days* come to life. It wasn't my event, but it was a lovely event, and I had my own sweet blessings ahead. More communities should host these events and get to know their neighbors and the lives they live—the atmosphere is Americana.

With a Saturday like that, who would have guessed I didn't have a home to go to? Tonight was the second night sleeping at my friend's house. It was lonelier without Kellie, but I knew she needed to be at her friend's house to feel a sense of normalcy, and a summer sleepover was very normal for her. Kerrigan didn't want to stay the night with me, but he was preparing to leave for a week at the beach with a family friend. It was summer as usual. God had planned back-to-back invitations for the kids, which included time at the lake, a week at the beach, and even a trip to a family friend's home a few states away. God had orchestrated summer camp, summer invitations, time with Dad, and brief lodging so as not to overstay our welcome around a trip I could not have planned better had I had six months time and $10,000 saved up.

Sunday was church day, so I dressed for church. When I went, with some apprehension, tears of joy streamed steadily down my face as my heart and voice offered abundant praise and worship. It was just me, the kids didn't make it up and out, and that was okay considering I was grateful for every minute I knew they had someplace safe and comfortable to stay, to keep us all from feeding our fear.

Breakfast after church was with a girlfriend, outside on the patio, enjoying the sun as if it were any other day of my life; that's what makes this the sweet life. God is always on His throne, leading me, loving me and guiding me, in spite of the circumstances of my life. Kellie went to her friend's for the weekend, just like she might do if we were in our own house. Weekend sleepovers for two days at a time were a normal part of summer break, so for us, it was life as normal. I just kept my thoughts at bay, banished anxiety as best I could, and ramped up my internal dialogue with God for peace and confirmation. This constant communication gave me the courage and confidence to face the moments and not worry about the future or my impending needs.

The weekend slipped by and quickly turned into week two, and I was getting slightly antsy. I knew I would be going; Oregon had already been confirmed. Kerrigan was at the beach a week, and Kellie was invited to a friend's grandparent's home up north. They would fly, which was always such a treat for her and made it all the more special. An entire week for both of them to enjoy their summer as kids and not worry about where their clothes and belongings were or how their mom was going to fix this one. I just kept reassuring them, "God has a plan, trust me. He promised me He would have a house for us if I would just trust Him. Look, everyone has a place to be, friends to share summer with, and trips to take; let's relax and not worry about it for now." They sure had a lot of confidence in me as their momma to keep with the flow.

I was out of money, but then my rental house deposit from my former home was released to me just as I was wondering how the next leg of the journey would be funded. It wasn't needed just yet for a rental deposit. I was feeling pressed to keep traveling, so I assumed it was meant for funding the next leg of my journey. It was just enough to get to the west coast and back if the first leg of the journey was a guide, at that time not having a clue how much traveling I was getting ready to do.

I took my 95-year-old senior citizen friend to the grocery store for a short trip since I knew I'd be gone a week and he depended on me so. While we slowly shuffled through the produce, I coordinated my flight plan by phone with the friend who issued my buddy pass. We pushed the grocery cart to the café and soon found a seat at a bistro table at the coffee shop located at the rear entrance of the store, and I confirmed my flight. With this, I felt my schedule for the week fall into place. God was mapping out my travel plan, even while I grocery shopped. Be the hands and feet of Christ for others, and God will work out the details of His plans; just be willing, flexible, and good at multi-tasking.

# CHAPTER SIXTEEN

# WINGS TO THE WEST COAST

• OREGON • ALASKA • UTAH • IDAHO • WYOMING

With a buddy pass in hand and a small reserve of cash from my deposit, I went all in and headed to the airport. I had one suitcase and at the last minute had thankfully traded my purse for my son's Swiss Army backpack. What a great move. That pack was a lifesaver on the entire summer excursion—the straps were solid and it carried my week's worth of belongings.

I was glad I got an early start because early mornings are the best time to catch a non-revenue seat, especially in the summer. I was a little sleepy still, but got on easily and was soon on my way to the West Coast. It was an exhilarating feeling to be airborne, but I was also torn that I was going on this trip without having a home and not able to bring my kids along on this adventure and knowing they were scattered about in the care of friends and their families. It was just God and me. It was crazy, for sure, but I knew so profoundly it was what God had been preparing me for the last decade of my life. It was for His purpose, and I was surrendered to Him.

It was June 9, and I had made it to state number 39—Oregon. When I was in college, one of the other America's Junior Miss scholarship recipients who attended the University of South Alabama with me was Miss Oregon. Now, all her stories of home seemed to come to life. I couldn't believe I was on the west coast; I couldn't believe I found the nerve to load up a backpack and jump on the plane—alone, with no one in my family knowing, just the two children in my charge. It was the boldest, wildest thing I had ever done; it was a crazy leap of faith.

Immediately, I felt a rush of joy flood my spirit as I walked through the airport, with my backpack on my back—a backpack on my back, that was an oddity. I'm a red Pullman with wheels, wearing high heels, carrying a latte in my right hand kind of girl. I knew that wouldn't work flying standby, and I had to adjust my traveling gear for this trip. So, I repacked my suitcase and pushed it all into the one backpack.

I had to pause and enjoy the wall of honor for our military when up above the vaulted ceilings in the main lobby there was an American flag posted and under its covering were large, beautiful seals paying honor to all five branches. "The Port of Portland Honors Those Who Serve Our Country." I liked Portland, Oregon already.

After snapping a photo, I headed straight to the rental car counter. There were quite a few choices, so I went to the familiar chains. I was nervous knowing I didn't have a return flight guaranteed and no national credit card, both stipulations to rent a car. How would I rent a car, and what if I was stuck there without transportation? I wasn't going to doubt for a moment. I prayed as I walked, approached the counter with complete confidence and a smile, and talked my way into an upgrade, a map, and rental car that would serve me well for the week. I was beyond elated. Thank you, Lord, for being my tour guide.

I set my GPS for Bend and marveled at the scenic 200-mile drive I was privileged to enjoy. The highway went on forever, meandering through the Deschutes National Forest and past miles and miles of tremendous Ponderosa Pines and other beautiful flora and fauna. I didn't anticipate it being such a long distance between Portland and Bend, and to be honest, I'm glad I didn't know in advance because it may have deterred me from pressing on. Midway, I found a traveler's rest and made a quick stop. It was clean with lots of brochures and informational material. I was a little unnerved that I might make headlines of "woman traveling alone found attacked and left for dead," but those fears were unfounded. Everyone I encountered along the way from the roadside stops to the multiple Starbucks, was down-to-earth, nice, and friendly. Covered under His wings and in our great, hospitable land of America, traveling was a breeze, and my confidence increased with every mile.

I did keep an eye on my gas gauge and my map, though, because help would have been miles away. From the rest stop, I began calling for overnight accommodations. I like to do that before I see any hint of the night sky, just to ensure I have a place to lay my head by dark.

God seemed to have every detail already worked out for me. I called what seemed to be the most popular bed and breakfast from the online chats and feedback only to discover they were sold out. They referred me to their sister inn downtown, which reduced the price to an enticing figure of $80, including breakfast, with only one caveat—the air conditioning was out and it might be a tad warm. That was a hard one, considering the June humidity in the air, but I wanted a confirmed room and the price was right on my budget, so when the reservationist told me she only had one room left called "The King's Suite," I knew it had my name on it; my Father had already made the reservation for me, it seemed. At least I could drive on in peace, wondering about what the accommodations that awaited me would be like.

I had to drive through a much older section of town, past insurance companies and doctors' offices in former, older homes; my doubts were rising about these accommodations until I turned the last corner and saw the beautiful Tudor-style inn with a circular driveway, arched entry, and wrought iron accents. I was delighted. My heart raced in anticipation. I quickly parked and pulled out my sack, entered the key code, and opened the entrance door to a lovely appointed sitting room with a very fresh decor. Up the hardwood winding stairs, holding on to the wrought iron handrail, I came to the arched bedroom door that mimicked the front entrance. I opened it with my iron skeleton key and gasped at the beauty of the King's suite, fit for a queen and reserved for me, just like my redemption. Oh, that sight felt good, and my spirit leapt.

It was a suite in gray and beige tones with a claw foot tub, vintage tiled floors, and crowned prince frogs and regal bronze crown wall ornaments. It was dreamy and, yes, a wee bit hot, leaning toward sweltering sauna as in a day spa. But, it was the King's Suite, it was mine for the night, and, I was delighted.

I met the other inn guests, young adults of the "Now Generation," traveling around together, who enjoyed the details of my story and applauded my boldness to journey America and share. Though our values and our spiritual beliefs were different, we shared a love for America and the joy of walking out one's passion and life's purpose; they were quite encouraging.

A nice walk to the center of town brought me to a chic, urban restaurant, Zydeco Kitchen on NW Bond St. The restaurant was bustling, but the bar was empty. I chose to sit at the bar, anyway, to at least chat with the bartender, and hopefully others would soon come in. The bartender was fairly busy, so it was dining alone, or so it seemed. And, then a party of six couples came in, full of laughter and life, to have a beverage while waiting on their table. They sat around me, "including" me in their party.

"Where are you from?"

I said, "Atlanta," and then I added, "Well, you wouldn't know it, Peachtree City, really."

She laughed, "I own a home in Newnan, GA." Newnan happens to be the next town about 20 minutes south of me, where I often shop. The world is small, America. We laughed at that. What are the chances? I travel all the way to the West Coast to meet new Americans, and here I am chatting with my neighbor from south Georgia. We shared a sweet southern social before they took their seats at a table. I was soon joined by other folks at the counter. We exchanged niceties and southern hospitality, and they pointed out that I did not want to miss some landmarks in town.

One of the highlights in Bend was discovering McMenamins, the former St. Francis Catholic School, which had been renovated into a multi-room restaurant and lodging for guests. I discovered walkways, hidden lounges, outdoor fire pits, and intricacies of surprise at this unique establishment. It was like a secret, magical garden made for a beautiful night of exploring.

The next morning, I about skipped out on the breakfast included with my B & B lodging and headed to the airport, but I am sure glad I didn't. The breakfast was served at the original inn, The Mill Inn, as the "sister" inn was not yet opened for breakfast. There was, of all things, a mini model of the Statue of Liberty in front of the restaurant as a lawn ornament, and the food was organic, amazing, and likely, the best food I had on my excursion to the West Coast. You won't want to miss it. I can't wait to go back and slow down to truly savor the experience when I enjoy it on my next journey there.

Within 30 minutes, I headed to the Portland International Airport, turned in my rental car, and was left wandering the terminal with my backpack, unsure of my next direction. I was jumping through hoops again trying to imagine this journey, mapping out possible destinations and airports to connect me to wherever it was I was supposed to be going. Fifty-by-fifty is a rather vague travel plan. I pressed in to hear God's leading.

I had thought to drive north from Portland to Seattle, Washington, but I had already been to Seattle—I loved the memory of the open air fish market and the organic beet salad with feta cheese. But the drive east toward Coeur d'Alene, Idaho seemed like a lot of miles of highway.

I finally found a seat at a high top table to perch on and continued to plot my travel options. Go back and get the rental, I pondered, drive north, then drive east; no, forget the rental, try a flight to Seattle, check the flight loads, give up that pursuit and head somewhere else to a different location altogether; round and round I went. An hour and a half into it, I slammed down my pen and proclaimed, "Enough!" How ridiculous that I was wasting precious travel time lamenting. "Lord, you will just have to show me where to go! I have got to get going in some direction."

That was bold. I packed my map and papers, slung on my backpack, went out to the airport lobby, and gazed at the military seals posted high on the entrance wall that had welcomed me only yesterday. Let's face it; I was buying time. I had no clue where I was going next, until the Holy Spirit nudged me to the Delta Customer Service counter, just behind where I was conveniently standing. There was a lovely Asian representative working at the counter, with no customers standing in line. How convenient. How unusual. How perfectly designed by the Holy Spirit.

I felt it in my spirit like a parent nudging their child into kindergarten class toward the new teacher. "Go ahead, you'll see, she will help you." I didn't want to go. I felt the resistance in my spirit. After a few lingering seconds, I took a deep breath and headed to the counter. When the agents are busy working with their head down, the last thing they want is someone interrupting them, especially a non-revenue passenger—that's what the red service phones are for, not the live agents. They are usually firm to tell you they can't offer you service. But, the Holy Spirit was nudging me, so I acquiesced.

"Hi." I smiled extra brightly as I approached her counter, hoping to warm her, but to my surprise, I didn't have to—she radiated warmth and returned the smile. I was so relieved. I placed my notes up on the counter in front of her at eye level. "I know I am a stand-by passenger, but can you help me verify a flight, if you have a minute? I'm just not sure where I want to go and I need more information."

She agreed right away. As she was looking, I was being nudged again. "Go ahead." Another deep breath from me as I took another step closer in toward the counter.

"I just flew in from the East Coast yesterday. I went to Bend; it was gorgeous," I gushed. She smiled and typed quickly on her keyboard. "I'm an author," I offered. She smiled and shook her head up and down exuberantly as she continued to make a search on her computer.

"I'm traveling the United States on a buddy pass, writing a book about my journey," I was nervous, but I decided to just dive in. "I was lucky enough to get on the plane to Portland first thing, in spite of being a non-rev status. I need to get to all 50 states before I'm done, in fact, I haven't been to Alaska, but I know that's too big of an ask with a buddy pass, right? So, how about Seattle?" I slowed down and smiled like a kid again. I knew at any moment she was going to snap my head off and send me to a red phone. But, again, she just smiled and said, "You want to go to Alaska? I can do that."

"You can? On one buddy pass?" I was incredulous and petrified that she would actually make that happen. My kids, my family, heck, even my mother didn't know where I was. I'm not sure I had enough money to take care of myself in Alaska; that seemed like halfway around the world. I was on a *buddy pass*. What if I got stuck in Alaska? This was June; no one uses a non-rev pass in summer due to the possibility of getting wait-listed due to the full-fare summer travelers. I was shaking inside and out and God was just grinning, saying, "I know, go anyway."

So was this lovely, helpful gate agent; she was eager to help me along. "Sure, I can do that. I'll just route you through Salt Lake City—it will be a stopover and then on to Anchorage, no problem."

"Did you just say Salt Lake City—as in Utah? Because I need to get to Utah, too!"

She smiled, happy to accommodate me. It was as if she was in on the plan all along and God had called ahead to make my reservations.

I had wanted Alaska to be my 40th state, a milestone, and now there was Utah. But when I later looked at my ticket, the flight there was a touchdown, not a stopover, and thus, I could not count as my 40th state and so Alaska would be my 40th state, after all. Not that I was going to turn down this gift if it didn't line up exactly as I had imagined, but it was an extra bonus when it fell into place just as planned. This was another lesson to not jump to conclusions; sometimes the details go differently than they appear, and the story always works out as it should it in the end.

Just as she was finishing up, another agent stepped over, and then another. "That's not possible, you will have to pay additional fees," said the first agent to arrive. "You will need another pass," said the second agent with equal authority.

The original agent looked up and said firmly as she continued to click away, "Yes. This is how you do it." She pointed out her process with assuredness, just to prove she was making the reservation according to the regulations.

Then, she looked at me with satisfaction and said, "Here is my personal cell phone number if you get stuck. And, if you have any problem once you are in Alaska and you need another buddy pass, just call me and I'll give you one of my personal passes."

Only God could have lined me up with this agent and worked

out every last detail and provided me with her personal cell phone number so I didn't feel like I was going to be stranded. Isn't He amazing? Thank you to the wonderful Delta agent with the big heart and the surrendered spirit. You gave me so much peace on this leg of my journey, knowing I had a safety net. Plus, I love sharing with everyone your good nature and generous spirit; people marvel at it every time I share.

I took the leap of faith in spite of the absurdity. I was on my way to Alaska. I was both elated and scared out of my britches! I clung tighter to the straps of my backpack and to the coattails of Jesus. My kids were a continent away. "God, please protect them. I'm trusting you—for everything," I prayed. Four of the five kids were over 18, but I was still the momma, and the youngest, Kellie, was in good care, so her needs were addressed. But still, she was so far away. It was a great, big leap of faith. It was a magnificent spiritual journey that is really quite difficult to share. My internal fear, the fear of my flesh and rapidly thinking mind was real, but the peace of the Lord, the one who helps me walk in His righteousness, was real and bigger, and I was compelled to make the leap. I knew, without a shadow of a doubt, He was leading me, guiding me, and prompting me; I knew He would let no harm come to me. I was under the covering of His protection. He is my shield and my fortress. Walking it out is still like walking a rope bridge over the raging Amazon—don't look down; just do it.

I touched down in Anchorage, Alaska pinching myself. Hello, state number 40. God is awesome and *all things are possible*, how could I ever doubt again?

"Lord, thank you! I don't know what I'll do or accomplish while I'm here, so just surprise me, Lord."

At the entrance, I was greeted by an oversized stuffed moose with tremendous antlers; he had to be 800–1000 pounds when he was free range. I felt the call of the wild as I passed other displays of taxidermy of Alaskan wildlife showcased along the corridors of the airport.

I especially liked the tribute to the military. "Alaska welcomes our troops home. Thank you for your service to our country," was emblazoned on the exit wall of the terminal. I loved the patriotism that was so clearly displayed as far away as Alaska; we are, indeed, all connected and united as America.

Since I carried my pack, there was no luggage to retrieve, so I walked outside to catch a cab at the sidewalk. I knew I didn't want to drive around Alaska. In my mind, there was too much wilderness and incline and risk of running into wildlife or out of gasoline. Years back, my mother had come to Alaska for a summer with a girlfriend and they "rented a wreck" and came back with stories about how they almost drove off a cliff in Denali National Park. As a solo traveler, I didn't want to bring back similar stories.

It was late when I arrived, and, thankfully, my cab driver was very congenial and knew right where the bed and breakfast was located. It was so late, in fact, the inn keepers were already asleep for the night. They had given me a code to the front door and left a note on the stairs for me to take the room at the top of the stairs. Here I was a stranger, walking unannounced into another stranger's home late in the night, albeit an inn. It was a little eerie, but spoke to the nature of the state and the environment I was in. I quietly crept up the stairs, let myself into my room, crawled into the deliciously comfortable king-size bed, and soon fell fast asleep.

Atlanta is four hours ahead of Alaska, and direct flight time from Atlanta is about 7–8 hours, meaning, regardless of where I had just flown in from, my internal clock was all out of whack. I just kept pushing ahead on my journey and wasn't too terribly out of whack from it, but sleep would have been a nice reward.

It was difficult to awake so early in the morning, but I didn't want to miss a moment. It turned out to be a very good decision. After a quick shower, I made up the bed and packed up my things.

I was struggling with guilt for being in Alaska, over-thinking the cost and internalizing that I couldn't stay long. Though I had hoped for three relaxing days and time of pure enjoyment of the perfect bed and breakfast I had discovered, something gnawed at me to run quickly! After all, I had made touchdown and today's adventure would make the count. Downstairs, I met the innkeepers, such delightful folks. And guests who were proud to say they were Christians gathered for breakfast. It was a delicious omelet; I was saddened to leave the inn behind.

When I mentioned to the innkeepers I wanted to see the fjords, they quickly arranged a cab and a seat on an organized tour. I was disappointed to leave the best cup of English tea I had tasted all week as the cab was already calling for me from the door just minutes after I took my seat at the banquet table. I was offered the mistress' coat and binoculars for the tour as I was walking out the front door. In haste, I told them I would likely be leaving and not staying the second night, though, it was such a shame to be in Alaska such a brief time at this lovely inn, but I had packed my bag and left it waiting at the door of the room. I hastily said goodbye to the table guests, and together we agreed I should return to celebrate my 60th birthday at the inn since this was officially my

50th celebration trip. I couldn't agree more and secretly hoped I would be celebrating with a life spouse as my traveling companion.

The cabbie took me downtown where I connected on a shuttle; the driver warmly greeted me by name and made me feel like an honored guest. The shuttle took me to the ship waiting at the dock, but not before stopping at a bakery on the side of a mountain where they served the largest oversized freshly baked pastries I have ever seen. The baker was from Montenegro—I had never met anyone from Montenegro before. It was a fun, brief exchange. The sweets were feasts for the eyes and the tummy. I would go back to Alaska for that pastry alone.

Once inside the shuttle, we picked up a driver trainee, and since I was early, I sat close to the front. I caught the trainee's ear while waiting for the other tour guests to re-board the bus and shared about my book. It turns out he was a close acquaintance with prominent evangelist Franklin Graham and enjoyed my story, saying that Mr. Graham likely would too. That would be nice. I smiled at God for yet another confirmation along the way of what was to come from this journey and my story. I agree that Mr. Graham and his followers would likely share an interest in what God was doing with this journey and the story He was writing. I had yet to discover that I, myself, would be following the Graham Decision America ministry tour in less than six month's time. God was weaving quite a story.

On to the port we went, stopping at water pools and mountain peaks and nature trails along the way. The tour driver stopped the bus a few times to allow us on and off to take photos. He was eager and delighted to share the beauty of Alaska with us. And I was glad to be capturing the details of this journey to share the beauty of God's America with readers everywhere. The landscape was breathtaking. I have previously been to Norway and could relate to some of the views as quite similar, but Alaska was grand and part of America, which made it all the more an important impression on my spirit. Alaska is a treasure, a part of America's crowning glory that we should all have the privilege to visit once in our lifetime. Of course, I was in the Kenai Fjords National Park, and even in the mist and the low ceiling due to fog, you could feel and see the magnificence of this national treasure.

I am inspired to ask. What is holding you back? Money, circumstances, handicaps, or obstacles should not keep you from exploring the landscapes of America—God's gifts to His children. I pray that you would pledge today your very own 50 X 50—to see all fifty states by your fiftieth, or to begin where you are and make a plan for all 50 in the decade ahead. Make travel a possibility for your children as well. I know mine was a supernatural walk, and traveling is extremely expensive. I am just gently nudging you to make it a priority; make a plan and discover and see as much as you can. It's vital to our minds and spirit and to our country to enjoy and preserve it. Seeing and experiencing it, makes the fight for freedom more personal.

When we arrived to the ticket window, God delighted me even more. Remember that prayer I offered upon landing in Alaska?

The name of the ship was the *Prince William Sound Surprise* from the Major Marine Tours line. God was unwrapping the desires of my heart one beautiful "surprise" after another. This was some jubilee celebration and some adventure He was taking me on—a walk of intimacy I couldn't wait to share with the world.

I brought a copy of a few local magazines, including *Fayette*

*Woman* magazine, from my hometown and had the souvenir photographer snap a photo of me next to the ship, in spite of the mist that was falling. I wanted proof I had been there, and I wanted to use this story to encourage women everywhere to believe in their dreams and to not look at their circumstances, but instead, to trust a big God, who would deliver them in spite of themselves.

"All things are possible." Repeat after me. Say it often. You don't have to remind God; He is waiting for you to claim your birthright. "With man this is impossible, but with God, *all things* are possible" (Matthew 19:26, emphasis mine).

We were off for the day to enjoy the views and the cruise touring Prince William Sound. There was Beloit Glacier, Blackstone Glacier, and my favorite, Surprise Glacier, and, no, I had no prior knowledge that this existed. We saw swarms of Kittiwake in a rookery that together made the sound of a rushing waterfall. We saw sea lions, a humpback whale that showcased his tale for us, and, God's sweet surprise of trees filled with American Bald Eagles—the national bird of the United States, and more. It was a delightful surprise. I especially enjoyed the National Park Rangers who gave educational presentations on board and encouraged the younger attendees to participate; it's so important to educate and encourage the next generation. Those kids will talk about that experience their whole lives, especially the ones called on to participate. I wished my kids were there to take this in. Perhaps, one day, we will be blessed to return on a family trip. Alaska shouldn't just be a once-in-a-lifetime trip for retirees; it's an adventure the whole family will benefit from and love.

And, yes, I talked with everyone on board, sharing about my books and my testimony and left with lots of blessings from the experience, meeting still more people from my sweet state of Georgia and exchanging business cards. Considering the icy wind, the mist and the cold, I wouldn't have made it without the coat— what a thoughtful thing for her to offer. Hospitality and kindness take so little extra, and the warmth extended goes so far. It allowed me to go outside in spite of the brisk wind, to take a few pictures around the deck, and to have a closer look at the amazing landscape and wildlife.

I couldn't leave Alaska without King Crab, and I had just an hour to grab some at The Glacier Brewhouse, a bustling restaurant down the street, following the end of the tour. I made friends with the other patrons who were intrigued with my story, one who shared that his young daughter had recently written a book and who was pleased by the inspiration and encouragement of my efforts. God continued to align me with strategic partnerships where I could share, encourage, witness, and in turn, be encouraged, as well.

I made it back to the inn only to find everyone had withdrawn for the night, and with that, I grabbed my suitcase, left the coat on the foyer bench, and jumped back in the cab to the airport. Including the inn, the tour, the cabs, and the crab, I was quick to spend $700 on my 24-hour Alaska adventure and knew that my budget would not allow me to linger the three days I had hoped for. What if I could not get out on my buddy pass? Stranded without money was not an option. I knew I had to make Alaska, the trip of a lifetime, a 24-hour experience. There would be another time, I told myself; there was, after all, my 60th birthday to celebrate in a decade.

That's the beauty and flexibility of a non-revenue pass. With a small fee, I was able to change my flight and head back to the mainland with ease.

I slept on the plane and arrived in Salt Lake City at dawn. At least I didn't have jet lag to contend with. Too bad I couldn't stay longer in Alaska. But I had no time for regrets and savored the experience I did have—grateful for it. So many people dream to go there all their life, but in 24 hours, I managed to get a taste of so much from locals to tourists, from patriotism to Christianity, from nature to the politics, and I was surprisingly satisfied. There was something special about Alaska, and it got stuck under my skin. Deep down, I hoped I would get to come back to celebrate my 60th birthday and better enjoy the inn and that delicious cup of tea I barely sipped.

I had a lot of territory to cover on this next stop: three states in two days. I hopped in to a rental car out of Salt Lake City and drove a beeline north to cross the Idaho border. States 41 and 42 came in the same day, though I knew I would return for a better look at Utah on the return journey. Where was I headed to in Idaho? What was even in Idaho? Well, the slogan says, "hidden gem," and I discovered it to be true. I loved Idaho and could see coming back for a spell to discover even more; no wonder some of my southern friends were claiming it for their retirement moves.

I drove to Shoshone, just North of Twin Falls, and looking for some lunch, I jumped at the Five Guys hamburger I spied, even though it's a chain and there was one near my home. I was craving a good, quick burger and needed Wi-Fi to plan the next leg, so it fit the bill. Twin Falls looked big enough and Boise was much too far west, so Shoshone it was.

I approached two businessmen in suits, under the assumption

they traveled for work, and asked about potential next destinations, and they directed me to Pocatello and Idaho Falls.

Only because time before sunset didn't allow for me to make it further west or north and since Wyoming was tomorrow's destination, I turned back south toward Twin Falls as my first stop. I figured I'd be back to Idaho in the future, on a trip to visit my sweet friend with whom I had graduated business school and who had, with her husband, purchased retirement property in Coeur d'Alene. (Let's get that on the calendar, Liza).

I found a remark on Trip Advisor before I headed out that directed me to Dierkes Lake, and there I stumbled upon a beautiful setting. There were stunning views and so much recreation to enjoy, but because time was of the essence, reading the educational boards, taking in the panoramic views of Shoshone Falls (the Niagara of the West), and a few selfies were going to have to count. Now I can say I have been to Niagara Falls of Canada and of the West. It was a great outdoor space with families enjoying picnics and the beautiful day at Centennial Park on the grounds. It was a fun, beautiful stop and a perfect follow up from the vistas and water views I was missing from Alaska.

Onward ho! Sun Valley was a must as the businessmen had described it. I'm so glad I chose it as a destination. It was like a 30A of the North. 30A is my favorite beach area in the panhandle of north Florida. (Read more in *eLph*, book two). There was beautiful sun and fun shops and cool shopping. It was trendy with lots of pedestrians just enjoying shops and good eats and their sweet life. In fact, I stopped in the beautifully landscaped quad where people were enjoying freshly scooped ice cream, melting down the waffle cone from the heat of the glistening sun, and enjoyed a chocolate mint scoop myself. It was clean and pretty, and there was just a magical ambiance in Sun Valley. My favorite find was Atkinson's Market—yep, my maiden namesake. I was compelled to go in and peruse. I walked out with two great finds: A reusable canvas Atkinson tote and some picnic-size tastings of cheese for my car travels. There was so much to enjoy in the local grocer, I had to remember I wasn't taking my purchases home. I love to visit the local markets when I travel; they always have great "snackies" and delights.

I absolutely loved this stop on my route and cannot wait to return; both summer and winter would be great times to visit, as they are known as a ski resort. I went into the visitor information center, chatted at length with the nice ambassador who greeted me, and walked out with a dozen brochures of fun outdoor events to enjoy, if only I had more time and resources. As reassurance I would return, I drove around the neighboring area and took notes of the names of accommodations and ranches so I could research them before I returned—I loved this stop.

I drove east in order to make Wyoming by the morning, heading for Twin Falls, but opting for Moore, Idaho when I was having difficulty finding a hotel or a bed and breakfast and found one with availability at a good price, including breakfast.

Moore, Idaho was a long, lonely drive from Sun Valley, and for a very long stretch of the road, I was the only car and driver on the road. God and I had a nice, long chat, and I was very grateful for His care because if anything had happened here, no one might have discovered me for days. It would turn out that I felt the same about my evening accommodations.

I drove through the downtown of Moore, a town population of

less than 200 and about two-dozen rustic painted buildings; many were empty. I felt a tumbleweed would roll by at any moment, but I continued to follow my GPS. I went up a hill with a dirt road, definitely off-terrain when the GPS went haywire. I was driving down a dense neighborhood with wire fences and curious faces from the residents.

Dang GPS, I did a U-turn onto a gravel drive and went back down the hill. Where is this place? With a house number of 3258 and a street address of 3350, there were lots of numbers and nothing I was seeing matched up to that information, just an industrial town with nothing much going on from first glance. And, I was staying here? Alone? I turned right at the bottom of the hill and drove a good stretch when the GPS picked up again. Then I recognized house numbers on the mailboxes and sensed some progress until they began to spread in numerical distance one from another, and before very long, it was farmland. Gheesh! Then a mobile home park came into view and a fork in the road. I made a sharp left turn to get off the highway, but just as I did, I saw a sign. I was doing a few 360 degree turns back on to the highway to read the sign, find the road, and get back on track, but once I saw the sign, "King Mountain Bed and Breakfast," I was sure I had the right place and God had made the reservation.

That was until I saw the long gravel driveway and the log cabin on the property. *Gulp.* "God, are you sure this is the place?" I had quick nightmarish flashes cross through my imagination and prayed that God would keep me alive to get back to my children. Horror movie titles flashed across my mind, but it was getting late. It was the only accommodation choice I had, too far to the border and too lonely back in reverse, so I went down the drive, pulled in front of the house, and with the car running, climbed the three steps and gingerly knocked on the door. "Stand firm; trust God," I kept thinking in the waiting.

I wanted to bolt. A barking dog sounded from inside. I was standing in front of a screened porch and the door was opened by a man in a white sleeveless tank and jeans and a wispy, country smile. My spirit leapt for me to "high-tail it home, Jackie!"

I introduced myself, and the homeowner said "Yes, we were expecting you. Go around the house and park in the back. Use the back entrance and pick any room you want downstairs."

Like I was going to stay? But, I had nowhere else to go, I reasoned, and the Bed and Breakfast was King Mountain. And he did say *we* were expecting you, so I knew it had God's fingerprints on it. I said another prayer as I drove and parked behind the back of the building.

When I got out of my car, I took in the mountain views, the luxury of the exterior of this mountain cabin house, and the pure awe of the property. My vision was coming in to focus; I was going to give it a chance.

Out of the few empty rooms downstairs, I picked the panda bear room; my college sorority, Alpha Omicron Pi, adopted the panda as our mascot, and so, I determined it yet another sign of confirmation. Everything was done in a panda bear motif from the blanket on the bed to the shower curtain in the shared bathroom.

I was very delighted when the hostess of the house greeted me at the top of the stairs with a smile. I laughed at my unrest as I climbed the stairs. When I got to the top of the stairs and took in the view of the main floor, I was taken aback. It was a beautiful, immense luxury home with great views of the mountains. The owners were wearing bright smiles and happy to greet and host me. I immediately got whisked to the kitchen counter, and bowl after bowl of food was placed before me—a very comforting experience for a weary traveler. I was quickly put to ease as they dished out the hospitality.

And the rest of the night unfolded with a clear distinction of God's orchestration. There was witnessing, sharing, and prayers for family in need and encouragement. There were stories exchanged that were salve to the spirit. And, then, much to my surprise and delight, the evening's entertainment was karaoke freestyle dancing in the living room accompanied by laughing and pure, free joy. It was ethereal. The three of us enjoyed fellowship and dancing until late in the night and agreed it was the absolute best night we had enjoyed in a long while. God was full of surprises on this trip. It was hard to say goodbye to these beautiful hosts. Just before I left, I was handed a business card and the cell numbers of the owners and was told to call if I needed anything down the road. They were just good, American folks—what a delight and a surprise. This is America, my friends; these are the good folks I encountered along the way across our great and amazing country.

I had angels with me on this trip, for sure. A little ways down the road, I stopped in to a truck stop. There was the clue of the large Jack Daniels sign for sure, but it was broad daylight. I didn't realize the gas stop would have a "biker bar" in full swing. Those dens of uncertainty, likely filled with retirees and veterans enjoying the open roads and a rest stop with locals, but looking intimidating to a single, female traveler.

As I was entering the building to find a restroom, a clean cut gentleman, wearing a collared golf shirt and khakis, came along side of me from out of nowhere and opened the door for me and pointed in the direction of the restrooms, like he was a regular. From the first glance of the customers on the bar stools, he didn't look like a regular. Where did he come from, and how did he know where the restrooms were, let alone that I was looking for on? I am sure he was an angel sent to protect me. That was the quickest stop I had made in a long time, and I was soon driving down the highway again laughing out loud at my choice of stops and marveling at the doorman God sent.

It was a beautiful ride, and I was praising God with every mile. In no time, I had entered Wyoming and was soon headed north toward Grand Teton National Park, though I was only going as far as Jackson this trip. I knew I would be back for a longer trip maybe in the next summer or two when I could really enjoy the National Park, so I settled on just seeing Jackson Hole. I was truly enjoying the curvy road, the miles of praise, and the mountains when the road snaked around and took a little dip. I caught my breath, barely able to keep the pressure on the accelerator. I was following the Snake River, which originates in Yellowstone National Park, as I understand it. The sun was glistening off the water that was at the basin of these majestic mountains, and in the moment, taking in every inch of the Snake River Canyon, I was completely blown away by the Master's design. Literal tears started streaming down my face from the beauty, and I just began a litany of praise and thanks for our country, for this landscape, for this trip, for this opportunity, for this moment. It was deeply moving to see so many natural elements in harmonious relationship and giving off waves of beauty and life and light. It was pure gratitude. You simply must experience that for yourself.

Into Jackson Hole, Wyoming, I rolled, and I loved it all the more. This little rugged town, nestled into the valley surrounded by the mountains of the Grand Teton National Park, has a unique charm. I parked in front of the Jackson Hole Chamber of Commerce and stepped inside to grab a handful of brochures for planning my return trip. I struck up a lively conversation with the Chamber representative, and we talked about my upcoming Chamber interview. She wished me well. I meandered down the wood-planked sidewalk, crossed the street, and posed by some oversized stuffed animals like Bison and Elk. I sat on the iron bench, took a selfie with a bronze statue lookalike of Albert Einstein, and posed on a bench; how quirky and amusing. I stopped passersby to take my photo under the famous Elk Antler Arches in Town Square.

According to information provided by the Chamber, Jackson Hole is home to the

National Elk Refuge, and because male elk shed their antlers every spring, there is an abundance of antlers near Town Square. Boy Scouts and The Rotary Club were responsible for gathering and eventually erecting the distinctive arches.

Though I wanted to rustle up some wild game for lunch, I had to settle on the newest Tex-Mex restaurant in town for location and speed. It was already time for me to head south after a fantastic afternoon in Jackson Hole. It was my first time ordering chicharron (fried pork belly) and perhaps my last, but the enchiladas and slightly spicy enchilada sauce were a big win.

It was a long, windy way through Big Piney and Kemmerer toward Evanston, but a beautiful view and an extended flavor of Wyoming treated me before I crossed back in to Utah. I had called the University of Utah housing office to arrange for a room in the summer guest quarters, typically residence halls, so that I would have an overnight stay in Salt Lake City. I had been president of the university residence halls when I attended the University of South Alabama and recalled that we made rooms available to guests. It was more affordable than a brand hotel downtown and offered a unique experience and availability.

I headed downtown to find a good meal in the city. I parked at the outer edges of town, hoping to walk in to a corner seafood restaurant I saw, but with a closer look, there wasn't a good vibe, so I started checking my About Me app and targeted another restaurant. I had to walk for blocks only to discover the restaurant I was searching for had closed, perhaps relocated, but I didn't have the energy to search it out. I was getting hungry and frustrated when I saw a rickshaw type commercial bicyclist cycle by and without passengers. I called out to the driver who gladly picked me up and took me to a very hip joint—the Red Rock Ale house. It was the best steak dinner I have had in some time.

I was in heaven. While I waited on the steak to arrive, I took notes on my idea to bring commercial bicycles to our re-urbanization project back home to Fayetteville, the neighboring town looking to attract and retain Millenials. Salt Lake City had a great night vibe, and I was totally comfortable walking around, passing Temple Square and several other buildings brightly lit in the night.

I was happy to make the drive back to my college room after such a fun night downtown. The university offered a pleasant stay with a buffet breakfast, which I shared with about 50 athletes attending a summer program on campus. It was a little noisy and rowdy, but a lively experience.

And, with that, three states in two days, I had had a good taste of the National Parks in this neck of the woods, the mountains, and three more states of my America. I was now ready to head to Texas to meet my international pastor friend Miguel and visit my sister for the weekend. I could use some sister time. But, I would soon learn, God had other plans.

## CHAPTER SEVENTEEN

# REROUTED FOR
# A PATRIOTIC SURPRISE

There was no time for friend visits in Colorado or sister visits in Texas this summer.

Salt Lake City International Airport was bustling with people. It was mid-June, and summer travel was obviously underway. That would be a problem with my space-available buddy pass, but I didn't anticipate it to be a problem for me because I was headed south to Houston, Texas. I checked the flight, went to the gate, took a seat, texted Miguel to confirm our rendezvous for a prayer event, and checked in with the Holy Spirit on His confirmation for this leg of my journey.

The Delta representative called stand-by passengers for seat assignments and boarding passes. I, naturally, stood up. Mentally, I was asking God if I was in the right direction. I was simultaneously texting my sister, who was looking forward to my arrival, and the minister, who immediately responded, "Jackie, I'm sorry, the prayer meeting we were to meet at didn't transpire. We will reschedule." Reschedule? I was standing at the gate, ready to board. They were calling passenger names. Okay, don't panic. I'll just visit my sister, I reasoned. I quickly texted her again, and in just a few exchanges, I could feel that she was suddenly lukewarm for our visit. A lunch meeting she had planned so I could meet someone she knew in publishing didn't transpire, and that left a nice, quiet sister weekend for us, but I could sense she coveted some downtime as well, since she had just come off a high intensity workweek and grandma's weekend with her little grandkids; she "understood if I didn't make it." What? Was I imposing? Oh no! Time to make a decision, Delta was calling my name.

"Father? Hello? Am I supposed to go to Texas?" No answer. Okay, I'm going, anyway. It's a place to stay for the weekend, be pampered, and enjoy my sister.

I reached the Delta counter and the gate check to receive my seat assignment, and the Holy Spirit says, "Sit down."

"Sit down? I'm going to Texas."

"Sit down." A seat assignment on a plane, heading out of Salt Lake City, with my name on it in the middle of summer and The Holy Spirit says, "I know. Sit down." Oh, how I didn't want to, but I knew better than to debate. He is in control, and He always has a better plan. So I reluctantly told the gate attendant I had changed my mind, not mentioning my little conversation with God, of course, and just sat down, dumbfounded and wondering where I was going.

Little did I know, His plan would include a 12-hour delay in the Salt Lake City Airport. Yep. There were no flights going out with empty seats, and my buddy pass was no good out of Salt Lake City now. Yes, I anguished over the fact that I had a seat on a plane headed to Texas just hours before.

The first few hours, I played the non-revenue charade: switch gates every hour, use the red phone to change flights when another airport looked like it was opening up, chase the flights, until I surrendered and asked the Holy Spirit what I was doing and to clearly highlight my travel plans. Simple.

He had assignments and prayer opportunities one after another to lead me and delay me to the flight I was to be on. Paramedics were called in for the man in the corner gate; he was down for the count. Rather than crowd the space, I prayed from afar. I'm sure angels were sent to take charge over him. He seemed to come around before being taken out on a gurney.

Stories were shared, folks were encouraged by my testimony, and questions were asked and shared about the temperature of America; there was a purpose for my delay. And, then there was the lady in the wheelchair who was next to me as I waited to speak to yet another gate agent about getting out of Salt Lake City.

The general consensus for my ticket fare was "you are not getting out anywhere for at least two days." This was not welcome news, but the lady in the wheelchair was bursting out in tears, and I was an arm length from her, so I reached out and comforted her as she spoke to the gate agent, who was doing her best to offer compassion. "I'm so sorry you missed your flight. We don't have anything going out for hours."

It turned out her daughter in California had been in a car accident, and she was trying to get to her. She felt helpless, and I can only imagine that this feeling was enhanced as she sat there in

172

a wheelchair, traveling alone. I knew God had me on assignment. Delta wheeled her over to the waiting area close to the wall and told her they would be back to check on her periodically. That wouldn't do. I took up residence next to her and comforted her and offered prayer and companionship for several hours, offering to get her food and drink in the interim, as well. She offered me a prayer she kept in printed form in her purse. I now keep it in mine. It was beautiful inspiration. I was trying to lift her up, and she was looking for a way to thank and encourage me. During our time together, she shared many life issues her family was facing, and I was able to pray with her, encourage her, and offer her family's needs to God in prayer later, as well.

When she finally made a flight at about 7:30 p.m., I knew my work in Salt Lake City was finished and I was free to make a move. Where else could I go? I frantically looked at all the destination boards and caught Kansas City, Missouri out of the corner of my eye. It was almost time to board the 8:15 p.m. flight, but I still had time to change the destination on my ticket. I headed to a red phone and was able to make the change as they were finishing up the boarding at the nearby gate. I got a seat assignment and waited for them to call me onboard. As quick as I could, while waiting at the gate, I searched for a hotel in my landing destination and reserved online. There was barely time for the website to cycle through and accept my payment when it was time for me to board and for the agents to close the gate door behind me. This last-minute travel seemed to keep working out, but it was a bit stressful trying to use every second to secure my plans so I wasn't landing in a strange city without a place to lay my head well after dark.

"God, I don't understand. I have just been to St. Louis, Missouri last week with Kellie. Why am I going to Missouri again?" I asked once in my seat on the plane. "I don't have time to waste on states I have already been to," I anguished—not that it really mattered. I was happy to be getting out of Salt Lake City to somewhere, anywhere; two days there with dwindling funds would not have been welcomed.

Then, I overheard someone talking, and the light bulb went off— Kansas City, Missouri shares a border with Kansas City, *Kansas*, yet another state I have not been. God was so good to orchestrate my journey. I arrived very late, near midnight, into the airport—state number 44—and knew I had just 15 minutes to exit the plane, run to the curb, and catch the hotel shuttle or I would be taking a cab, and at this point, I really didn't know how many dollars I had left in my account; I was going on trust the whole way.

"Lord, you are going to have to help me here." I made a mad dash and caught the shuttle just in time. That was lucky. Thank you, God. The driver brought me to the hotel I had secured through Expedia online. I shuffled on and off and on again as we realized there were two locations for the brand hotel I had secured and I had a reservation at the other location. It gave the driver and me time to talk about his great city. I shared briefly that I was an author, writing about patriotic topics.

He said, "Oh, well in that case, you ought to go downtown. I hear there's a memorial or a statue or something patriotic you might be interested in." He was a youthful driver and hadn't seen it himself.

His brief, casual comment would turn out to be the highlight of my trip and the main purpose of my 12-hour delay. By rerouting my trip, God was aligning my schedule with the calendar at this particular location. Tomorrow, I would discover, would be a very important day for me. But, tonight, I had more important things in mind, like where would I find a cozy bed and if there still was money in my checking account when it was time to pay the bill.

When I arrived, dog-tired, just after the midnight hour, I leaned on the counter and mentioned my journey and delay at the over-crowded airport, and the Spirit of the Lord moved on the clerk and she said, "Oh, you are a stranded passenger? We have a special rate for that." Thank you, Jesus. Yes, I was a stranded and nearly broke passenger, grateful for a bed and the courtesy of this newfound discount.

I had the desk clerk call a shuttle so I wouldn't waste any time, and she was accommodating to keep my backpack for my day's excursion. It was nice to be free from that weight. The shuttle driver arrived and invited me to sit in the front seat as he guided me through his city. He pulled up in front of the "small memorial" the shuttle driver mentioned; however, I was taken aback by the great expanse and prestige of this memorial. The "small memorial or something" turned out to be *the only* World War I National Museum in the United States, a massive, architecturally-beautiful marble-designed building. And, to this former Army spouse and patriotic writer, on this day, June 14th, the 240th anniversary of the Army's birthday and the observance of Flag Day, I was pretty blown away. God is awesome. The whole time I was stuck in the Salt Lake City Airport, I was on assignment, being His hands, feet, and mouthpiece, yes, but He was preparing a way to reward and bless me with something better than I could have imagined. That's a pretty awesome God I serve, wouldn't you say? I pray for stories and experiences and blessings like this for you, too. Trust Him. He doesn't have favorites; we are all His favorites. He has blessings like this for you too.

The most amazing design of the building is a clear glass floor of a bridge which allows you to see through to the level under your feet, filled with 9,000 poppies, the memorial flower of World War I veterans—each one representing 1,000 combatant deaths. It was intimidating to walk on this unique, transparent walkway and humbling to see so many poppies for so many American lives represented.

The massive amounts of red poppies I was looking at was symbolic of the famous poem "The Flander Fields," written by poet, physician, and Canadian colonel John McCrae, who was intrigued that the poppy could lie dormant for years and reappear in greater number. He associated that with his veteran patients and deceased comrades. Walking on the glass flooring was like walking on water, and the poppies were images of the fallen from World War I.

The museum was a maze of many nooks and rooms, so something informative and emotionally touching was around every corner. I especially like that God had surprise after surprise for me, like one soldier's personal letter home to his wife and family on Christmas. As a former military spouse, that resonated with me, having experienced deployments and separation over Christmas and other important holidays. It was heart wrenching.

I enjoyed the religious relics on display and took a photo. And I was thankful when I went into an alcove and found the entire Uncle Sam campaign, including a patriotic Joan of Arc. It was as if God was delivering the public relations plan for my books I was writing and showing me the charge I would lead. There was a plaque that outlined "the birth of modern public relations," down to the speeches, posters, and pamphlets needed to run a successful plan. It was then I laughed at the realization that my patriotic program, *Spirit of AMerica days*, shared the same acronym as Uncle SAM. God had planted that in me back in the fall/winter of 2001. It was exciting to see it unfold nearly 15 years later.

One of the last displays was a beautiful wall art of every Army insignia, including the 3rd Infantry Division patch I think my former spouse wore. I didn't see other branch insignia displayed in this grand manner; it was a special recognition for me.

At the conclusion of my beautiful tour, I took the opportunity to connect with a retail member at the bookstore and introduce *The Military Family* book and the possibility of including it in their retail bookstore. I bought a poppy lapel pin to always remember. I could never forget this special day, but we all need to remember. Americans need to remember, more than just on Veteran's Day and D-Day and Memorial Day. We need to remember the cost of freedom always.

The building was massive and also had an outside observation deck with awesome city views. I walked down a bunch of stairs and down a long street to the old train station where the Kansas City Trolley car was waiting to take me on a city tour. I had phoned the trolley company only to have the driver answer, and he held the tour a few extra minutes while I walked the distance. What a sweet life gesture!

This was one of the most patriotic cities I had encountered, and on Flag Day, of all days, I got to be a part of it. God was delaying me at the airport, and there I praised Him and served others, only to be blessed with a grand ol' blessing like today. I was thrilled and delighted. It makes the waiting, the stumbling blocks, and the delays more palatable when you know God and trust Him to have your best in mind. Rather than moaning, groaning, and waiting in angst, we can release, serve, and praise Him and bless others, knowing our amazing God will reward us according to His perfect plan.

I greeted the tour guide and could see they were actually waiting on a few guests to purchase their tickets and join the ride, which made me sigh in relief; I hate to keep people waiting and delay others because of my tardiness or selfishness.

God had saved me the very front seat. There were two guides on the bus as they were waiting to change shifts. It set the stage for a magnetic entry where I began pouring out my witness. The tour guides joined in with rich contributions that shed light on the Christian and patriotic temperature in Kansas City. The off-going tour guide was able to share that his neighbors had indeed asked him to take down his American flag when he posted it recently, yet he refused. There was stimulating conversation from every tourist seated on the bus who agreed he should stand firm and the American flag should remain. I was getting excited with my conversation and testimony and added that it was the 240th birthday of the United States Army and as Americans we should do our part to be aware of these observances. A few people called out from the back of the trolley, "You should give her the microphone. She should be leading a tour." God is always generous to "give me the microphone," like this.

And, all that transpired because God had delayed me and the tour just the right amount of minutes to have both transferring tour guides onboard and an opportunity for me to have the floor and the front seat as His mouthpiece. Be bold for Christ because others are yearning to hear it! Be patient with delays because God's timing is always perfect. Be encouraged because Americans do care about our heritage, our flag, and our country.

What a great tour. I saw American flags waving, a host of small businesses, and culture galore. There were museums one after another, art on the lawn, and sculptures—this Kansas City was one amazing metropolitan place! I determined to come back in the winter and celebrate at Kansas City Plaza for the lighting of the Christmas lights. I'm sure it would be dazzling.

My prayer warrior back in Georgia had been praying I would be on TV to share my testimony, and don't you know that when I got off the trolley, there was a newscaster on the sidewalk doing interviews. God answers prayers, even across a continent. I approached with reluctance as I didn't want to intrude and I only had an hour left before my shuttle driver would arrive, furthermore I had not eaten a morsel all day and wanted to savor some famous Kansas barbecue. It was for God's glory, so the newscaster took precedence and I headed toward the newscaster and decided to forego the barbecue, but just as I approached, his interview appointment of Kansas City Royal players showed up. I changed the direction of my path and made a beeline for Jack Stack Barbecue, Freight House, on foot and let him attend to his scheduled interview, knowing, with satisfaction, God had created the opportunity and had, indeed, answered our prayer for television exposure; there would be another future opportunity, I was sure.

Walking through Union Station to the freight house back alley was an experience in itself—with interesting people, fixtures, an obscure, rickety elevator, and an exhibit. I love cities that intentionally add design and education to highly trafficked areas.

I was so excited to be at Jack Stack; I actually had the waiter take a picture of me with the menu so I could share on Facebook because my friend back in Georgia just visited the popular barbecue joint last week while visiting family at another location, hence my discovery of this great gastronomic delight. She and I seemed to walk in tandem, arriving at destinations one before the other. This visit was for Brandi as much as for me.

The crown prime rib beef tips and shredded pork barbecue made a hefty combination from their "remarkable menu," just like it says, with cheesy corn bake; trust me, order it. This was another "royal" meal, with crown burnt tips in the city of Royals; I was smiling at the irony of this trip King Jesus had planned for me. I threw in a slice of their famous carrot cake to go as I spoke with and breathed life into the young server behind the bar, a single mother. We talked about her future, her destiny, and her education plans. I was a well-fed body and soul when I got a tap on my right shoulder. My shuttle driver had taken time to come in to the restaurant and summon me to leave. Who goes the extra mile like that? I might have to start replacing "southern hospitality" in my vocabulary with "American hospitality."

On the 30-minute drive back to the hotel, I shared my story and day's experience with the driver, who actually seemed to be listening intently and genuinely happy for my experiences. I was telling him my quest for 50 states and how I ended up in Missouri twice, but without a car to get to Kansas this trip. At that moment, he grinned ear-to-ear and said, "I can fix that." I have a choice on the return trip to go back the way we came or to take the bridge. It's a little longer, but it goes back by way of Kansas City, Kansas.

And, with that, he willingly escorted me through my 45th state.

It might not have been the full experience, but considering the limitations of time and resources and what I saw of the bordering state, I was fully satisfied to count it. He said there are shootings there every night, and he only brought me because it was still daylight and we were just driving through. It made me sad, and I jumped on the opportunity to pray silently for the spirit of poverty and lack. I prayed for the devil's lies to be broken. I prayed for the children and the homes, that the fathers to rise up and lead and for God to shake the town out of their complacency and darkness. Nothing is lost to Jesus. It was a valuable side trip.

As an extra tip, I let him know I had brought back a take-out box of Jack Stack barbecue. I had put it on a clean side plate prior to digging in, seeing the portion was too large for me to eat alone and brought it home in a container, rather than waste it. God already had a plan for it. Do you know, he was delighted to receive what would have been discarded. He said his wife was sickly, and he had gone through a hard time and making ends meet was a challenge, especially in regard to food. I was glad it was a fresh portion and happy that he would receive it as a blessing. The Lord provides for the sparrows, and He also provides for His children; it was a blessing to be part of the giving. It was also humbling to think of my abundance. I prayed for his increase.

And, with that, I went back to my room, replayed my amazing, patriotic day, proud of the USA and loving my amazing God. I took a few satisfying bites of my carrot cake slice, disappointed I didn't think to give that to my kind shuttle driver too, although, I did leave him a satisfying tip, in addition to the meat portion. He provided for me so much more than a shuttle into town and another state for my list.

# CHAPTER EIGHTEEN

# STANDING FOR CHRIST UNDER PERSECUTION

It was time, God's time, because in spite of a crowded airport, without delay, I got on the flight home to Atlanta. And, there he had set up a divine appointment, as well. Arriving home, I had expected my son to pick me up at the airport in my car—the one I had filled with gas and loaned him for an entire week while I was away. But, the rage of a teenager led him to depart from what he knew to be right. After a great deal of angst and back and forth with him on the telephone, I decided this was God's battle and not mine and when he refused to meet me at the airport because of the long drive. I went curbside for a shuttle to take me to my car, north of Atlanta, so I could drive myself home, south of Atlanta; it was a good two-hour journey or better in total.

Yes, any other good day and there would have been war, consequences, and good parenting. Today, without a place to call home, weary from supernatural, supercharged travels, and in the midst of spiritual battles within, I let go and let God. It was a great choice. God has His way and had a spiritual appointment for me, too. He would reconcile this situation down the road.

Having decided my ground transportation once I arrived, I took my seat in the back of the plane and asked God to cancel any assignments so I could rest. I was tired from my long journey, delay in the airport, carrying my pack and such, and ready to be home, in my bed that is not waiting for me. God laughs from heaven. I no sooner sat down than a female passenger took the middle seat next. Catching a glance of the cross pendant around her neck, I knew I was in for a flight with a loaded conversation ahead. We exchanged names.

"Valerie Miles of Acworth, Georgia. Nice to meet you." And when she heard I was a Christian author on assignment for God, she got so bubbly and happy and exclaimed, "Thank you, Jesus!" See, God had an assignment for her, too. She had been praying to meet someone who could help her write a book churning in her. And, I was an author's coach. God had arranged the whole flight.

I was pondering my transportation options home. I wasn't sure my son would meet me; I didn't know how much an Uber would be, and I was sure I had less than a few dollars left. I wasn't worried; I knew God would work it out. We continued our conversation, feeling like we needed to meet again to work out the many ideas we were trying to exchange and heard the wheels touch down on the tarmac. We had landed in Atlanta once again.

Without much thought, she whipped out her checkbook and handed me a $100 love offering. "I am feeling good about this. This is sewing good seed." I was touched. "You know, my husband

and I were supposed to sit together, but they couldn't work it out; he's sitting up front, but I knew God had a better plan and I didn't mind, at all."

God did have a better plan and now I knew my transportation plan home, too. I lined up for the speedy shuttle vans at the curb. The shuttle driver was from South Africa and very open to the testimony of my trip. Deep into it, he revealed a God encounter with a former pro-athlete passenger. It was then that I leaned in from the back seat to make a point and my eyes landed on his King James Bible which he had sitting on the front dashboard. It was a beautiful moment of discovery. He said he used his shuttle business as an opportunity to witness for God. He shared an amazing story from one of his passengers, and I retorted with a victorious "Yes!" and, claimed that God had a monumental win planned for me and this book. At that moment we both laid eyes on this massive billboard with the words "Believe!" emblazoned on it, from Morgan and Morgan, of all firms. Morgan, again, was my family name, my mother's maiden name and my second son's middle name. God was confirming blessings ahead and the cleansing of generations. We were both laughing and pleased, and he slowed long enough for me to take a great snapshot of it on my phone. At that moment, we both believed in God's miracles ahead.

I was able to get to my car and hold my tongue from scolding my son; instead, I went to fill my car because of the gas he had used. I purchased him a gas gift card to get home in his own car too. It's what moms do. God would work it out in his spirit. There was a lot being asked of him.

I was happy to get to my car, fresh clothes, and what resembled my home. I had one storage unit that was only partially full, and it became the home base for rotating clothes and, in extreme cases, quick changes. My air had gone out in my car just at the start of June—and what would be the hottest summer on record in Georgia. I was driving around in misery with no air conditioning, thankful for the sunroof and the windows I could roll down. It was miserable. I had brought the car in to get fixed, but they were unable to order the part for it and there was a long delay. I was still happy to have my own set of wheels back. It was particularly uncomfortable, though, when I had to dress up and head over for my interview in the sweltering heat.

I was cutting it short on time but had to stop at the storage unit, digging for where I had packed a résumé and leather portfolio in advance for such an occasion and pulling out hanging clothes one at a time looking for a reasonable business blouse and suit. They were pretty wrinkled from the move and the heat, but I put my hands on a group of clothes that had recently come from the cleaners and not yet been worn. I was able to pull together a suit and business look and head out with just enough time to get there. My hair was whipping outside the window, tying itself in knots as I drove down the highway. I was reviewing notes from my résumé trying to remember what the job position entailed and what skills I had that might fit the role. Did I have any business skills left?

I aced the interview like a rock star, I might say, considering all the odds against me, but times were different. I had the mark of Jesus all over my résumé and website. I was given many questions to test my business acumen and defend my professional experiences, but the one I couldn't overcome was the repeated inquisition regarding my books.

"I see you are an author and your books have a Christian theme," was a repeated leading statement.

"Yes, I am an author; my books are about my spiritual journey of faith. I have been paid as an author. I will forever more be a Christian author and, undeniably, a Christian."

They asked if I would shut down my website and stop promoting my books if I were offered the position. This was getting dicey. This amazing position, with the big title and the awesome salary, when I had not even a home, nor air conditioning in my car, was enticing. And they were dangling the solution right before me, if only I would deny my sweet Jesus and walk away from being the person He made me to be. Satan did exactly that to Jesus. He offered him everything in his material kingdom. "All this I will give you," he said, "if you will bow down and worship me" (Matthew 4:9).

I replied, "Writing is what I do, like how you go fishing, and you see grandkids on the weekend; I write. And, no, I can't stop writing; it's who I am and what I'm called to do. I'm a Christian author. I'll always be a Christian author." I also reassured them. "I was a military spouse for 23 years. I have worked with all cultures, ages, and types of people. I know protocol. Business is business. I am a professional. I understand the sensitivity of certain topics in the workplace."

I was like Daniel in the lion's den, and this was modern-day Christian persecution at best. I knew I wasn't going to be offered this position, but I defended myself and my calling and vied for the position best I could, in case it was truly what God had for me. Each board member continued to say how well suited and well qualified I was for the position and how they could see me in the position, but there was a lingering hesitation over my books with the Christian perspective.

I intentionally brought my *Military Family* book and placed it on the table as we talked. I write about solid values and American patriotism, as well. "This book talks about what America stands for. Though there might be a few references to biblical verses, that's not its main focus. And, if American values aren't how you do business, I wouldn't be a good fit for your organization, anyway." I stood firm and gave them a balanced view of my work.

I walked away with confidence that each board member saw me as competitive for the Executive Director position, knowing this would be an excellent fit for my experiences and my personality. I would love the chance, if offered, but I knew that God had a different path for me.

And, true to my intuition and the Holy Spirit's calling, I never heard back, at all.

I was a hot potato no one wanted to touch in this changing business culture of ours. This was the land of opportunity and the home of the free and the brave because God has established her and blessed her, and now He and His followers were a hotbed of trouble and best avoided, especially in the work place.

I was okay with that. That position wasn't the answer, but I know God had one for me; I just had to persevere. And, I was proud that when under fire, I stood firm in front of the enemy and the interrogation and stood for Christ. I was rock solid. "Deny me before men and I will deny you before my Father in heaven" (Matthew 10:33).

And, after all that, I got to drive back to my storage unit in the sweltering heat and eat some more humble pie. There is joy in suffering with Christ, the Bible says. And, there was. It was sweet to be so close to my Savior, held in the palm of His hand and knowing my redemption and my opportunity lie ahead.

There's a saying on the wall of Mimi's Good Food, the local diner my kids both serve at. It says, "Not all those who wander are lost. – J. R. R. Tolkein." This saying is particularly true for me. I once was lost, but now I'm found, as the favorite hymn "Amazing Grace" says. And when I wander, I wander with purpose for my Lord, waiting for His direction. He is always my true north, and I am never alone.

If He wanted me to have a job, even an Executive Director job, He certainly could make it happen and open that door. He had just clearly proved that, but I could feel it in my spirit, and the interview was clear to indicate, that there was another plan for me.

Now I had to address sleeping arrangements that I was back in town—yes, there's that on top of everything else. I take this one day at a time, always thinking ahead and considering two or three possible options but trusting the Lord to nudge me in the right direction. I texted a few friends, and with a quick response a friend offered the guest room for a whole four days, what a luxury not to have to go from bed to bed for so many days.

Kellie discovered a turtle on the lawn when we arrived, and it was just like any other summer day. Staying at someone's house was good comfort; it felt like home or like we were on a summer vacation visiting aunts and uncles. The problem came when I was handed a key and didn't have to use it until the last day, only to discover I had misplaced it. We combed the grass, cleared the car, unpacked all that was packed, and determined the turtle must have trotted off with it. That was a painful $80 mistake as my resources were so depleted, not to mention that it was an embarrassing event to have to take responsibility for. I don't recall ever losing a key. How could I be such an inconsiderate guest? Why did this have to happen to me now? Mistakes happen and the devil loves to keep me caught up in chaos. Too bad for him, I stay close to God in prayer when turmoil comes. You know, I take that shield of faith and deflect his fiery darts with God's promises. That helped for a week or so, but still there was no key, and I had to make good on the lock change.

To top that little mishap off, the body shop offered me the air conditioning repair bill that included a compressor, a recharge for the system, and a flush and supplies. The bill was hefty—an astronomical number, according to my bank account. Oh my word, I guess Satan wasn't too happy I stood up for Christ, and he wanted to push me to see if I'd cave. Nope. I just kept trusting God for provision and thanked Him for all that I did have: a great car, a great town to live in, my healthy kids, and great accommodations every night. I recalled all the moving miracles and the amazing journeys. Nope, I knew God had His hand all over my life, and it was for His good purpose. I repented a lot and sifted through my conscience for things gone by. I prayed for my family tree and asked God's blessings on all 1,000 generations to come. I didn't want to be the reason my blessings were blocked. I figured there was a huge price tag for that kind of ask. Yes, I know it is finished; Jesus was the price tag for all my sins. It is *His* redemption, no redeeming of mine can pay the price, but I still believe there is truth in the book of Leviticus and sometimes atonement and offerings are required—I was, after all, pursuing a clean family tree for generations before me. And, yes, I am a New Testament follower, but through experience, I can tell you atonement and offerings have been part of my walk. Not inspired by a guilt-ridden conscience or from a sinner's perspective, but an act of obedience, a fragrant offering to my Lord.

God is in control; that's all I know. And we are to accept the good with the bad and to be content in all things; it says so in the book of Hebrews. Surrender because God's in control anyway. It's the only way I know how to do this life. He certainly had the resources to fix my air conditioning if He wanted to, which, thankfully, after three long, hot weeks, He did. Hallelujah.

# CHAPTER NINETEEN
## A HOME ON THE HORIZON

In the midst of juggling kids, daily sleeping arrangements, travel plans, storage units, and keys, I still had a small piece of me wondering about my future housing arrangements. Kellie, being the youngest of five, was bent on graduating from the same school as her four older siblings, and Peachtree City had become home after 12 years. I prayed God was bringing us back. In the days between trips, I searched for rental property in her school zone. Due to an influx of new folks to town due to the Pinewood Movie studios, inventory was low and prices were high—not a good situation when you are jobless, homeless, and walking on faith. I continued to comb the market, drive the neighborhoods, and put out my feelers, without fully divulging my crazy situation. Not that I had any pride left, I just wanted to maintain normalcy and not always explain the whole leap of faith.

As soon as a rental went on the market, I'd be there, along with four other families looking for housing. One time, Kellie was so frustrated, I told her to fleece God.

We prayed for a house with a view in the school district. The very next day one with a lake and golf course view, in our price range and school zone became available. So she put up her own $50 for a rental application fee, but the house went to another family. I was not yet finished with the journey, but I wanted to show her if God wanted to give us a house, He could. That was brave for a 14-year-old with less than $100 in her account. I knew God would provide at the right time because He takes care of the sparrows, and He was my provider too. It was a good lesson for her.

And, now it was three weeks into June, and my funds were locked down. Having been through all the June income and extra provision God sent, the bills, needs and travel schedule still demanded my attention. It was during these times I would become vigilant to solve the problem.

With the interview out of the way, I was intent on finding something for our home, just in case they made an offer and I had to start July 1. I would need a house and would have to move out of the way as fast as possible. I saw a sign go up on the corner, and I passed through the neighborhood. It was my friend's home, the home where my son occasionally spent the night. I called her up right away, and she let me pop in. I walked into the foyer, loved the open-air ceilings and the "feel."

I said "Great. I'll take it."

Then I took a speedy look through the rest of the house. It had a very small kid's room and a nice size master with a walk-in closet; I lucked out there. The view was a small patio with a retaining wall that had greenery cascading over it. Sold. I didn't even know if my belongings would fit. We would squeeze. I had at least sold the baby grand, which God already knew wouldn't fit here, and it was a continuous process to shed material things, so I would make it work.

I called the landlord immediately, and we met at Starbucks. He had four appointments lined up to see it first thing in the morning, but since I saw it first, he gave me first right of refusal. Now it was time to do my show-and-tell and pray for the Holy Spirit to show up. I told him I wasn't credit worthy. I didn't have a job. My last landlord might not give me a favorable report, though the neighbors would. But I explained that I was writing a book on a journey of faith. I said that I was a single mom with dependable child support and would make it work and take care of his house. When he learned I had been a friend of his current tenant for 10 years and that we were both part of the same church, he said, "I don't know why I'm doing this, but I like you. I'm going to take a chance and say, ok."

Boy, was he taking a chance, and I was so very grateful. I didn't have the first penny for one month's deposit or rent when we spoke, but I knew in my spirit, the Holy Spirit was prompting me to jump in faith, and He would provide it. I filled out the application and encouraged him to save his time and my money and not officially run it through the credit check. He wouldn't like what he saw in print, and to my relief, he agreed. I left with a lease to complete, and he left with a promise, guaranteed by God.

So I prayed, "Lord, you are going to have to do something. You have me on this journey and I am walking in faith, trusting you. You are going to have to provide for this need."

And, in not so many days later, He confirmed His faithfulness.

He sent someone my way who listened to my testimony and wrote a check for one month's rent which would serve as my deposit just at the right time. God is so good. Thank you to the kind person who cared enough to bless a single mother and her family. Where would I have been without that grace? Where would I be on any given day without God's blessing and provision?

It confirmed to me God would make good on all His promises. I was humbled. Of course, I spoke of this to no one. To this day, my children have no idea how precarious our situation was or how much I relied on God's provision. He is a good and faithful provider. He said He would, and He did.

The house wasn't available until August 1st, but it gave me great relief. Besides, if God wanted me to move somewhere else, it would present itself. At least I knew I had a back-up plan. August 1st was a long way away—forty-two more days to go. Now, what?

There were still those other five states lingering. There were still a stack of bills I knew were mounting. The mail had gotten all screwy in the move. I placed a temporary hold order, and my disgruntled landlord placed a "vacant" sign in the mailbox so no mail could be delivered. Technically, since I had no house, no hold is permitted. On the second week, a mail carrier pulled the hold order and my mail went to outer space for a while. I got a post office box, but that was another expense I didn't need; it was all so unfortunate. It took weeks for the mail to catch up. And, then I was moving into the rental house and had to re-forward it. It was a maze of paper trails and so unnecessary. After all, I had hand delivered mail for over a year to both the former rental tenant who had relocated locally and my homeowner every time it arrived. Sometimes you can do nice things, but it still doesn't flow your way. Do the right thing anyway.

Oh, well, no mail, no bills, right? That was my outlook. I called when I knew particular things were due and paid by phone, and I lost contacts along the way. It was another cost of doing life God's way.

I had no money coming in, no place to station myself for projects; I had no control to work or produce income during this transition. All I could do is depend on God as my provider. The few days after that second trip turned into good productivity as I had the job interview, secured the rental house, and then was waiting upon God's prompting to depart again. It was nine long days of lingering, shuffling, wondering, and angst. I tried to think of creative ways to fund the last leg of my journey. I was so close. How could I come this close and not finish? Finally, I had fresh inspiration.

Recall from my 50th birthday how I received a ticket to anywhere in the world? *Anywhere.* I was dreaming of Bora Bora and French Polynesia. Well, sometimes higher priorities come along. I knew that God could find a way to replace it and make even that happen at the right time, but I needed that golden ticket now. It was trying to get my courage up and not let the cat out of the bag about my recent travels; that was the hardest part. I finally reached out to my brother, the gift-giver.

"I know you might have been thinking of using your points to fulfill my birthday ticket to anywhere, but do you think I could cash in my ticket for a cash value? A ticket to Bora Bora is easily $1,700 and up. I'm in the middle of an adventure, and I'd really like to finish. Would you consider some reasonable cash amount instead?" I was humble and hopeful, and I drew in my breath with a big Cheshire grin over the phone.

I gulped. He pondered it and said he needed a few days to think of it. A few days? Sigh. Well, what's a few days more? And besides, what other option did I have?

In the meantime, I marked time with my daily routine and made it to Friday when the faith-based movie, "Max" was released. I was glad to see it the night it came out. I'm personally thrilled faith-based movies are becoming so popular. It means America is starting to stir and wake up. There is a wave of faith-based movies since 2015. "War Room" and "God's Not Dead" each grossed over $60 million dollars. "Noah," with Russell Crowe, grossed over $301 million. I'm personally happy that America's eyes and ears are stirring and searching for truth. I have several film-ready, faith-based books I can't wait to show on the movie screen for the world to see. Hello Kendrick brothers!

God has positioned me in Fayette County, GA, home to Pinewood Movie Studios and perhaps, the faith-based inspirational film capital of the world in the near future, if prayers are answered and more films are attracted to use the movie studios here. America needs to see the miracles I have experienced and hear these amazing stories I have been a part of. God is amazing, and I know I didn't see and experience all of this just for myself, but to share with the world at this very time. Many folks are visual learners, and we need visual reminders. Besides, seeing the landscape I visited on this journey on the movie screen would inspire many to travel America and connect with her again. It's a true adventure I hope to share soon. Get your maps ready and clear your calendars. You are going to want to take an adventure for yourself very soon.

When I saw "Max" was directed by Boaz Yakin, I smiled. Boaz is the character in my second book, and Kyle, the main character who played the son, is also my oldest son's name. And the date on the tombstone in the movie was my parents' wedding anniversary. Was it a coincidence or spiritual nuances?

I thought if America can be inspired by a military dog, my family's true story, *The Military Family: A Casualty of War*, would surely be an inspiration to many. I was hopeful for the future of my story and for the journey still before me.

Inspiration and confirmations were good, but I was very restless and ready to roll. Let's do this trip so I can get back to my life and settle in a house.

My brother finally sent a text, having arrived at a number, a number I knew God could stretch to work, and I was grateful for his generosity to fuel my dreams and celebrate my jubilee. I thought it was perfect. And he did it without knowing that he was seeding my 50 X 50 dream. It was from him I got the mindset and the inspiration to set my original goal of fifty states by fifty years. Nine days later, the day after "Max" was released in movie theaters, I was grateful for my brother's gift and finally released to go too.

I had to ask my friend for a second buddy pass, but she happily issued one. She wasn't sure why I was doing all this traveling; she thought it peculiar I wasn't looking for a job and a house. But she had agreed to issue me one, and she did. Her irritation was becoming evident in her voice. I felt the disapproval, but not everyone gets this unusual walk I'm on. It's my experience, not theirs, and I can't say I blame them. I just keep smiling and walking in the direction I know I'm being called, grateful for every seed sown to help me on my way. It's a lonely walk, but I know it's for God's purpose.

I put my hope and my trust not in myself or anyone else, but in Him.

# CHAPTER TWENTY
# MY JUBILEE CELEBRATION

### • MISSOURI • KANSAS • NEBRASKA
### • SOUTH DAKOTA • NORTH DAKOTA • MONTANA

June 27 coincidentally was my sister's birthday and the date I finally knew it was time to head to the airport. June was the heavy summer traffic season. Where would my buddy pass get me? I tried to get to Colorado to see my good friend who was fighting Lyme disease. At least there I would be able to stay a few days in one bed and maybe figure out what was next. But, after two attempts where I couldn't get a seat, I caught on, asking the Lord where He was sending me this trip and what route I would take. I chose Kansas City, though I had already been there twice, in order to get an easy in-and-out airport and a point I could pick up a rental car and drive the northeast/northern states. I found a quarter on the floor and knew I had made the right choice.

> "Be still before the Lord and wait patiently for Him"
> —Psalm 37:7

I got on the flight to Kansas City without delay. When my seat assignment popped up, I had been assigned a first class seat. I knew that God was going to make this a special leg of the journey.

As it would turn out, on this day, my sister's birthday, I would be officially celebrating my 50th birthday, which had been impacted by finances and turmoil eight months earlier on the actual day. It was funny how things seemed to resound with a pattern and a nuance I couldn't quite understand, but it was familiar. I knew it was for me because the funding came from my actual birthday ticket I had cashed in, and God had just put me in a first class seat to confirm it. The events of the week ahead would further confirm it again and again, too. It's as if the first week of this journey was for Kellie, with Mall of America, the second was for Him, with a walk of faith to trust Him all the way to Alaska, and this, the third leg, was to celebrate me, my Jubilee. God was so good to me. Have I said that yet?

When we landed, I had not a clue as to what I was going to do next? "Okay, Lord, please show me." As we were gathering our things, I heard my seatmate, who was in the music event business, said on a phone call, "I couldn't even get a ticket for myself."

After he hung up, I had to ask. "You must be in the music business. Is there something special downtown tonight? I was after all looking for something to do."

"Yes. The Rolling Stones are in concert tonight, but I couldn't even get a ticket for myself."

"The Rolling Stones? How cool." The cool thing was only that The Rolling Stones were important in Book Two that I had released last year, and I remember thinking one day that if I took my summer trip I might miss the opportunity to be available for The Rolling Stones—important to the person in the book, not me. And I thought, many months earlier, "It doesn't matter. God could have me anywhere, and they could be traveling, and I could get to see them still." And, here God had delivered.

But, it was silly. I was on a limited budget. They were playing tonight in downtown Kansas, and I had already seen downtown Kansas and needed to be heading north to Nebraska. I was fleecing God and asking if I should go. Once I got my rental car, I decided to "just drive by the Coliseum to just see how the crowd looked." Who drives into concert traffic to just see? And on the way there, God confirmed it with a sign He always gives me, and I knew to go. I was two hours early for the concert. Unplanned, just off a plane from Atlanta, the timing couldn't have been better.

I had to park. Uh-oh, I had $27 cash in my purse. I pulled up to the lot attendant taking cash. He announced parking was $25. I had just enough to pull right in; all I could think is how God always perfectly plans every detail. I saw all the tailgaters, the vendors and the fans *with tickets* and I just kept walking toward the coliseum like I belonged. I went to the gate and asked if there were any tickets, but they doubted it and sent me to guest services (fully around the entire perimeter of the Coliseum). I saw a security guard and shared my story; he doubted there were tickets but wished me luck and directed me to guest services. I continued on my walk of faith.

At the window, I discovered where people had paid hundreds of dollars, and, yet I would be getting a seat with a ticket price of

$35.00. It supposedly had an obstructed view. While I was high in the stands, I had the greatest view of the stage, in my opinion. I was pinching myself. Why was I going to this concert, anyway? I found my seat. It was great. I took a few selfies—who would believe I was here at The Rolling Stones? Crazy for me to be here. Crazy venue. Crazy music. Crazy story. Crazy faith.

I left my seat and walked the arena inside and smiled at everyone, wishing that since I was back in Kansas City, where I could have some Jack Stack BBQ again. Looking for food before the concert started, I was grinning ear to ear to find the satellite stand of my favorite BBQ joint right there in the Coliseum. This was an amazing game of Candy Land. I was having a great Jubilee celebration, and it was just starting.

I went back to my seat only to realize I had originally taken the wrong seat; I was actually two sections over. When I got up and took my seat where I belonged, there were four young adult men in their mid-20s to early 30s. Had they seen me sitting there where I belonged, they likely wouldn't have taken the seats, so the Holy Spirit had me entertained with food while they chose those particular seats. I arrived and they admitted, "These aren't our seats." But, I encouraged them to stay and said I didn't mind.

I introduced myself, mentioned I was an author and had stopped spontaneously for the concert. The young fellow next to me said, "I was going to offer for you to go smoke weed with us." Remembering that I was at a Rolling Stones concert, I chuckled. "Well, I didn't mention, but I am a *Christian* author." He blushed.

"That's okay," he answered not hindered at all, "But why do I keep meeting people like you?" He was referring to people who want to talk about Jesus and their faith.

I laughed. "What's your name?"

"David." The other boys were shifting in their seat and not as engaging, but an occasional yes, head nodding, etc. as I took off like lightning with engaging stories.

"Oh, David. David was a man after God's own heart. God loved David and He loves you. He is pursuing you, and He won't give up because He has plans for your life," I gushed.

For quite a long while, David let me witness to him and speak life into him. He confided that he was a mentor of young boys (high school or college, I can't recall) and that he had wanted to make a change, but it was his peers—he pointed to the crew next to him—that seemed to hold him back. He wanted to leave and make better choices, but he felt responsible for them. He tried to fit in to hang with them and influence them.

I assured him that God loved them too. I explained that walking away from friends was tough, but God had a plan for them. And sometimes being a good friend meant holding others accountable, telling them like it is, and walking away, if necessary.

He let me talk on and on, so hungry for what I was saying. It's such a small world; we discovered we had a distant mutual friend (I don't recall the connection now, but it was by name). The concert had long started. It was exciting. People were hollering, singing, and dancing to the popular band's music. In between, I kept on rolling, hoping I was making an impact on him. The friends got restless, ready to find a private spot to inhale, I imagine, and he waved them on ahead and sat next to me for more. After a while, he had been filled and was ready to find his friends, but before he left, he thanked me profusely.

"I know there was a reason we came here tonight. And, I know there was a reason I met you. There's a little white church down the street from my house. I'm going to it Sunday morning. Thank you for coming." He jumped up, headed to the stairs and paused a minute to look back at me with a very satisfied look, shaking his head in amazement and marveling to himself as he walked down the stairs.

I thanked God for bringing me to this crazy environment, saw the slide show start to the music, and knew I had stayed long enough for my purpose. I was likely the only Rolling Stones concert fan to leave after just one set; this wasn't the setting for me. I was happy to get out of there, to have had my assignment, and to have met David. I'm still praying for him.

People might judge. Why would I, a Christian, go to such an event? Jesus sat with sinners. We can be the light anywhere we go. And, I know I was meant to meet David and speak life. He was ripe for the harvest, if only he knew there was someone who wouldn't give up on him, someone to speak truth to him. Who knows if he also influenced his buddies present that night? Or maybe he went back to his team of young fellas a changed man and they wanted to know why or how and chose to be more like David? God can use us wherever we are. Never be afraid to follow His prompting.

By now, it was very late, and Nebraska was three hours away. It would be a challenge after a flight, a late night concert, and a testimony, to drive the long distance; God would have to be my co-pilot, for sure. I picked Lincoln as my destination, since it was the capital. Somehow, those roads became deserted and the drive was longer than three hours, closer to four. I was starting to fade, but could not find a hotel stop. I was getting a little nervous and frustrated that I was over-tired and hadn't planned this part of my journey very well when I had to make a full stop at a four-way stop sign. "The Lord is my strength and my shield; my heart trusts in Him and He helps me. My heart leaps for joy. And with my song, I praise Him" (Psalm 28:7).

I started up a late night chat with my co-pilot, reviewed all the places He had safely taken me to, and paused to begin calling hotels for a room. Booked. Booked. Referred to a "sister" hotel. I had so many notes, using the overhead light on and off, while I drove, I wasn't sure where I had made my reservation or when I had crossed over into my 45th state, Nebraska, but I knew when I had finally arrived in town—it looked collegiate, with a late night wedding party walking down the sidewalk having enjoyed after-hours celebrating. I wasn't the only one celebrating at three in the morning.

Happy to find my hotel in the Haymarket District, I parked curbside and hoped for the best for my car through the night. The staff was overly friendly and the room turned out to be the right one for a great night's sleep. I received a discounted rate for reserving online and a ticket to a lovely morning breakfast with a window seat. It had been a very eventful night, but a proper cup of tea in a porcelain cup and a delicious corporate buffet put me back into a chipper, adventurous mood. God knew how to woo me.

Nebraska turned out to be a surprise state that went on forever. There were so many surprisingly interesting things I wished I had time to stop and see (like Indian Cave State Park and Chimney Rock National Historic Site). I had originally wanted to go to Minden, Nebraska to see Harold Warp's Pioneer Village, but the hours didn't coincide with my departure, and I eventually decided

I wasn't going to make the out of way destination, so I headed west through the longest part of the state to get to South Dakota, where I wanted to spend a good amount of time. I didn't really have a magnet destination drawing me in Nebraska, but God had a surprise planned for me here.

I drove through beautiful countryside, maybe even past the historic Sandhills or the Chimney Rock I saw pictured on several tourist brochures. It was just beautiful landscape. This state went on and on and on and on—no, really. It's as if God had elongated time, and I was on a merry-go-round and couldn't get off. I had wanted to take a side turn to stop at Indian Cave State Park but missed it and decided to just forge ahead in spite of it. Eventually, I was getting antsy; why did it seem like this road would never end, and there was no destination in sight?

I saw a sign that indicated there was a veteran's memorial ahead, and I took it as my opportunity to deter off the main road to scout it out and find some relief. I headed to North Bend, Nebraska on Sunday, June 28. Just as I arrived in the center of town, I realized that God had planned a Fourth of July parade for me! It was minutes from starting and the entire town was gathered in anticipation. I was over the moon with excitement. This certainly explained why I was on the road to nowhere as He aligned my arrival with the start of the patriotic parade.

I took time to walk around the military memorial. The entire roundabout of memorials was lined with American flags, waving at attention. Bronze statues of gunmen dotted on the lawn and benches with words like "freedom," "courage," and "honor." There was a tribute to fallen soldiers and every military branch. There was even a tribute to women in the armed forces at this Memorial Park.

The parade was starting, and I took my seat on the lawn, in spite of my cotton skirt, by the curb and the corner stop sign. It was a great vantage point for every entry and the point where the town sheriff would post himself and make himself available to hear my story. There were flags and fire trucks, vintage and new; there were queens and musicians, candy throwers and puppies, too. It was a spectacular slice of Americana, and the whole town, young and old, was out to enjoy, honor, and salute America. God bless America. He certainly has blessed me. My very own Fourth of July parade and I still had the one in my own hometown to look forward to on the actual Fourth of July.

I crossed over the train tracks, tried to chase down the entrance of a golf course, but abandoned the pursuit to find my way west again when I couldn't find my way to the course. Traveling in the direction of South Dakota, my next destination, I did make one u-turn in Oakland, Nebraska, to take a picture of the Swedish Heritage Center for my Nordic friend with whom I pray often and whose husband helped me move on the final day, though I had never met him. I think I had been driving in the wrong direction anyway, so it allowed me to get back on track.

Time seemed to then resolve, and another five hours of driving found me in Midland, South Dakota. Having spent the entire day crossing Nebraska, including the hours that seemed to go nowhere in a way that still perplexes me, I passed into South Dakota and discovered 1880 Town, with 30 buildings and replicas of a town from 1880–1920. I couldn't help but stop and walk about and take a few pictures. It was very rustic and another slice of Americana— Chevy Chase's Vacation. There was rolling prairie, an iconic train, and a Conoco convenience stop. Admittedly, it was deserted like the Wild West, but I'm sure, in its heyday, it made for great family memories.

Having spent my day driving, I decided to turn in early and found a motel-style Best Western. It was old style, but the staff showed sweet hospitality. The desk clerk assured me I'd be safe in Murdo. It was the head of the Northwest Cattle Trail lead by Murdo Mackenzie in 1880. I'm sure if the pioneer woman made it through, I would, too. As a child, my mother often marveled at the pioneer woman, and now I was one. Isn't it ironic how life turns out?

I got an early morning start across the prairie landscape. With the rock cliffs and flat mountainous ranges in the foreground, the drive was brilliantly different than anything I had yet experienced. Soon I started seeing the Wall Drug Store Pharmacy billboards. It must have been some sort of landmark because there were signs counting down from at least 100 miles. My curiosity was up, and I knew it would make a great stopping point. I loved every minute of the whimsical shopping town.

I took photos and found surprises around every corner, including The Travelers Chapel, where I stopped to pray. Imagine a chapel in a shopping store—just for me.

In one shopping alcove I saw a sign that said, "Let your smile change the world but don't let the world change your smile"—that was a good one. I smiled at everyone and struck up small conversations at every chance. I loved changing the atmosphere with my smile and the message I shared everywhere I could. I found a beautiful, long wooden box with a patriotic design on the lid; I knew the box had to make the trip home with me. It was cedar and signed by a local artist.

I got a kick out of the Jackalope lore in every store. My ex-husband called me "Jackalope" when we first met and here it was at every turn. And outside, in the courtyard, sat an oversized, stuffed version. I asked someone to take my photo—a Jack-a-lope by the original, if fictitious, Jackalope. He would have liked that. There was a Jackalope hunting permit on display along one aisle. He would have liked that. I was not sure if I would have been the game, or not—tongue in cheek.

There was a T-Rex hiding behind bushes and a replica of Butch Cassidy's Texas hold 'em poker game. I posed by a stuffed bison and a covered wagon with a flag, got my free cup of water (which they boast of in every store), and had a jolly good time with the whimsy that abounded. It was a multiplex of entertainment, with plenty of shoppers to keep the doors open. I was delighted with my discovery to this cheesy, touristy slice of Americana.

I managed to track down book retailers and managers to get a point of contact to send my books to, as well. When you stop for a visit, ask for a copy.

I was ready to head in to Rapid City, South Dakota, but first I needed a few minutes of being "normal." I took a coffee break at a long-awaited Starbucks. Ah, my classic chai tea latte with foam—how I missed it. I saw an older retired couple with a map open, contemplating their journey. I knew there was socializing ahead. I was happy to join the community table and strike up a conversation. I was a little starved for human camaraderie with all this isolation in the car and traveling alone. God's a great conversationalist, but I tend to talk too much, and He tends to be a little less frequent with His responses. I was craving contact, poor couple. Actually, they heard my traveling story and were inspired, but I'm sure they would have expected privacy for their own trip planning discussions. It was very encouraging to share with them, as well as hearing about their journey and letting them encourage me on mine.

I passed picnic tables and American flags at a park and snapped a photo. The excitement was building as I was excited to finally see the Mount Rushmore of American history fame. Along the way, I discovered an important stop that I had to detour for immediately— America's Founding Fathers Exhibit at 9815 South Highway 16, en route to the Mount Rushmore Memorial. There was a Liberty Bell replica and an American flag on the lawn, beckoning me to stop. I parked to take a photo. This was an unexpected gem that fit perfectly in my schedule and would inspire me on my patriotic adventure. The owners claim it is a premiere Black Hills exhibit where art meets history. Everything about it was premiere, informative, educational, inspirational, and enjoyable.

I was like a kid in a candy store. A docent led me in to an exact replica of artist John Trumbull's rendering of the meeting where 56 patriots gathered for the signing of the Declaration of the Independence, making way for history and the birth of our nation. It was complete with autobiographies of every signer and life-size replicas of 47 of the men who risked life and limb to take a stand for America.

My favorite signer was Samuel Chase who rode 150 miles by horseback, through the night, as Paul Revere once did, over two days time from Annapolis, Maryland to Philadelphia, Pennsylvania, to bring news of his authority to approve the deciding signature to vote for independence. It was his action that gave the deciding vote. It was his signature that made a difference. *The signature of one man made a difference for America.* This is why I write with Paul Revere fervor, through the night, when it seems as no one will notice, to make a difference for my country, my America. I am the Paul Revere of this day, crying for an American Revolution—crying for my people to rally together, to *rise* and *unite* for America's freedom. I challenge you, my fellow Americans—Ignite *The Spirit of America* with me. Wake up! Stand up! Take action for America, for God and country!

It is one man, one book—this book, one voice—perhaps, my one small voice, one vote, that will make the difference in these dark days, my friends. I encourage you to make a visit to South Dakota, one of the most inspiring, patriotic places to visit to take a look at this important exhibit. Read all about our founding fathers, who, at their mostly young ages, made a difference for our country for over 200 years to date. Connect with them, study them, and decide to follow in the footsteps they first forged for us to take action for America. They sacrificed more than we remember.

According to an article I found online (http://www.barefootsworld.net/doi1776.html), five signers were captured by the British as traitors and tortured before they died. A dozen had their homes ransacked and burned. Two lost their sons in the Revolutionary War; another had two sons captured. Nine of the 56 fought and died from wounds or the hardships of the Revolutionary War. One was forced to leave the bedside of his dying wife. These were real people, real Americans, and true patriots who have sacrificed for the freedoms we enjoy today. Let their lives and efforts not be wasted. Let us honor their sacrifices and appreciate all the liberties we have today. To God be the glory for the sacrifices of these men.

This is an American Revolution I am suggesting our country

is in need of, just as it was then. If we look away now, where will America be? Who will America be for your children and your grand children? I encourage you to get to know the signers, identify one who resonates with you, and follow in the footsteps of some who forged the way for our freedoms.

I applaud the creator, furniture manufacturer Don Perdue, and the artistic team who executed the creation of the "Declaration of Independence" painting into life-size replicas, all who had a hand in this magnificent exhibit who recognized the importance of solidifying history for many to see and enjoy. You simply must plan a trip for your children to learn, grow, and be inspired for America. Our history is so rich and important and must be shared with younger generations. Kids enjoy the exhibits free; you won't be disappointed with this 20-minute presentation and learning experience; you will be doing your patriotic duty. They are open 9:00 a.m. to 4:00 p.m. daily, seven days a week through September. Our future is dependent on each of us waking from our complacency and taking action, honoring our heritage and preserving her legacy.

Learn more at www.foundingfathersblackhills.com.

I was full and feeling patriotic as I drove to the Mount Rushmore Memorial, through the town at the foothills. It is a lively, bustling town. I made a quick, unexpected turn and drove up a steep hill to the top where a sign advertising helicopter tours was leading me. If I'm going to see the presidential faces, I want to see them up close, so why not by helicopter for a very memorable experience?

I had, after all, added some unique experiences to my 50th wish list such as: trail riding, zip-lining, fly fishing, hot air ballooning, kayaking, Yolo boarding, and riding a bi-plane, and now, adding a helicopter ride to that list seemed very appropriate. It was time to be adventurous. I just hoped I could face my fear at the point of entry.

As a former military aviator's wife of 23 years, I was quite familiar with the cyclic, the controls, and emergency procedures, should we need to auto-rotate on the way down. The chopper appeared to be a like the TH-57 my Army husband took his check ride in more than two decades ago. I remember watching his solo flight, praying I wouldn't be a witness to his crash landing. This helicopter was only slightly bigger. It would hold a pilot, a co-pilot, and two passengers; it was barely bigger than a "squash bug."

The crew and staff were super encouraging and fun and patient with me as I contemplated the thrilling adventure. It was slightly out of my comfort zone; I was slightly afraid of heights. Plus, I was somewhat reluctant to pay the premium for a solo flight, so I passed on the first few flights to go out while I was there. I was chatting about aviation and military experiences when a nice couple came in and I was quick to ask if I could jump on with them. They heard snippets of my story while waiting for the chopper to be ready and then they insisted I sit in the front seat. Wow. God placed me in first class on my helicopter ride, too. This was a birthday adventure indeed.

The helicopter ride was so much more than a firsthand look at Presidents George Washington, Thomas Jefferson, Theodore Roosevelt, and Abraham Lincoln, it gave me a God's-eye view of Mount Rushmore National Monument. I had the added bonus of taking in Crazy Horse, a tribute to an Oglala Lakota warrior and equally as important to my history and the healing of my family tree. All of this came from the unique, firsthand view of my former husband's perspective as a helicopter aviator.

# My Jubilee Celebration

I gained perspective into the joy he had while flying high, the intricacies of his job (which involved skills like interpreting all those instruments and managing the sensitive cyclic). I felt the exhilarating freedom of flying from the cockpit and the boldness and confidence it must have took him to properly suspend the aircraft in thin air. I am surprised they allowed me in the front seat because there was nothing to hold on to during the turns, and I was more than once tempted to grab the cyclic, which would have been disastrous for all onboard. I carried on conversation with the pilot, the passengers asked questions, and internally, I was praying over my former husband, asking forgiveness for any judgment I passed and blessing him for all he did, the risks he took, the missions he ran, and the flights he managed. I was grateful I had overcome my fear to jump in the hot seat. God had an assignment greater than the flying experience, even while I was enjoying the scenery. It was a historic moment on many levels for me, and I was grateful for the ride. The best part was when I landed. Truly, I felt freer than an eagle while in the air, but I was still grateful to have both feet on the ground.

After my flight, I took a little drive on the meandering road through the adjacent neighborhood. I had observed a nice restaurant during our descent and wanted to try to find it from my car. Instead, I stumbled upon Our Lady of Mt. Carmel church. This was the name of the church we went to when we were a young family and our oldest three children had gone to Catholic school for a year. It was bittersweet to stumble upon this now. We were front row Catholics during that season of our family, active in both the school and parish. I would have gone in to pray, but it was locked up, so I took a pause in my car to pray and reflect over my family and my faith. God was undoing the knots along the way and healing another part of my heart and my family tree, I was sure of it.

There were more patriotic sites to visit, including a tribute to the presidents at the National President Wax Museum, but my time was running short, and I had taken in all I could experience on this short trip. I could hardly wait until the day I could return with my children for them to soak it all in. I think every American family needs a trip to South Dakota, just as important as the Smithsonian Institution in Washington, D.C. and certainly before The President's Hall in Walt Disney World. Okay, maybe kids need to experience the Magic Kingdom first, where they can be mesmerized by the Disney princesses. But once they reach school age, they should be taken to the Black Hills next to be mesmerized by America and her heritage. Families need to connect with these important landmarks and our country's history and continue the conversations of our heritage for the next generation—for our children and their children.

I enjoyed driving along the Blue Star Memorial Highway, a tribute to the Armed Forces for defending the United States. There was a beautiful commemorative plaque at a stop point overlooking beautiful lake views. Sponsored by the National Garden Clubs, there are many such highways across America, and it would make a fun addition to spot them along your drive. It's one more reason to fill your heart with gratitude for America, her beauty and those who volunteer diligently to preserve her.

Since I was in South Dakota, I decided to make the route to Sturgis. I had long heard of this town, made famous for its motorcycle rallies the first full week of August. On the hillside were Hollywood-style letters and not many bikes in sight, but plenty of biker stores for gear. It was actually the Sturgis Dinner Theatre I wanted to stop at for the famous Chuck wagon dinner and show, but I was losing daylight and really wanted to get to the geographical center of the United States before nightfall, so I kept my "pedal to the metal" and left full-throttle down the highway.

I arrived in Belle Fourche, South Dakota, with just enough time to enjoy the museum full of early pioneer heritage and chat with the staff. I especially enjoyed the vintage nurse uniform on display, since my oldest daughter was currently enrolled in nursing school. I pondered her future and the plans God had for her. I reflected on those who had served and marveled at the many scenarios they must have encountered.

I was encouraged to be quick as the museum was soon closing. I asked the gal at the souvenir counter if there were any place I should visit next. I was advised to have gas, which was good to know in this rather sparse area. And, almost as an afterthought, the cashier asked if I liked outdoor theatre. I was a theatre minor and played the leading role in several productions from high school to community theatre, even winning a prestigious acting award, so this was quick to bring stars to my eyes. She suggested a town north of the museum, called Medora. Medora, North Dakota would prove to be the pinnacle of my birthday celebration and leave a lasting print on my spirit.

The museum closed, and I scurried out, but I was welcome to walk the grounds. Around back was a beautiful courtyard of American and international flags—just like the display I had once designed for my Spirit of America Days presentation at a patriotic

215

home site in Orlando, Florida once. I was delighted to see my vision fulfilled here.

On the walk to the flag display, there was a beautiful Korean War display, not often seen, honoring all branches of the military and a lovely memorial, a tribute to their "fork in the river" location. The memorial depicted peace flowing like a river. A good walk down the path, at the center of the flags displayed was an oversized, 21-foot diameter structure made of South Dakota granite with a 12-inch bronze marker. It depicts a map of the United States and marks the geographical center. It was a spectacular memorial.

The theatre production started within three hours from the museum closing, and I didn't know if I could make the drive, get a room, buy the tickets and make the opening number. But, I had determined I was going to try. I crossed into North Dakota, state number 46 and another pushpin for the wall map. "North Dakota is Legendary," according to the state welcome sign, and it is true. I had to come to a full stop on the desolate highway road for a deer to cross to grassier land. There, he met a friend, nature at best.

I entered Theodore Roosevelt's sanctuary of escape during his presidency, the very place that shaped our conservancy efforts today, the Theodore Roosevelt National Park. Wild bison greeted me on the highway from their gated open preserve. The vistas were rugged and patchy and unique, a combination of prairie and rugged badlands, and it was evident I was entering a land where time had stood still. I pulled into the area dedicated for Bison. There were bison in the paddock, and I watched for a time and then became motivated to see more of Theodore Roosevelt National Park and locate my motel.

I drove past horse stables and saw the Badlands Motel sign,

where I would sign-in for two or three nights. The hotel registration desk doubled as the town's convention bureau, and they had a slew of information on things to do. I was disappointed to know I hadn't quite made it in time for the outdoor musical and dinner, but there were several other options for eating in town.

I was well pleased with my simple, slightly rustic lodging. The bed was comfortable and luxurious with a wood log headboard, and the mountain view from my front step was one I could drink in for a long while.

I took a driving tour of the town. It was easy to get around, and I felt very comfortable getting to know the lay of the land. It was pretty late by then so I decided to go right to Theodore's Dining Room for dinner. There were still diners, but the server informed me I would have to order right away before the kitchen closed.

God had saved the best for last, and a quick look told me this would be my birthday dinner meal. My favorite entrée was the night's feature, *ossobucco*, made from bison, of course. There was a beet, apple, and feta salad, which made my tummy sing, a glass of fine pinot, and the finale being my dessert favorite of crème brûlée. It was a birthday feast, planned with me in mind. God had orchestrated a beautiful evening in North Dakota for my birthday finale. It was my Jubilee year, indeed.

The whole evening was just magical. There were only two diners left by the time I got my food, but the server and I made an instant connection and were friendly throughout dinner. Her name was Jella. She was from the Philippines on a summer work visa. Our spirits immediately connected, and we continued to share, witness, and breathe life into one another the entire night. I believe God set that assignment up because in last August, Kellie and I had finally adopted a Compassion International child. She was randomly assigned to us, but it was not so random, more like hand-selected by God. Jamierine V. is from the Philippines. I said it would be great if my two daughters and I get to the Philippines some day to visit our adopted girl. Now that I have also met Jella, perhaps we have greater inspiration to go, and when we are there, Jella can be our guide. In any case, I believe our meeting was divine that night.

It was a fun dinner, and she helped me celebrate my belated Jubilee. I was so happy when I told her I was a traveling Christian author, and she said, "I'm a Christian, too." In the South, we take this for granted, rarely asking or stating this identity; we just are, and those who are no longer practicing were typically brought up as a Christian in the traditional church and share a common language of understanding.

Through each course, she told me how she admired my faith and how I was an inspiration to her; we mutually shared and witnessed. She asked me to come see her again tomorrow, and I did first thing, for breakfast. She was outwardly delighted I came.

She told me then she was thirsty to meet more Christians but, "There aren't many in North Dakota." What I would learn is that Holy Spirit had guided me there to connect her with other Christians who were feeling the same and working just down the street from her in tiny Medora. This was a good testimony to one of the problems we face. Christians need to be bold to speak about our faith. If we take a chance to connect, we will find other believers also looking to connect, and if we take that one courageous chance, we may find an assignment God has waiting for us. If we fail to speak out, we miss opportunities for fellowship, sharing Christ, and strengthening our own faith. Oftentimes people are just wobbling in their faith because they have faced a life obstacle without other Christians to help strengthen them on the journey, they often grow cold, complacent, or abandon their Christian path.

At the USA Mercantile, the manager and I would share at length. She was an encouragement to my journey and said, "I have been praying for God to send someone like you for a long time." She was thirsty for this message of spiritual revival in America. Even she did not know the sweet Jella I had met the night before, though they worked on the same street. She actively pursued her faith *at home*, with a small group of fellow believers. I was delighted to be the thread to bring them together and tell each of the others. It is time for every Christian to face their fear and speak about their faith boldly. This is the time we need to come together in unity with our neighbors, fellow Americans, and sisters and brothers in Christ. United we stand, America.

This town was alive and it made me come alive just by breathing the air; my spirit was awakened as I walked around town, first visiting the shops and mercantiles, then sharing my testimony, connecting the Christians on the block, and then visiting the Harold Schafer Heritage Center, a tribute to the man with the vision for Medora. He was just an honest workingman with good values, and he shared his philosophies with many.

I loved and adopted his favorite saying found on a wall of the heritage center: "Some day I'm going to have all the money I want to spend." Indeed! Tongue in cheek, of course. God is my reward and my pursuit, not money. Money is a tool in this society. Money helps us enjoy a different quality of life, but I have experienced the manna and the miracles that come from God alone, making the pursuit of money lifeless and droll.

One day when money does flow my way, I will be quick to delve it out to support others on their God-given journeys. An open checkbook is a good thing, if used for the right purpose. I do agree that Mr. Schafer had the right idea, and I think it's a good motivator for some, a good philosophy to motivate those just starting out.

And as a result of my stopping in, I learned that I could come back for an entire week and give back to this magical place, this patriotic town, this heartbeat of America, and volunteer to see it thrive. I couldn't get to the information center fast enough to sign up to return next summer. And, lucky me, the Theodore National Park would be celebrating its Centennial Anniversary—100 years of Theodore Roosevelt's vision to preserve parts of America for her citizens. It is a Sweet Life USA, and this is one primary reason. I invite each of you to make this your summer destination, too. If you're a senior, remember to apply for your Senior Pass online at the National Parks site and enjoy.

The National Park Senior Pass is a lifetime pass available to American citizens 62 years old and over. It's good for use at over 2,000 federal recreation sites and all the National Parks. It's a benefit of citizenship—it's your birthright—so go explore and enjoy. There is a $20 processing fee, but the pass is free and obtainable online at www.nps.gov. With it, you have 2,000 ways to spend your retirement years. I think I see another adventure ahead for me, too!

After visiting the USA American-made Mercantile, I encountered a live remote on the lawn. My friend must still be praying for my message to be on TV, and God was still trying to answer. I did meet the anchor Kevin Stanfield, North Dakota News for NBC. He listened to my story and shared his card; I'll follow up at the right time. God had provided yet another microphone for me.

It was time for one of my favorite pleasures: trail riding. When I got there, I laughed to see the news team had traveled from the quad on the lawn to the trails to shoot footage. I suppose I was on camera, in the foreground of their story; God was determined to answer Sandra's prayer and not let me miss the blessing! "Man can establish his plans, but God determines his steps!" (Proverbs 16:9).

The trail ride put me a good mood. The Lord directed the way when the guide went off trail to show me up close the lover's rock that sweethearts used to carve their names into. The two girls riding just ahead and I seemed to have a connection. It turns out they were summer volunteers for the mission camp around the bend. I can always recognize His light. We had good testimony as we climbed up and down the dusty trail, stopping to admire flowers and landscapes along the way.

A quick change and I was off to the Bully Pit driving range. A little sprinkle couldn't dampen my courage to get to the famous golf course, but my skills weren't yet ready for the drop on the 15th tee box. Congressmen and Senators played these courses. Theodore Roosevelt was certainly a visionary when he mapped out this land. I looked forward to sharpening my game and returning, but I was proud of myself for dressing out for the driving range, nonetheless.

My full day was almost over. I returned back to check out of the Badlands Motel and catch the Theodore Roosevelt reenactment. It was an amazing portrayal with rich history. I was fully alive watching his flawless performance, and, with so many monologues to remember, I was fully impressed. I recall when I was in 4th grade being selected to be a "member of the press" and how I interviewed "President Theodore Roosevelt" and had prepared questions when he called on me. God really does work together all your experiences for His purpose. Following the performance, the audience offered where they were from. The entire front section of the theatre was from Maine, and I knew that was an indication for what would be my next destination.

Theodore Roosevelt re-enactor, actor Joe Wiegand, and I snapped a photo as I shared my charge for patriotic revival. He was very encouraging and wished me "Godspeed." In fact, he offered a tidbit: while in office, former President Roosevelt would go by canoe to Bible Point, Maine and there, still today, he would sit at a desk and read a Bible. He offered to arrange a visit when I arrived. What a beautiful gesture. It is a small, sweet world we live in, America; don't let life, politics, and news jade you. Dare to discover and make connections.

As I headed out of town, I got a double scoop of fresh creamery, mint chocolate chip and maraschino cherry because I never get a double scoop, but the Sweet Life I just experienced deserved to be celebrated. It had been a double portion, indeed. I was sad to leave Medora; a piece of me wanted to stay and felt like I had found a new home.

> "'For I know the plans I have for you,' declares the Lord, 'To prosper you and not to harm you, plans to give you hope and a future'"
>
> —Jeremiah 29:11

I wasn't homeless; I was being spoiled by the King with first class seats, a trip across His kingdom, and favor. I had found favor with the King and a home under the covering of His wings. This journey was an incredible adventure.

I still had to drive to the Billings Logan International Airport by morning, and it was a state away in Montana. I stopped for gas across the border and encouraged an entrepreneur from California I met at the pump. I laughed when I made a u-turn in the small town and found The Beach, founded in 1909, but there was no water. I drove through the cute little Montana town and celebrated state number 48. I had the delight of "racing the train," that was pumping along on the tracks parallel to the highway. I was fascinated by the views as I drove along the highway. The moment I got to experience the sun up on my left view and the moon up on my right view, I was touched by His majesty once again. How was it possible to have them both in sight simultaneously? There is nothing more exhilarating than being on the open road in America and to experience the wonder of our country. He is a good God to make such a masterpiece for us to enjoy. It touches the very core of our existence. Meeting others and seeing how they "do life" touches our humanity. Traveling across our land is a must. *This land was made for you and me!*

Montana just didn't get a fair shake, and I can't wait to return again for a better experience. First, I decided to take a detour to Spring Creek campground and see if I could go Trout fishing—fly fishing was still on my list to do, but I would equally enjoy a catch and cook camp before I flew home. I chased the signs and the camp down for a full three turnarounds from end to end of the town and eventually had to drive on the gravel road and cross the cattle grate to find the fishing lodge. It was quite an effort.

The owner met me at the door of the office cabin and looked at me like I was absolutely looney. This was a peaceful, calm camp where men came to fish, and I showed up a little too dolled up, wearing high heels, asking about trout fishing. I think he thought I was out of my element. I made small talk, took a photo of the life-size wood-carved black bear, gave my excuses, and fled, laughing all the way back to the highway as I headed to the airport. The things I did amused even me.

The airport was a little obscure, and I had to make a turnaround to get to it too, but not before I found a beautiful white, rustic building with a tremendous American flag nailed to it—a beautiful site. It was like God took me past my turn just to show it off to me. It was a sweet slice of Americana draped on that old building.

It had been a long, beautiful journey, and I was willing to skip waterfalls and additional adventures in Montana to head home without delay. I know it's a great state, and I have a list that goes beyond my La Quinta Inn and Denny's dinner experience when I return.

Turning in the rental car was a bit tense as they were unsure of my final bill because I had changed departure airports. It left the balance outstanding until they reconciled accounts. Well, leave it to God, because my account had just enough for one "last supper" in the Billings, Montana, airport, and, with the rental car not charged out, room to spare.

The views were spectacular, and it reminded me of the first time I took a trip West to Boulder, Colorado, when I was in college.

I had determined then to be a motivational speaker and inspire thousands, and all these years later, 30 or so, I was finally building a story to do that. My view of the mountains looked about the same. It's funny what sticks with us; where we begin is where we sometimes end up.

As for my flight home, you would think after a first class ticket to start, it would go without a hitch? There were 38 open seats, and I was rejoicing until the agent said something about weight and balance loads and that there might not be any non-revenue seats. I was not amused. I would have no money for a hotel and my rental car was already turned in. I approached the bench and plead my case. I turned up my southern charm, gave the Delta agent a big, hopeful smile and told him I'd be praying for a seat. I sent a "911 text" to a prayer warrior to offer prayers of agreement. The minutes ticked by, the time for the flight to close was almost here, my heart was racing, but I was ever hopeful. I was sitting nearly motionless praying deeply, and just a few minutes before final boarding, the agent called my name and assigned me a seat. I was shaking with excitement.

"Thank you, Jesus!" I was going home.

I had a seat assignment. Now I hoped God had the rental car bill covered before I landed and before it cleared. I was checking my account about every ten minutes while I was in the airport because I had used up every dollar of my birthday funds through that last lunch in the airport and was waiting for an automatic deposit to clear to cover the rental car until I could replace it with new money when I returned home. It happened the moment I landed in Atlanta, not yet off the plane; I checked my account one last time, and the deposit had been made. The coast was clear and so was my rental car invoice. This was living on the edge, for sure. God never let me drop. He was my tour guide leading the way, and he was supernaturally financing this trip.

I had gone on this journey using one love offering and some heaven-sent tithes, the original rental house deposit written two years ago and recently refunded, and a birthday ticket to anywhere, received eight months prior before this adventure was known and cashed-in at the last minute. God had a savings plan in place for my big adventure when I didn't even know it was being funded.

I landed in Atlanta, July 2nd. I had made it an entire month. My kids were happy and had been on beach trips and lake trips; Kellie had even been snorkeling to the Keys with her dad for a week and flown on a plane to New Jersey. Except for lacking a home to lay our heads in, it was a great summer. God had just brought me to 14 states in 18 days. I began with $2.12 and ended with about the same. One financial miracle and grace after another kept me going (many I didn't share here, but they were astounding); only through prayer did they happen.

When it is God, He makes a way. I was exhausted from the travel, carrying a pack, schlepping all my belongings, and, in spite of God's warning, worrying a time or two about what might lie ahead. Our new home was one month away. If we had made it one month, we could make it two, but where would we sleep and how could I keep juggling kids as if it was no big deal?

By now, my 18 year old was angry enough at me to spit nails, and deciding that he had a job, a high school degree, and a good head on his shoulders, I left him to figure it out and grow up a little. It was time for him to realize life can be hard. It hurt a lot, but I knew God had him in the palm of His hand. I either texted him every couple days or relied on his sisters to tell me what his social media posts were indicating and ensured that, at least, the siblings were texting and knew where he was day to day. He was safe. He always reached out when he needed the storage unit key and, in our small town, I knew where he was working and, most nights, where he was sleeping. It was Kellie I had to keep calm and under the covering of her momma's wing while showing her what it was like to trust God for His promises and ensure she had her emotional and physical needs met. She was a trooper for the most part, and when she had her moments, we just rode out the storm. And I prayed and cried harder when the lights went out at night. Mostly, I walked as if this was the normal way to walk. I heard His voice and just kept following. "Whether you turn to the right or to the left, your ears will hear a voice behind you, saying,

"This is the way; walk in it"

—Isaiah 30:21

# CHAPTER TWENTY ONE

# THE DECADE-LONG DREAM INTERRUPTED

My second day "home" from my adventure, I was invited to meet with my Christ Renews His Parish (CRHP) sisters from Holy Trinity. Funny timing. We used to meet regularly, weekly, then monthly, but after awhile, we went our separate ways except to wave to one another at church. We had not formally gathered in about two years, I'd say. And here it was seven years later as I was just finishing my journey to Mall of the Americas, the same one I had planned in 2008 when God showed up to change that plan, place me at the CRHP retreat, and bring me back to be a speaker and share my life story as a testimony. It was now July 2015, seven years later! Perhaps, the Lord was clearing the land and I was getting a "do-over." It was, after all, my Jubilee, when, biblically, all debts are cancelled. It was sweet to share with my sisters what God had been doing and how I had experienced the Holy Spirit showing up. They had prayed often for me as we met regularly and listened to my unique stories of favor, even then. It was good to share the fruit of God's rewards.

And, the next day was time to celebrate the Fourth of July, again. I had enjoyed every moment of my own private parade in North Bend, Nebraska, but was doubly glad to be "home" for our Fourth of July. It's quite the big deal where everyone in town plans to come and show up in decked out golf carts to watch the morning parade. In Peachtree City, you are either in the parade or watching it, if you are not at the beach on the Fourth.

This year, sadly, it rained; either it's sweltering hot or raining on Fourth of July every year, it seems. We stayed in our guest beds and skipped the parade that was still held in spite of the rain—how's that for spirit? I was now gladder than ever that I had enjoyed a patriotic parade on my travels. I love Fourth of July parades. I used to organize them through our neighborhood when we were stationed in Virginia, pulling kids in red wagons and cheering and waving flags. I think every neighborhood should organize a parade. It creates great *espirit de corps*. Organizing neighborhood parades is one of the 52 action steps in *The Spirit of America Days* program. Parades bring everyone together.

When the rain settled down to a drizzle and a bunch of puddles by mid-morning, just after the parade had come to an end, we headed out to other planned community events. High on my list was the Fun Day events where Bull Dog Golf Carts was teaming up with the local retail center, giving away a golf cart—a brand new golf cart and it was red! I was shaking; I was so sure we were going to win.

The music DJ for the festivities was even rooting for me and gave us beads and hula hoops to participate in the organized games while we waited for the drawing. There was a good crowd, and we were doing our part to be festive, wearing red, white, and blue. Kellie and I had patriotic stars painted on our faces, and I was sporting patriotic toe polish on my toes that peeked out from my shiny red patent Guess sandals.

Good thing we have healthy legs because we weren't going home with a golf cart. Our names were not pulled in the final drawing. God is a giver of dreams for His purpose, but that doesn't mean that every material thing will come our way, and it didn't include this shiny red golf cart today.

We cannot pursue God for wealth and prosperity, as some modern believers might preach. It doesn't mean I couldn't put my name in the drawing and offer a prayer for the golf cart, if it was God's will. He knew our need and our desire. It turned out we knew the family name of the winners, and we were happy just the same. Having the thrill of the possibility of winning a red golf cart gave us hope and encouragement that God had heard our request and saw our need, and we had the joy of possibility of that being fulfilled and somehow, that was enough for us today. Our turn would come, in time; I was sure of it. I had to sell our golf cart to pay for rent to participate in this crazy journey of faith. God would bring one back my way at the right time. I was sure of it.

It turns out we didn't need that golf cart, anyway. Where would we have stored it for a month? We had been invited to go to the mountains at Fontana Village, North Carolina, for four days by some sweet church folks. It was so nice to have a reprieve from the struggling to find accommodations several nights in a row without imposing on anyone and to have a mini vacation, to boot.

## The Decade-Long Dream Interrupted

I tried to limit the overnight asks to a day or two to any one friend and not more than once or twice to the same friend to ensure we weren't a burden. In the end, it was only five friends we asked for a night's stay and not more than one-third of the entire summer without our home, about 21 days in all of the 64 days without our own home. As it worked out, we were gone mostly the entire summer, and it wasn't really a burden to anyone, but it was still nice to have a break from the juggling and the stress of wondering if we were imposing, whom I would ask, and where we would stay.

The mountain views were beautiful and so was the fellowship. Located in the Great Smoky Mountains National Park, the Fontana Dam is the tallest concrete dam east of the Rockies. The history of the Fontana Dam was rich and historic. It was the power of the dam that produced energy for multiple uses for the good of the nation during wartime. The building of the dam was one of the largest engineering feats in history. Even on this surprise getaway, I was finding patriotic tributes. With the American flag flying high, I was proud to explore this new spot.

There were hikes, a day on the lake, trying to outrun the rainstorms and enjoying old-fashioned s'mores by the fire pit. This was a place for good, clean American family fun. It was nice to meet some of my neighbors from different states.

And, to ensure I was being the best mom I could, I left at four in the morning to head to Milledgeville, Georgia, to meet my son for his freshman college orientation. He might have been angry over our living quarters, but he was surprised and his face gave away how truly pleased he was that I had made the nearly five-hour trip to support him.

The college campus in this historic town seemed a perfect fit for him. We stopped to take a photo by the classroom his business classes would be held in, Atkinson Hall—my maiden name again. Isn't it funny how things kept going full circle?

I drove back to Fontana Village so as not to miss out on the planned weekend festivities. A lot of extra miles passed along the way, but my children are that important to me. I believe kids need to know they are loved and their lives matter. What's a tank of gas and a day of driving for such a milestone?

Hands-on parenting makes a difference. I have five great kids, three Eagle scouts, three college graduates, honor students, leaders, and hard workers as proof. On the day of orientation, his older brother took a day off work and showed up to support him and mentor him. That's the kind of family we are. Family matters. This summer was a different kind of test for us, but I knew good seeds had been planted, and we would make it through.

After a nice long weekend and enjoyable mini-vacation, I was beginning to wonder where our home base would be next. "Lord, I am so tired. I really need somewhere we can stay for at a stretch, a week or so, just to relax and unwind." Where would that be?

I was on my way to the next town to check on the records for the upcoming school year when I felt the Holy Spirit prompt me to go to Panera Bread. I wasn't hungry. I didn't want to waste time or money, and I said so. But the prompting came again, so I stopped for a green iced tea. I was on the way to the restroom to say a prayer and figure out why I was there when I saw my good friend at the beverage station. We chatted, connected and caught up about our busy summers.

I said off-handed things like, "Yeah, we moved out of our house, and we're looking. But it will work out. The kids are so busy this summer on and off with friends."

I was not really making it out to be a problem and never said where we are actually staying, not addressing my house or income status, and she said, very nonchalantly, "Oh, by the way, we're heading out on vacation right this very minute, and I have a work trip following that. We'll be gone for ten days; if you and your daughter want to stay at the house. I'd prefer it actually, that someone was in the house."

My heart soared. I minimized it, so I didn't look desperate, but I was overjoyed. "Well, that's so nice. We'll see. But, just in case, how would I get a key?" I didn't want her to offer and then be down the road with the only key. As it turned out, she has a code for entry and gave it to me right there, standing at the beverage stand at Panera Bread. Just like that. That's God. He always had our hotel accommodations covered. And, finally, ten whole days of stability and peace in the midst of chaos was just around the corner.

I texted my son right away to tell him that I had secured a house for the family for ten days, that he would have his own room, and that I would cook for the family. But his anger, and maybe the freedom he was enjoying, got the best of his judgment, and he replied that he wouldn't come back until we were in our own home and he was in his own bed. Ouch. My heart sunk instantly, but I couldn't resolve that today, so Kellie and I went, determined to just keep inviting him over for dinner until we moved into our own new home just a couple weeks from now.

Coming to the house was especially poetic. I had already determined with this gift of time and stability, I would finally write book four, the final book in the *Eat, Love, Praise Him!* series and then begin the book regarding this journey. This house had special meaning as my friend had purchased the house from someone close to me—he was in book two of my series, where my heart was shattered.

I recalled helping her move-in and offering to help her prepare her new home, without thinking who the previous occupant was, and then it clicked—the unique history of this home. I laid down my pride and cleaned and prepared the house anyway, praying over every inch of the house, blessing the comings and goings of all owners, occupants, family, friends and guests, trying not to think of its history. And, without knowing, just four months later, that I was actually praying prayers that would cover my daughter and me as well. God has a unique perspective on life; this one left me shaking my head in disbelief. I was just so grateful for a place to call home.

We were greeted with a box of home-delivered organic fruits and vegetables on the kitchen counter that she insisted I eat since she would be away to prevent their spoilage. God had provided a home and a bountiful harvest, which was a good thing, considering my current finances. It was an amazing feeling to cook that first night, just like being normal. I love the ritual of planning, chopping, simmering, and plating pretty food and enjoying every bite. It was especially sweeter, considering the circumstances.

But, the calm from the storm I had pursued was elusive. I set up shop to write, but time kept escaping me. From the former relationship I mentioned previously, I "inherited" a 95-year-old man who was in good health, at the time, but with two grown sons who lived out of town and out of state and was lonely for company. So I showed up to visit him about a year and a half ago every week to ten days, just to be a good citizen and brighten his day. Now that he had given his car up this year to a granddaughter, he was no longer able to drive and asked if I might be available occasionally. I agreed to take him to the grocery store and increased the frequencies of my visits to about two to three times a week. It cheered him up tremendously, and I felt it was the least I could do for a senior citizen and a veteran. One of his sons was a missionary in Iraq, and I considered my visits kingdom work until his son returned.

Settled at my friend's house, I was asking God when I would finish the last two states of Maine and Hawaii, and I kept feeling as if it was imminent. I went to Starbucks one of the first few days, and I was waiting for God's answer. I was drinking tea and on Facebook, ready to like the post of an acquaintance when he walked in the door of the coffee shop at that very moment. I laughed as I rarely saw him there. He came over and said hello and then sat down in the empty chair next to where I was sitting for a brief chat; we have never had talked at any length before.

I chatted and freely shared that I was on an adventure for God and was traveling across America on a buddy pass and that I just got back in town. "I am supposed to go to Maine next, but I need a buddy pass and a money tree," I laughed.

Without missing a beat, he said, "You need a buddy pass? I'll give you a buddy pass. My parents have some, and they so often go unused. I'll arrange it." And, with that, God had just made a way for the last leg of my journey. It was so well orchestrated, I marveled at that meeting for a long time.

I had planned to go to Maine at least three times in the last five years, always about this same time, and for various reasons, the trip kept falling through. I don't know why I couldn't get to Maine. And, I wouldn't get there this time, either, as it happened. What happened next would delay my decade-long dream of going to 50 states by my 50th birthday, as another event would become a higher priority.

I stopped in to visit my senior friend at his independent living center, and he didn't sound right. There was a wheeze in his chest and a shuffle in his step. I mentioned it to the front desk administrator and she arranged to have his vitals taken. They didn't sound good. I knew he would have to go to the doctor's. I left to retrieve some things from the storage unit and prepare to repack for Maine.

The center where he live called. He had gotten worse and needed to go to the hospital, but refused to go in the ambulance. His sons were out of the area; I knew I would volunteer to take him. I rushed right over and talked him through every breath all the way to the hospital, 25 minutes away. They admitted him right away and you could see the fear on his face.

He kept asking, "Am I going to die? I guess I'm getting old." And, then he asked if I was going to leave him. He looked so vulnerable and overwhelmed. He trusted me. I couldn't leave him. So what that I had plenty of my own demands and a buddy pass to Maine waiting me? I couldn't leave him. I arranged for my daughter to sleep at her friend's house for a few days, and I stayed on the family couch at the hospital to help care for him through the long night of wheezing and vitals and nurse care. He was diagnosed with congestive heart failure and had to stay for four days. I drove back and forth from my new temporary lodging to the hospital at least nine times and stayed overnight and during most of the days until he was on the mend. So what I didn't have my own house and I had a mountain of problems to solve? Jesus came to serve and not be served and so I also was called to serve.

This is a good opportunity for a soapbox moment, one I have recently got to see firsthand from all the seniors I have encountered. Elder care, abuse, and neglect is such a huge problem in our country. I contribute it to the breakdown of the family, the ones who formerly provided this care. The elderly are a forgotten generation. My heart is full of compassion for anyone in a helpless state, in need of care and concern. What if each of us looked to our neighbor to the left and to the right and offered good cheer and occasional companionship? What if we simply started in our own family to ensure their needs were being met, through the church, through volunteers, through a shared family system, or through home health care, senior companions or facility assistance? I know we can't help the world, but we can begin where we are when we see people in need—for the pure humanity of it. Honor our seniors. Begin by honoring your parents in their old age and pray your kids will do the same for you. Our elders need love and care.

Back to my situation in July, yes, there was a cost to extending kindness.

I didn't get my book written, I didn't get to Maine, but I'm certain I was blessed in the midst of my service; it was an honor to serve, and I planted good seeds for a future harvest. As I was in the middle of a major Godly mission, I know I was likely taking on more than was carved out for me.

The next month, I would wake up from dreams that were vivid; in one, a rubber stamp emblazoned "URGENT" was prompting me to get back to writing and finishing my journey and my book, but I continued to offer care to the senior and concern myself with my household needs and unpacking more than the book and delayed my final travels without a plan.

Good thing I don't have to be perfect or make perfect decisions. God can always work out our waywardness. I'm just saying, this book has an important message for a time such as this, and I likely wasn't meant to delay its release. I should have drilled onward for a God-sized mission, but I know there was a human being in need, and I chose to offer care over my priorities. It's what God would have wanted me to do, I'm sure. Maybe I got off track from my destiny and God's priority, but it's the choice I made.

It was rewarding to extend care and compassion, though there was a cost to my mission for that detour. My mission was not fulfilled in the predestined timeline, but it wasn't taken away, simply delayed. Instead of moving into a house with "the view" I had in mind and reaching my 50 X 50 states goal, I moved into a temporary home and delayed the completion of my journey by ten months, seven months longer than my dream goal. I had a mindset for a decade; I could have made it, but I had a tender heart and chose a higher priority. I hoped I was still honoring God and He could see my heart and the book would still be a blessing for America. What would Jesus have done? What would you have done?

> "Stand up in the presence of the aged, show respect for the elderly and revere your God. I am the LORD"
> —Leviticus 19:32

1 Timothy 5:3–16 also has a lot to say about the service to the elderly and good deeds; it's how I'm wired. Jesus came to serve and not be served (Mark 10:45), and our circumstances shouldn't keep us from service and acts of kindness. In spite of having no home, I could offer my time.

Yes, perhaps, that's the point. Elder care isn't simple or easy, but I can assure you, it's rewarding and it's the right thing to do.

My senior was released home after a week of hospitalization, and the demand of companionship and care seemed to increase as I helped him recover his health and strength. I learned to work my visits in between coordinating the move, fleecing God for the next leg of my journey, and searching for ways for new income, but none came. He insisted on paying me for my time and my constant care, but I was leery. He was in need, and it was my Christian duty to offer help. I knew God would take care of my needs. I also felt that because I was in a precarious financial position, people would judge me and assume I was there for the wrong reasons. In spite of the truth, people talked and wondered, anyway. Do the right thing, anyway, and don't take advantage.

Just as God had promised, in spite of the hiccup and the stall in my mission, He provided a home for my family and me and just in time—in His perfect time. We moved in the day before my daughter started her first day of high school. And that first night we moved in, my son was sitting at the family dinner table, and peace was on the horizon. God is good. He is faithful. Trust Him in all things.

We had arrived at the new house just as the former tenant, my friend, was pulling out of the driveway to move. We gave a final farewell and walked in for our walkthrough. We got keys and were finished in less than 15 minutes because what was there to debate, really? So what the cabinets were chipping a little and the light bulbs were missing from the fixtures? I was grateful for the home we now had.

The carpets were still damp from the shampoo service the night prior, so we postponed our movers until Monday. We tested the air by sleeping on blankets on the floor the first night. The house was fine, but our bones paid the price. And, finally, after 64 days of following the Lord on this incredible journey and trusting Him for a new home, we moved into our new home on August 3rd. It was a rental and yet another downsize for us. We had now gone from 4,100 square feet to 2,400 to 1,600 square feet, moving three times in the five years post-divorce. God had me shedding a lot of materialism and baggage along the way. I was hoping to springboard into more, but God knew right where I was.

With the movers on their way, I first had to make a run to the Board of Education in order to reenroll my daughter in her school—the one her four siblings had previously graduated from and she had been in attendance (in the same school system since kindergarten), but that was another lovely glitch of not having a home address and having our mail suspended due to the "vacant" note in the mailbox; my daughter had been disenrolled, and it took six weeks for the notification to be forwarded and find us.

The proper records were filed, but we would still have to make a trip to the high school and plead our case to have her schedule released to us before Meet the Teacher night to ensure she was actually scheduled for classes. Her friends were getting their schedules, and she had to wait to be a part of the excitement.

> "Join with me in suffering, like a good soldier of Christ Jesus"
>
> —2 Timothy 2:3

There were a myriad of obstacles and issues that had to be mounted and addressed every day. That one behind me, I could meet the movers and begin the monumental task of unloading and clearing four storage units. At least the weather was clear—until the last day; it was reminiscent of our initial move to Peachtree City, 11 years earlier. And, when it was done, even three boxes were moist from the rain of the day. I overlooked that the first few days, and they sat in the dining room, unnoticed. I was quick to get them to the garage and air them out when I discovered their condition, before any mold truly festered. But, somehow in the move, the large box that contained my two silver fox furs and my ladybug coin box was missing. I know it was stacked near the now discovered wet boxes. Was it yet another shedding of ill-gotten gains or was it still lost in the shuffle?

The move was hot and hard, but went off fairly well. We moved two full storage units, and I was left with work to do. It was just in the nick of time. The next day was Meet the Teachers, in spite of the mounds of boxes to be organized and unpacked. Following that, we headed to the store for our annual ritual of supply shopping. So much expense on top of expense and task after task, we just kept moving, one goal at a time. I tried not to look at the whole picture, but the line item in front of me.

And, with determination to bring my family back together under one roof, I cooked up dinner following the day of moving, and we ate around the boxes stacked everywhere except the stove and the sinks which I had cleared. With the three of us seated at the table, we melted back into the comfort of being a family together once again. It was all I could do to carry on a conversation and not let the tears flow from the blessings and faithfulness of my Father. Our home and our hearts were finally restored and at rest.

# CHAPTER TWENTY TWO
# THE WALLS OF JERICHO

O n the first day of school, we took the traditional snapshot by the door of our new house, backpack full, new outfit on, and headed back to the familiar routine of friends, school, and (yes, still) unpacking boxes.

Kerrigan was home, but his stowed anger was simmering and beginning to reemerge, spewing about. I could take no more, and on the first Sunday after we moved in, I was on my hands and knees begging Father to rectify the situation. His anger was now, in part, due to money I borrowed exactly one year prior. I promised to return it in time for him to leave for school. He would leave the following mid-week. He was afraid I wouldn't make good on my offer. And, he was likely right, according to my actual financial plan, but I fleeced God, stood on His promises, and knew He would provide; I was counting on Him.

By the end of that Sunday, I had the check for $1,000 in my hand.

Grateful that God had made good on His promises and moved the right hearts to respond. When we pray, our Father hears us, and if it is according to His word, He will come through. And, when I handed my son his loaned money back, the anger completely faded and the hardness of his heart melted. Father had restored it with one brush stroke of His pen. I melted with gratitude that night. The fear of going to college without enough resources also melted from my son's spirit. God is good. And I continue to live on His amazing grace, every day, trusting Him to meet my needs and the needs of my children, His children.

The first ten days in my new home, I was anxious, overwhelmed, and a bit disappointed. This is not what I had expected: mounds of boxes, too many belongings for too small of space, and where was my view? Yes, God had provided a house, but I was clearly disappointed and disgruntled, until I saw and heard myself and checked my spirit. I was grateful for having a house, but it wasn't according to my expectations. The spirit of disappointment was taunting me. I had to quickly adjust knowing it was God's will and that it was a house for my family, for goodness sake.

The lawn service had already been around for their weekly maintenance and in doing so knocked my rocking chair into the wall where some of the stucco crumbled to the concrete. I had a view of it through the window where my desk was positioned in the dining room. I was horrified it had happened to my new rental property and moved the rocking chair immediately; it wasn't the chair exactly, it was the carelessness of the lawn boy blowing the leaves that accidentally knocked the chair into the wall and caused the damage. But with the new view, I was quickly reminded of the walls of Jericho and how Joshua circled them, and after seven days, nothing more than faith brought them down. Maybe this was a temporary home, and the view was coming still.

One day the following week, I was sitting at my family kitchen table enjoying a quick lunch break between unpacking, and through the opened blinds and the tiny clearing in the woods behind the house I could see the American flag flying that was posted on the house on the street behind mine. I had found my view. God just wanted me to appreciate what I had and keep my eyes focused on Him. He had a quiet surprise and the perfect view waiting for me. Another sign of my sweet, sweet life and my good, good Father!

With the move, I was overwhelmed with the boxes and the tasks ahead, and I was physically worn from the journey; I kept pressing in for more of God and more answers and relief in my "bondage." Monday nights and Thursday mornings were One Life prayer and Emerge worship prayer groups with my sweet prayer warriors. Sundays I spent visiting churches where I could feel the Holy Spirit's presence and enjoy meaningful worship.

One Sunday, I agreed to attend church with a friend who had invited me several times before. I was happy to answer her invitation to attend. Hard to find, it was set back in a shopping center where there were several churches in a retail shopping area. It was small, but full of smiling, sweet folks. It was a soulful, mostly African American church, full of families. I sat down about the third row. We had beautiful worship, honored the pastor and his wife, and heard their daughter give a word. Then, he was back preaching and somehow, the spotlight was on me—a visiting member!

He handed me the microphone for a word. What guest gets the microphone the first time they visit a church? Not to mention, I had never been given a microphone at church before. I stood up and spoke boldly all that came out of my spirit and then I shared a vision I had while he was speaking—it was a flying monkeys meets storms on the horizon, Wizard of Oz type scene; I don't recall every detail, but I recall that he said it was very confirming and an exact vision he had gotten months earlier while on a trip in South Carolina. It had to do with the move of the Holy Spirit and how He was calling us to attention. Perhaps, it was even a reminder that "there's no place like home"—America. What should be pouring out of us is gratitude for our beautiful land and a heartfelt return for all that surrounds us.

It was so powerful. And, then he had a word for me and shared about great prosperity that was coming my way, 70 days of wealth and favor, great prosperity. It was a very uplifting word in a time of great trial as I was surrendering to the new house and what God had chosen for me, which seemed so different than what I had hoped for and envisioned, having moved out of my house and trusted Him across America.

It was a good reminder that He is my reward, and whatever falls in my lap, I am grateful. One morning, I had a vision of that verse, and when I awoke, I took a sharpie and wrote it on a box next to my bed that I had yet to unpack as a visual reminder

> "Keep your lives free from the love of money and be content in all things."
> —Hebrews 13:5–6

Funny thing is, after hours of unpacking, in order to recycle all my moving boxes, I posted them on a community Facebook board

246

for free pick-up. A young mother and husband came to retrieve them, and when she saw the verse, she smiled and commented, "I love that. I try to be like that. It makes me so happy to use the boxes now." Plant seeds; pass them on. I was becoming more and more content with my little house, less things, and passing on the blessings to others.

There were some disappointments for sure—my house with the view was not as I envisioned, but it was darling and the right size for us. After moving out of my house and taking the journey, I expected financial release where I could, at least, start earning money or enjoy a trickling cash flow—no such luck. I thought for certain my first few books would begin to sell and take off and there would be a blessing, but nada, nothing. For several weeks, I beat myself up. This must be my lot in life. How did I get so fortunate to get so stuck in my life? Hadn't I been a great mother, according to so many, and, certainly, a giver of my time, generous to others? Why were all the doors shut tight?

I was taking care of my senior every day and visiting and encouraging him, ensuring the med techs were giving him the proper medicines and care and nurturing him. It was a full-time event, and every day a list of items to buy, sort, clean, or attend to for him. Mostly, he wanted my company, and when someone is sick, that's always the best medicine—simple encouragement and kindness.

But there were upsets along the way that made the journey difficult. For example, we were getting a piece of medical equipment for home use, and he insisted that he should go with me. I was wearing a dress and heels, as is my usual attire. He was using a walking cane. The drive was on a slight incline, and he went to take a step to the curb, resisted my extended arm and fell backwards. In slow motion, I saw it coming, went back down off the curb I had already approached and twisted at the waist to brace his fall, extending my hand and cupping his head with my right hand to prevent a firm bang to his head on the asphalt. We were both very shaken. The administrator inside saw us from the window and came rushing to our aid. He calmed down and only had a minor scratch or two. I refused care, trying to attend to him and minimize the fall. On the way home, I stopped at the pharmacy and got ointment for it right away, but with the delay in attending to myself, infection set in.

My ankle was swollen and hurting for a full week and then I saw the inflammation; I had to get to the clinic. Without insurance or money, I walked into the acute care center I bring my kids to and inquired on the cost. It was well over $100. I thanked them and drove around in my car praying.

"Lord, my ankle is swollen and in pain. You are my doctor, my provider and my counselor, tell me what to do. I was just trying to be kind and helpful and being your hands and feet (for this senior). Please come to my aid."

A friend I had not heard from in a few weeks called at that moment. I answered their question, "What are you up to?"

"I had just come from the clinic with a swollen foot, but no way to get care." They immediately told me to go get it cared for and called in the payment, not taking my resistance as an answer.

God took care of my ankle and the doctor bill; too bad I had waited so long to go. It had turned to Cellulitis and staph, and it was inflamed. I didn't want to take advantage of my friend's offer, so I passed on the x-rays that I should have gotten. It hurt in my sleep and when I walked for a full seven weeks; I can still feel it get aggravated from time to time now. The cost of service was high.

All the confusion the during the first three weeks in my new home, instead of abundant blessings that I expected, brought me into a depression. I wondered what I had done to block the blessings or miss the promised land.

I had somehow felt moving from my home and giving up my home and many of my blessings was atonement for sin, for mine and for my family tree; it seemed like it was an offering, not just an act of obedience. I was unpacking boxes every waking hour that I wasn't performing nursing aid and managing my house and my daughter's school and life, and I was falling into a pit. That is also when I was given the "URGENT" dream but felt like I couldn't live in the chaos of the unpacked boxes to stop and write. I was being very hard on myself, and my future looked bleak as I also realized I was in a house but without income to pay for the demands of it. Moving and taking the journey had solved nothing for me in my household, and I didn't know how long I could endure the persecution and lack.

Then I read this familiar verse mid-August in a new way.

"Therefore, there is now no condemnation for those who are in Christ Jesus"

—Romans 8:1

If only I could get this. If only we could each get this. There is no condemnation. We live under a state of His grace, washed clean. And, I realized I was being too harsh on myself. God was not condemning me; He was setting me up for something bigger and better. Why is our first inclination always to walk in shame and blame and defeat and disappointment? God, our amazing God, always has something better in mind.

I began to accept where He had me; I surrendered. I repositioned my desk in front of the window. Yes, it looked out to the beautiful view of the blank, plastered wall, but with the crumbling stucco, I now knew that the walls of Jericho were crumbling with every day of progress and patience; I was merely positioned. Even my daughter began to marvel at our "wall of Jericho." It took only faith for it to crumble. I would have to keep walking in faith and wait for it to fully come down.

With my senior friend, I never anticipated serving for an extended period of time, just until he was on his feet and the doctors released him, which kept getting extended. A few days turned into a few weeks, which turned into more than two months and would eventually extend beyond that. I was ready for the release as I was also volunteering for an international minister, and the commitment was getting heavier as he tried to grow his following and spread his message and needed my support. All the while, I had very limited income, none that I was generating on my own—about 30% of what I needed to operate my household. I was juggling bills, lists, and needs one day at a time. Finally, in an effort to gain some peace, I made a detailed list of every need and requirement and the date they were needed, and I just gave them all to God. I often stood on God's word to be my provider and brought my financial needs to Him daily.

He would answer with passages such as,

> "You were sold for nothing and without money I will redeem you"
>
> —Isaiah 52:3

Acts 13:41 also came to me during this time: "And, Look, you scoffers, if I even told you what I am about to do, you would not believe me."

So, I kept walking in faith, gave my itemized list to God, and tended to juggling my busy life and serving everyone who crossed my path from my daughter to my senior citizen to anyone who needed an encouraging word, prayer, or helping hand. Yes, it was exhausting, but I was compelled to keep going and believe, and I knew my Father in heaven would not fail me. He had brought me to Anchorage, Alaska, for goodness sake. He had already shown me all things are possible.

I was thirty days away from my birthday, and it was time for the final doctor's appointment for him, or so I thought. The heart doctor exclaimed with delight, "You have the vitals of a teenager now. How did you do it?" I had given him just the right amount of care and intervention, along with his daily caregivers all working together to get him back to health, that he was now thriving. But, he had also become very dependent on me, and it made walking away impossible. Trying to reduce the frequency of my visits was a battle at best, and I realized I would have to find a balance to keep the caregiving going and managing my life and messaging. He needed runs to the grocery store, follow up doctor visits, haircuts, and daily visits. He lived in independent living, and there were staff to greet him and dispense medicine, but not necessarily the extra mile that

I went. My mother always volunteered for the Veteran's Hospital and volunteering was my platform as Mrs. Virginia International, so it wasn't out of the ordinary, it was simply a heavy load at a time that I had extreme pressure of unpacking an entire household, balancing a mountain of a budget, and making our transition work.

I was feeling forlorn that, with only two states to go, I wouldn't make my 50 X 50 goal. There was only money for utility bills, sometimes not until the last minute still, and groceries seemed to come by grace; thinking of Hawaii and Maine seemed very unrealistic, in spite of all the former trips, provisions, and unique experiences. It was odd, though, that in September, before my October 22ⁿᵈ milestone, several of my friends were headed to Hawaii. Everywhere I turned, people were talking of traveling to Hawaii. I think the Holy Spirit was encouraging me, but I couldn't leave the senior's care or take a chance like that financially then, yet I had all summer. Oh, why do we entertain unbelief? But, in my flesh I reasoned, I was in a house now, it was a regular school year, and the challenges seemed many and insurmountable. Perhaps, this is why so many of us give up on our dreams or fail to believe all things are possible—life seems too big of a mountain to move. Trust God. Wait Patiently. Dare to Believe. That's what I did.

## CHAPTER TWENTY THREE

# THE JUBILEE YEAR COMES TO AN END

My birthday came, and I celebrated having been to 48 states. My 15-year-old daughter took me to a Japanese steak house and paid from her weekend earnings. It was bittersweet, but the night brought lots of opportunity for witnessing and was fun. The next night, I stopped in to my favorite restaurant, Due South, where book two takes place and where I also spent my true 50th birthday the year before. God had arranged a birthday dinner of deep fried lobster and trimmings. I had stumbled upon a generous friend who picked up my tab as we chatted and laughed through the night. God always has a celebration lined up for me. My biggest surprise that week came when having been through my entire 50th year bucket list except a very few last events: fly fishing, a flight in a bi-plane, and a ride in a hot air balloon, plus the two states. God arranged one of these items in the most unique way.

I was taking my daughter to high school at 8:00 a.m. I had been going to this school for 11 years, since all of my children have attended this same high school. I have never before seen what I saw this morning—the most beautiful, colorful hot air balloon on the grounds of the elementary school. I caught my breath at the sight, like when the gorgeous array of stemmed roses arrived to surprise me at the restaurant on my 48th birthday. God can bring you to Alaska; He can bring your birthday wishes to you, wherever your life may bring you. Just relax.

This reminds me of First Samuel. God is in control, even when it looks like He isn't. I might have missed my birthday goal, but I knew that the dream would still come true. The hot air balloon was God's promise.

In October, finally, I got back to work writing on the book, and as a reward, God sent me a speaking opportunity at a fundraising fashion show held at Georgia State University. I was to be a fill-in for the speaker who couldn't make it. I had one day to prepare. Just to be ready. I wrote a 13-page speech. Yep, I was ready. My printer wasn't working, and I had to find a way to print it out on the way to the event. I stopped at two office stores, and they were both closed and unable to help me. God said in my spirit, "I know, go anyway." I could visually see my death grip on my 13-page speech that was not in printed form and God pulling it out of my hand. "Let go. Let me."

The whole way there, I rehearsed my thoughts, trying to memorize them. God was laughing. "You have what you need already inside of you. Let go, and let me speak through you." It was a crazy, scary place to be in front of a couple hundred audience members, but God was building my confidence for future events. He had already given me what I needed to speak; I just had to relax and trust that the Holy Spirit would show up and speak through me when I was on.

And, He did. He is faithful. It felt like I rocked it, even kept the show going when there was a gap in the performance. It was exhilarating—this was a new me. The audience said I rocked it, and they were inspired. The event coordinator gave me a shining testimonial online. She said that she "can't wait to work with Jacqueline again. She was a rock star." I had found my way, even without a written script. I just showed up, and God spoke through me. I loved it.

My spirits were lifting, but I was still dragging to find my way, 90 days in and now past my birthday. The financial struggle was real and the senior care demand was ever high; my future looked bleak. I had put on some pounds; nothing in my closet fit, and I was not a bit motivated to find time to reverse the path I was on. It was the first time in my life I can remember not wanting to be Cinderella for Halloween, but instead opting for Snow White. Had I taken hold and bitten out of a poisoned apple?

I pursued prayer groups and deliverance sessions and looked for answers everywhere I could and decided God must want me to walk away from some things and get back on track of my mission for Him; it was time to take inventory. You can block your own blessings, you know. Through prayer, I made a decision to walk away from volunteering for the minister as a start, but I had already committed to helping him host and plan a major holiday banquet and fundraiser in early December. The demand for my time increased with that. The pressure was real.

It was November, and I walked in to visit my senior when I saw him awkwardly perched on the couch. As I approached him, I could see he was on death's door, and he admitted it.

"I think I'm going to die," he said.

I immediately went to work getting his oxygen, water, calling a nurse to help, petting him, and bringing him back to life in a very matter-of-fact way.

"Well, you are 96 today. It's a good day to die. Your wife of 62 years is waiting on you in heaven, and Jesus will be rejoicing," I said very calmly, "But, you can't die today. I spent last night making you a chocolate crème pie from scratch, and we're going to go downstairs to lunch and eat it and share it."

He thought that was a good idea and after oxygen, medication, and a 30-minute rest, we did just that. And, in no time, there was an impromptu party with the balloons I had brought and two residents we invited to our table to join the celebration and share the pie. It's a Sweet Life, and we were going to enjoy every sweet minute of it. He recovered just fine. And I was honored to help him reach his 96th birthday.

I was hanging on every day through Thanksgiving, knowing Christmas was looming and the meetings for the fundraising event were increasing. Every minute was scheduled and used. In between, I was shuttling my daughter and supporting her as she committed to a very important school event. She had been through enough, and I didn't want her to miss out on everything, so I encouraged her to lay out her desire to God and trust Him to make it happen.

# The Jubilee Year Comes To An End

She had truly wanted to participate in her high school pageant. It was a very big deal here. Pageants, as I know very well, come with a very big time and financial investment, plus it was a Miss America preliminary and required a very polished talent performance. My daughter was a volunteer, an athlete, a hard worker, and had a big heart, but you can't perform that on stage. She would need an instructor and a performance.

She was in tears as the application to compete was due. The guilt of spending and needing so much money was overwhelming. I put my foot down. We had sacrificed enough. No, she was not giving up one more thing. I told her to sign up and ask God for help, and He did. He sent sponsors and friends to help, a loan, choreographer, and encouragement. With very little investment, she was able to put on a great performance. She made a great showing for learning a performing art in just a few sessions and for being a freshman competing against upper classmen. She also took the award for most ad sales. She has a great spirit to be a part of a team. I was proud of her. The time commitment was big—practice a few times a week, which probably added 40 more hours to our winter schedule. I was really stretched thin.

When the ministry banquet came, I was stressed to the nines. Participants and guests were cancelling last minute, program changes were being made; it was taking on a life of its own. At the same time, my bills were stacking up. Most critical, there was a block on my income in-flow for about 10 days. I could take no more. I nearly was a no-show at the event, but I couldn't do that when I was helping to lead the event. I went ashen grey when I arrived, two women of the church noticed, prayed for me, and within five minutes, the spiritual battle had been fought and a direct deposit I was waiting on was added to my account. Thank goodness for virtual and online banking. I breathed easier and was able to enjoy the event, plus I was one of the speakers. It was a great inaugural event for over 100 people, and the Holy Spirit showed up in a powerful way. With the event behind me, I could now focus on the Christmas season for my family and our traditions.

# CHAPTER TWENTY FOUR
## THE CHRISTMAS LEGACY

There wasn't going to be a traditional holiday in our house this year. My 15-year-old inquired twice the week before, and when I told her I didn't know this year, she burst in to tears. Christmas was always over-the-top special in our house, and I was trying to balance mid-month bills and holiday meals; I knew I couldn't stretch it to Santa stockings, too.

Just in the nick of time, children came home from work and college, and we gathered around the tree that my 18-year-old son—yep the formerly angry one—had cut down and paid for at a tree farm, with his younger sister. He put it up and surprised me one night when I was volunteering. I was so touched and grateful God had healed him.

The night before Christmas, instead of guilt and fear, I had peace. I had provided 26 years of Winter Wonderland, Martha Stewart, Deck the Hall type Christmases and now, not even one trinket. I ran to the store and managed to get everyone a gourmet chocolate bar and a lottery ticket, for fun. That morning, I had lots of surprises in store.

My son, yes, the formerly angry 18-year-old one, had spent his hard-earned money, upon hearing my plight, and bought stockings for all and filled them to overflowing—with his own money. So thoughtful and careful did he pick out every item; he was watching me all those years, after all. Tears filled my eyes as I saw how God had tendered his heart and showered His grace upon him. My work was finished.

My older college kids worked to get through college and yet spent a nice sum of money buying very nice designer presents for each sibling; it was not just one gift each, but three or four or five, and when it was through, it seemed as Santa had stopped, after all. When all the wrappings were strewn, I got up with tears in my eyes and handed each child a paper bag with a ribbon.

"This year's not like most. And, what's more, I'm not really sorry or sad because I realize I've given you so much more. I've left you more than material things; I've left you a legacy and shown you what it looks like to walk a journey of faith with God when it doesn't make any sense. So I leave you with five books of life and lessons and love. And, with that, I hope you will see that that is so much better than any Christmas past. God is good."

There wasn't a dry eye around the tree.

I do think it was one of my favorite Christmases ever. And, when we were done, God had provided enough for a bountiful Christmas family feast. There were laughs and giggles, love and cheer, and everyone had peace when the day had ended.

# The Christmas Legacy

I was quick to put away the tree, so ready for New Year's Eve and a New Year to begin. I exclaimed I was going to be Cinderella, ready for the ball, and I spent the day pampering and primping and pulling out my crystal shoes—the ones I had received for Mother's Day and kept tucked away.

## CHAPTER TWENTY FIVE

# CINDERELLA'S, AMERICA'S SECOND TIME AROUND

I had been given a complimentary ticket to the ball where friends were playing music. I texted a group of friends to join me, but one by one they cancelled or did not commit. There were two left, so I headed to my favorite restaurant, Due South and waited and waited and even they stood me up. Cinderella's night was not so magical after all. There was a lot of irony in this. Book two took place in this very restaurant, on New Year's Eve, and here I was two years later; the song the band was playing was called "Second Time Around," and I was hopeful. But, there was to be no second round for me this night. Good thing I know the wait staff well as they kept me company. New Year's Eve ended with a fizzle. But, I held out hope. I knew God had not forgotten me even though something just wasn't right.

Honestly, the next three months became a blur as my senior

citizen had a bundle of doctor appointments day after day and another bout in the hospital, which left us both weak and tired. I didn't even recognize myself in the mirror anymore, nor did any of the clothes in my closet. How life can change in a few short months. At the start of the year, my smallest sizes were baggy on me, and now my largest sizes were fitting snug. Maybe that's how we start slipping away, and our lives and world starts changing, small changes, unexpected events and plain old life. I was hanging on for God's release. I savored the memories of my adventure across America as I waited for life to turn and doors to open.

I couldn't see God's plan nor find a way out. And, God was so clear about me not earning any other income still. I had starter kits for new cosmetic companies and essential oil lines, and each time they came, God said, "Don't touch them; don't even open the boxes. I have something more for you." In fact, it had now been two years and my real estate fees were due again, and it was quite a large sum. My spirit was pressed, and I knew I must. But I got a phone call and knew in an instant, the Holy Spirit was prompting me right away to go and render my license and inactivate it—that hard-earned real estate license. It was so very humiliating to concede defeat, but I never had a chance. The Holy Spirit had tied my arms and every opportunity for two years and clearly told me not to sell real estate; He had *something else*. He really *did have a second time around on the horizon*. He was lining up the calendar and a bundle of major planned events to fully ignite *The Spirit of America* as I had so long prayed for, and He was setting it up so I could play a part in it. I would have to clear everything else out of my way.

All the while, I was trying this or that while pressing forward. I knew the book was the most pressing thing I needed to focus on. I had started it, but work was slow on it with all the senior care, child care, and household care. Why is it that no matter our highest priority, dream or goal, we allow everyone else's needs to take precedence? Why is it we get so easily off track? Why is it I couldn't make this single most important thing work in six months time or bring it to completion?

Thank the good Lord for grace!

Then the light bulb came on. God had placed *The Spirit of America Days* on my spirit 12 years ago, after the events of September 11th and resurrected it a second time in *The Military Family: A Casualty of War*, which had won a national Christian Author's category award from Xulon Press, just a year before, so I knew He had a plan.

And at the beginning of the New Year, He finally began to shed light on His grand plan. And, in spite of my delays and distractions, I was on course to be a part of His magnificent master plan. At the turn of the New Year, I began to see one after another prominent evangelists publicize a message of America and a call for revival.

God told me time and again, "You will not believe what I am going to do with this *Spirit of America Days* and this book; this is so much bigger than you are asking or can even imagine." He always has a bigger, better plan. I was humbled to be a part of it.

> "'Look, you scoffers, wonder and perish, for I am going to do something in your days that you would never believe, even if someone told you"
>
> —Acts 13:41

Still, I was paralyzed to make much progress from the demands of constant care and financial lack and juggling. I did the best I could to work around progress on the book, like on my website and making a flier and creating new business cards and going to local meetings to talk about it, but not actually sitting down to spit it out on my laptop.

Then I saw a press release online announcing a 50-state tour for Decision America by Franklin Graham, America's leading evangelist. It was like a lightning bolt ran through me and I knew it was finally show time. This is what the Holy Spirit had been leading me to do all along. I knew I had to go and be a part of this special event. I saw his schedule included Atlanta. Georgia, Columbia, South Carolina, and Honolulu, Hawaii, and each for their own wonderful reasons, I knew I had to go. I began making plans to be a part of the gathering.

Then I searched and found Perry Stone and Dutch Sheets were hosting Awaken America in Cleveland, Tennessee—a drivable distance. I knew I had to go to that event, too. Their patriotic logo resonated with me, and I knew God was aligning our messages.

And then, there was a lot of anticipation when Evangelists Reinhard Bonnke and Daniel Kolenda announced their America Shall Be Saved Crusade, and my publisher friend interviewed Bonnke for the cover of *Faith and Soul Magazine* in the spring.

The thread that tied each of these patriotic and spiritual events together for me was when I wrote the following in my journal:

> "There are so many patriotic, spiritual revival events and now I hear there's one in Los Angeles, the AzUSA Street Ministries 110th anniversary event. I better catch the wave and get myself there."

Funny thing is I don't talk like that; I don't "catch waves." And, the very next day on their marketing emails that came to my inbox, I read where they wrote, "Catch the Wave and plan to come attend." I knew that, in spite of my financial circumstances, I had to attend. In the mean time, the electric and gas bills had been missed and were in the grace period to boot, leaving me with the current month's balance due, a hefty number, to address first. I had to spend time balancing the inflow/outflow numbers and a trip to the West Coast didn't look possible. It was a personal killer to think I had graduated with an Executive MBA from a Top 20 college, one of only a handful of women in a class of men who were senior executives and, yet, I was unemployed, without income flow by choice. I was certain God had told me clearly that I could not get a job, that I was to trust Him for heavenly provision and the more. I wanted to be obedient to His calling with all my heart. It was a confusing calling, but He was consistent to provide and it kept me walking in faith.

I often prayed, "God, don't let me miss one blessing." I had to go the extra mile, I suppose, for that one extra blessing.

I pulled out a poster board and wrote the dates and events and websites and common words and theme of each of the four ministries, events, and their missions and could see it was like bread crumbs leading up to what I believed would be God igniting *The Spirit of America* and finally blessing my book and my journey for all of America to read. After all, *The Spirit of America* was designated to include a National Observance, Memorial Day through Fourth of July—May was my month. *Spirit of America Days* is a program of volunteerism and patriotism Memorial Day through Fourth of

July, including Flag Day and was the perfect time for *The Spirit of America t*o ignite.

"I am not a Reinhard Bonnke, Lord, I have no money and no platform; how will I ever get the message out? I'm just a mom," I implored Him. "I'm just a willing servant who wants to love you with my whole heart and whole soul and all my strength."

God started unfolding His strategic plan in a way I could see.

God had sent his leading servants, Dutch Sheets, Perry Stone, Franklin Graham, Reinhard Bonnke, AzUSA street ministry leaders, Johnny Enlow, Frances Sturgill, Tim Sheets, and so many more prophets to rise up and share heavenly words of revival for this time. Their presence and their heaven-sent messages all came pouring across my social media pages; they all endorsed a common theme of revival and saving America. This has been my battle cry for 15 years for a return to Americana, for America to unite and ignite *The Spirit of America.* God has brought me to the season of His perfect timing where the calendar and my message meet. He prepared me and planted a seed in me over a decade ago to sound the liberty bell, ride across America, and stir up His children, my people, America's citizens, for a revolution, for a patriotic and spiritual revolution and a season of revival. May your hearts stir along with mine. We were born for a time such as this.

And, now, revival is here. He is igniting the *Spirit* of America. America prayed, the world has prayed, and now, God is answering.

Will we respond? Are you ready to recover? A familiar theme in addiction recovery programs is that you have to first admit there is a problem, and then you have to surrender and agree you want to recover and get well.

This is our moment of choice, America.

When we are serious, we will want God more than this world. We will come together in one accord and plead to our Father for mercy and grace.

We will, finally, be ready to say goodbye to idolatry, addiction, materialism, self-satisfaction and pursue the one who created us.

God is ready to redeem us, America.

His very word says that all sins are forgivable, except denying the Holy Spirit. Let us not deny the Holy Spirit and His power and ability to turn our country around.

Let us begin by acknowledging the one true God in our hearts and from our mouths. Let us believe in the power of the Holy Spirit, and that all things are possible, and that He is capable of healing our land and saving America from its current demise. Let us acknowledge the power of the cross and the blood of the lamb that was slain for all sins so that all who ask may have salvation. Let us believe in God's promises and trust Him for deliverance.

All of these events, choices, occurrences, reactions, and callings, are the choreography of the Holy Spirit and the heavenly realm; He is wooing His bride. Our lives are not our own. We were bought at a price, America. Freedom isn't free, not just in our flesh, but our souls, our very lives, were bought at a price.

Remember, reconnect, rediscover, recommit, repent, and reconcile with our country and her maker in this season. The birthing pains have started, and the birthing season is here. Let this be the season of the rebirth of America. Let this be the season we return to or heavenly Father.

## CHAPTER TWENTY SIX

# GOD GETS A BIGGER MICROPHONE FOR HIS MESSAGE

For two years, our small Emerge prayer group has been praying for God's hand on the media. We pray that amazing things will happen in people's lives and our communities and the media can cover that for the world to see instead of all the skewed agenda and sensational news items that are now covered to instill fear and chaos in our spirits.

During one prayer session, we were praying for Pinewood Movie Studios since they are a local enterprise with potential impact for the kingdom through movies and media. To my surprise, a prayer warrior broke prayer, looked right at me and handed me a symbolic microphone, confirming to me that I would have a microphone—a voice and a platform, perhaps, at Pinewood studios. I humbly and gratefully accepted, ignoring the fear and, instead, thanking God for the elation of my spirit, excited at what was to come.

Not long after, I got a call and an invitation to be a co-host on The Christian View television show on WATC-57. Filming once a month in Norcross, Georgia, the show is taped in front of a live audience, recorded, and distributed on-air once per week. It is a great platform for godly messages. Oddly, last year I was an audience member on their set, and I had silently wished I could be a guest host on just one show, but God had something better in mind. Instead of just one show, He had established my seat for an entire year; I just had to wait for His timing. Additionally, it was one year prior on March 11, I had been invited to be the guest speaker at the Pinewood pre-construction meetings, and now one year later on March 11, I was taping for my first television show. God was giving me another opportunity to have a microphone, and it was getting bigger and better all the time. I was excited for the microphones yet to come.

It was as if God was giving me a do-over; this is redemption. He is compassionate, and He is merciful, giving us relief even in our bondage. Just like I had been to the masquerade ball in October when my original 50 X 50 date had originally been, I was now again extended an invitation to be an ambassador and volunteer at a NASCAR fundraising event, another masquerade ball. Everything was sponsored by my friend at Source Point Coaching for an exclusive night of fun. I was the belle of the ball again. I even had a fairy godmother (my friend, Chris G.) help me adorn my face with a glamour look and crystal makeup mask, instead of a cumbersome mask. It was fun to wear a gown and socialize with the elite and receive celebrity treatment again. It was another start-point for the finish and the finale of the fifty states and His book. God was so generous to me. He always told me to write "NASCAR" fast, and now He was illustrating it in 3-D!

Still, it was somewhat of a mask I wore that night, one that wasn't seen. I was likely the only one at the ball with $2 to my name. It was only the day before that my nails were chipping and I didn't think I'd make it for a manicure or other preparations for the night due to the cost; thank goodness I had a velvet ball gown tucked away that would be suitable for the night because critical bills were due and my checking balance was unstable again. Just like God, in the nick of time, a deposit was made a few days before its due date, and I got my nails prettied up for the ball just the day before my Cinderella night. I learned to walk a financial tightrope. I learned that with patience, He would reward me. I stood on His promises as a provider, and He was faithful every time.

I had just finished watching the new releases of faith-based movies such as

*Miracles from Heaven* and *God's Not Dead 2*. These beautiful, true stories strengthened my faith during this journey. In *Miracles from Heaven*, God healed a girl with a life-threatening illness and renewed the lead actress, Jennifer Garner's, faith. God is true and alive and real and faithful and can impact hearts, no matter how normal or how big your name is. Watching these inspiring movies makes it all the more real. They are refreshing to our faith and great reminders of our great God.

Follow Movie to Movement for updates on the screen. Check

out Theodore Baehr's Movie Guide, which plays a valuable role in helping viewers discern their entertainment. The Christian Film & Television Commission is worth following for its impact on media and media decisions internationally. Keep an eye on Kendrick Brothers Productions for their faith-based material. I pray they keep an eye on me.

CHAPTER TWENTY SEVEN

# HUNDRED DOLLAR
# HANDSHAKES

L ife is tough, especially when you are walking through the fire. Though these movies of faith were helpful and gave me strength for days beyond their viewing, I can't say my nerves were always strong and steady in the face of my financial battles, and I would often turn to Him for reassurance in prayer and in His word. One particular time stands out. I was desperate to tackle the mountain of demand, thousands of dollars short every month to address the needs of my commitments and my household (month after month for years now). For two full years, my income was about 35% of my need, and this year held an increase but still a shortfall. I fleece God often. I go to Him, like Habakkuk, with 100 questions and "why's" a day, thankful for His patience and mercy.

On this day, I went to the throne of grace and brought my substantial financial needs, thanking God that He cares to even hear my needs and for all that He has provided in months past. I recalled to Him that in prayer recently, a prayer warrior cried out for "hundred dollar handshakes" for me.

"$100 would be nice, but with thousands of dollars of financial needs, Lord, I'm weary, and I'm going to need $500 handshakes. This financial mountain looks impossible to me."

I got a phone call from a believer who said, "The Lord told me to sew a seed into your ministry, to transfer it from my bank account—His bank account—to yours. This is a gift—His money—to your account."

I was deeply touched; I left with a hug and a few tears and drove straight to my bank to deposit the gift without opening it. En route, the Holy Spirit reminded me of that $500 handshake conversation we had had just days earlier. I opened the envelope to complete the deposit slip while still sitting in my car, parked at the bank's ATM, and burst into tears to discover a $500 blessing.

He sees me; He sees us. He knows our every need to the last detail. How else would someone I barely know bless me—someone who did not know my exact need to provide exactly that amount, and such a large amount. Then, for God to remind me of that forgotten prayer until I was en route to the bank blew me away. God was funding this mission and providing manna and miracles for me to write about. These miracles and His provision are for you, too. Circumcise your heart for Christ; let the blessings flow.

The more I wrote and made progress, the more favor that would fall, the more doors that would be unlocked. This book is like the key that will unlock the spiritual gifts of the Kingdom for me, for you, and for America. I am so excited to see Him ignite the flames of revival and *The Spirit of America* from coast to coast. I'm truly sorry it has taken me so long to get it all said and published, but I believe it is released according to His perfect will and His perfect timing. I have done my best to be obedient to His calling in the midst of living my life. He blesses me with the desires of my heart in this calling. It is a beautiful intimate dance, if only I could surrender more in the walk. The journey is beautiful, but difficult. Frequent and abundant prayers are offered. His word does say blessings and persecution are to be expected. I fleece the Lord for cleansing of my family tree and often lift up my mother's heart and my children to Him.

Favor Falls abundantly upon my children during what I dub "#MarchMiracles." Children are getting job interviews, multiple raises, and selected for recognition and promotions that took two years to come; the favor comes, one blessing after another. I am inspired to claim "#AwesomeApril" ahead. God is in the details and the moments. The doors to financial flow are still closed; there is a mountain of money challenges in front of me, and I will soon find God had a different kind of awesome in mind.

I made a 60-day-to-graduation plan. Two of my children would be graduating college, and I would hopefully fulfill my fifty-state trip and claim it as my graduation as well. Trust me when I say, when we are close to the finish line and fulfilling our destinies, the heat gets turned up. Financial demands increased significantly; I would no sooner address one that my phone or inbox would remind me of two more demands. My landlord informed me he was increasing my rent 40 percent when I had just relocated eight months ago and had no plans or energy to move, two college graduates, and an impending creating its own financial demand. The heat was over the top. God kept stretching my faith still. I could feel the home stretch around the corner and knew I just had to hold on for the ride. This was when the phone rang with the announcement that champagne was chilling in the fridge in Maine, which I'll soon get to. I knew it was God's way of saying, *"Hold on. Celebration is on the horizon."*

As the senior care increased and I was pulling wardrobe and researching topics for my new television gig, and pressing in to make progress on this book, his family gathered to make a new care plan. But it was challenging; the senior had become too dependent on me and resisted any change. I hated to see him so miserable, so we made an agreement to try to find some balance. That was short-lived, but it did give me the opportunity to be away for nine days and take my biggest leap of faith ever with God as God would stretch my faith in finances to a whole new level.

# CHAPTER TWENTY EIGHT
# ALOHA! HAWAII HIS WAY

## Hawaii Makes Number 49.

Here it was, spring break. This time, it was not like the one two years ago when my heart was broken and shredded and I held out hope for Cinderella's ending. I wasn't at the beach, as was tradition years past. No, I had just dropped Kellie off to be with her friends, and she was headed to the beach for a week of fun with another family. I was returning home to an empty house with all my chores done and ready to receive direction for my week ahead. It didn't make sense that after my year of journeys God would give me nine empty days (as a single mom without my daughter at home to care for) with nothing in mind. I had plenty of clear time on my calendar and freedom from my household responsibilities and yet no plan or finances to travel anywhere. Maybe God was giving me time to finish the book, I reasoned, kind of like a child being put in her room to finish her homework assignment. Since I hadn't yet disciplined myself to finish the book, He was making it as unpleasant as possible—everyone in town off at the beach and me, banished to my house to write; that is what I surmised, of course. Oh, well, I accepted it. I deserved it. I hadn't finished the book, and he had given me nine long months—plenty of time to write a book. It mattered not that I had moved and unpacked a house, helped Kerrigan transition to not one, but two different colleges, and nursed a 95-year-old man back to health and his celebration of another year of life. It mattered not; nine months was, after all, enough time to have a baby. Certainly, I could have spit out a book under heavenly request. Albeit begrudgingly, I looked around and had a talk with "me."

"Okay, I'm gonna be here, might as well accept it, hunker down and burrow in."

I contemplated changing into my fuzzy socks, where I would sit on the couch or at my desk. Would I turn the music on to break the silence of the house or not? And then I got stuck a little on what I would eat, considering I had frozen every morsel of food, anticipating I would certainly be sent on my way somewhere. It was obvious now, I would not. Oh well, I need to focus on writing, not eating, anyway, I thought. I gathered my writing tools and plopped on the couch, reaching for my large paper calendar and the remote simultaneously when my phone rang.

It was my praying friend. I had mentioned to her that I was going to the AzUSA event and wanted to manage to weave Maui into the plan, to knock two birds with one stone, er, trip. She immediately perked up.

"My husband and I had long wanted to go to Maui," she said,

"but we never could manage the financial commitment. I never even thought of it, but now, maybe."

How cool is that? "God, I hope you get them to Maui for a honeymoon trip," I silently offered on their behalf. Maybe I was just meant to mention Maui so they could see it was a possibility for them. I was glad to be used to plant that idea. I knew now that AzUSA was out of the question for me; there was no foreseeable "wave to catch."

I had just spent an hour budgeting expenses for the month, and to the last dollar, all the immediate and important debts were covered through the third week of the month, which was typical and a bearable breathing point for me. Everything was attended to, with exactly $12 left over for the month. Whew! Everything important was covered; that was good news to me.

God laughs from heaven at the plans of man. "The One enthroned in heaven laughs; the Lord scoffs at them" (Psalm 2:4). In that moment, my phone rang, interrupting my train of thought and this verse, and all my accounting was blown out of the water, allowing me to "catch the wave" all the way to Hawaii!

My friend called me, and I explained that I was not going. In my flesh, I saw no way and had no funds to travel with.

She laughed and said, "Oh, you're going. Pack your bags. I know you are meant to be at Azusa Street Ministries (The Call) in Los Angeles."

I hung up and marveled at her certainty. And, I laughed aloud skeptically.

First of all, it was already 9:40 p.m., and I had not yet packed. I was getting tired and had already concluded that I was supposed to be writing this entire week. I was always finding a reason to procrastinate or take care of another priority, which is why I was here instead of on the beach for spring break, anyway, wasn't it?

"I'm going? Okay, I'll at least pray on it and ask Father and see."

Well, sure enough, every prayer returned a power verse of confirmation, the first one being Song of Songs, which is always God's code for, "I love you; trust me. Follow me. Go. Go *now*." A resounding "Yes!"

I laughed at the incredible thought of going to Hawaii with just $12 available to get me there. I don't have a ticket. I don't even have a buddy pass—*not even a pass, I reasoned.*

I kept moving. I wiped the kitchen down, emptied the trash, turned down the water heater, and generally prepared the house. I pulled out clothes and toiletries and threw them on my bed. Then, I went to the hall closet to pull out the Swiss Army backpack from my summer trip across half of America.

"Hello, old friend," I looked at it warmly. "It's time again. We're going on another trip."

It was my constant companion every mile across America. I debated between packing exercise clothes or a bathing suit, hiking shoes and jeans, and whether to bring a coat or a sundress. Los Angeles and Maui were experiencing a good 20 degrees differential. I determined to squeeze my computer and all 10 days of beauty and clothing needs into my one trusted backpack. Friends and family would not believe this feat I accomplished, usually over-packing and hauling a suitcase, carry-on, plus a shoulder tote or two, but I had just proved it could be done when I get determined to do it.

All packed, house prepared and in travel order, I fell into bed and prayed God's will be done. "But, God, I don't even have a ticket." My spirit didn't budge, so I asked.

"Yes, Father, I know I can ask someone for a buddy pass, but the hour is late and I have to leave before sunrise. I will go to the airport, but you have to make it happen. Just let me see someone in the lobby of the Atlanta airport I know and let them just offer me a buddy pass. I don't know what else to pray. I'm going on faith because I believe you are telling me to just trust you. It doesn't make sense to me, God, but I know when the world says "No," You say, "Yes," so I'm going, but I need someone right there in the Atlanta airport lobby to offer me a buddy pass." I prayed firmly, also hoping God would not think my request too pushy. After all, I know a lot of people in the aviation community, and it was slightly (one in 80,000 people at the Atlanta's Hartsfield Airport) possible I could see someone I knew at the airport who would have it in their ability to offer me a buddy pass. A mustard seed of possibility and faith; it's all I had to go on.

There were a few short hours of sleep before I headed to the Atlanta airport and parked in the Park-and-Save lot. At $9 a day, I was proud of my effort to walk a bit further to the terminal and save and ignored the fact that was nine of my $12. When God prompts me, I know better than to worry about the details. That's His department, and He always works it out. My faith was firmly founded on that history with Him.

At the airport, I went straight to the self-help kiosk and checked in, as if I had a paid reservation. You never know, God can do anything supernaturally, and I had to rule that out, but the screen screamed back at me, *No Reservation Found*—like I was a complete fool.

I met up with my friend and her husband, on their way to Maui, and we sat in the lobby, checking flights, talking about finances, His provision and promises and waiting for the Holy Spirit to show up, basically. "Lord, where is that person you are supposed to send right here in the lobby?" I did know quite a few Delta employees, it was possible, ever so slightly possible, that I could encounter someone I knew in the lobby, so I kept scanning the crowds; there were no familiar faces.

About an hour and a half into our wait, I said, "Well, I don't see anyone here I know. It's 7:00 a.m., and I suppose I can make a call now. I don't even have a buddy pass, you know; maybe I could call a friend of mine who has offered one previously and might have one."

My friend turns her head on a quick spin and looks at me stunned, "What?" You need a buddy pass? I thought you had one or could get one. I didn't realize you were looking for one."

And then she said those God-sent words.

"I have a buddy pass you can have."

Right there in the Atlanta airport lobby. I saw someone I knew, who simply offered me a Delta buddy pass. God answered the very prayer I prayed.

Folks, she doesn't work for Delta. She is a *nurse* and was on a companion pass; I had no idea she had access to a buddy pass, and she didn't realize I was waiting on someone to offer me a buddy pass. God had sent me help and it was right under my nose. God sends His children for us to help one another.

When God tells you to go to the airport without a buddy pass, ticket, or fare—just go. Let Him work out the details of the trip. We laughed our heads off as she issued the pass and listed me.

We found our departure gate and headed west to Maui, Hawaii, via Los Angeles, so on the return, we would make The Call event, which was to be held in Los Angeles, California, at the end of the week; it was perfectly planned.

We cleared security and were on our way, or so we thought. Little did we know that during spring break, Atlanta Hartsfield Airport would support 80,000 travelers in one short weekend, and we would be wait-listed on our buddy passes for three days in an epic tale of persistence.

On the first day, we were in the airport for about 17 hours, going from gate to gate, concourse to concourse, after every missed flight, about every hour. We took stairs, trams, shuttles, and the escalator. We concluded God had us on the move to take every inch of airport territory in His name, so we prayed everywhere we went. We occasionally stopped and prayed for others—a lady with arthritis, a young child, a woman seeking the Holy Spirit. It was all God-ordained and satisfying to be used in the waiting. We were praying for seats and for God to make a way as we walked, carrying our packs from concourse to concourse, expectantly waiting for Him to answer our prayers.

Along the way, we passed the Interfaith Chapel and went inside and prayed. The Holy Bible on the podium was opened to Psalm 91, a favorite of mine, and Mark 16:17, "And these signs will follow those who believe; gifts and signs will follow them everywhere they go."

As I left, I felt a darkness so severe I had a lingering, piercing headache, and I had to stop to lean on a post outside the chapel. My friend felt it too, but faced it head on by walking back into the chapel. There was a man in the rear of the chapel, who I had overlooked, getting ready to bow down on a prayer rug and a lady kneeling in prayer. My friend offered to pray with the woman and was witnessing to her. The man was frozen, like a deer, listening reverently and interested, hanging on every word and testimony of God's promises. He never did fulfill his prayer ritual, but quickly left at the conclusion of the testimony. The atmosphere was changed at the chapel.

Eventually, we waited for the last flight of the night and the gate agent called my friends up, but only offered one seat, which they declined to travel separately. I was up. I had a seat to Maui! But, it was 11:00 p.m. and I had no provision and no place to stay. The gate agent looked directly at me and offered me the seat three times. Finally, I said, "I can't take it. No." I had no place certain to stay. It was too big a leap.

I drove my friends' home and promised to return in the morning to take them to the airport again. I was glad to be home and sad to not be on my way to Hawaii.

The next morning, I had made the decision that I wasn't going, but I followed through on my agreement to drive my friends back to the airport and wait with them for a flight or two. After I missed the first flight, I switched to a Honolulu flight, thinking that's where I was supposed to go and that must be the reason we weren't getting out and they stayed on the circuit for Maui. They got on their flight as soon as we separated. I did not. I headed home early in the day, dejected; again I was not on my way to Hawaii, but glad that perhaps I was the catalyst in my friends deciding to go to Maui.

I had the afternoon to finish errands, get my nails done, since they were in chipped and pitiful condition, and relax over a bite at the counter at Longhorn's Steakhouse, where God had already planned a divine appointment. There I would meet a Delta employee who, thrilled with my adventures, would offer his storehouse of buddy passes anytime I might need one for future God-adventures.

"I've never done this before," he said, "Well, actually, once, and it didn't go well, so I decided not to again, but you seem trustworthy. Call me if you ever need one."

Just like that, God had added to my journey. I knew now Jerusalem, Bora Bora, Thailand, and Australia were all possible. And, at the very least, I had a buddy pass for my trip to North Dakota where I planned to volunteer for a week at the Theodore Roosevelt National Park the last week of May. God just kept taking care of things. So, I went home, repented for not taking the late-night flight and made a promise to God to abandon myself to Him and catch the next flight He offered.

"I'll go back to the airport." I prayed. "If you give me another seat, I'll get on, in spite of my finances and just trust you to take care of them."

Third time's a charm. I went back to the now familiar Atlanta airport and waited in the lobby. I was rolled over on the first flight. "Rolled over? I was repentant and obedient!" I was indignant. "Okay, it is spring break. One more attempt—just one."

I was listed at 42 on the stand-by list. Then I rolled over a flight, but at the same gate, so I lingered in my seat, and was listed at 22. Number 22 was not very promising. They started calling passengers; it wasn't looking good. I prayed fervently as my courage was waning and confusion was taunting me.

"Lord, *all things* are possible. You said *50 states*, not 48 states. You sent me back to the airport for a third day in a row. *Three days.* Either you want me to go or you don't. I could be writing."

I stood up and inched my way closer to the counter. Still number 22. Waiting passengers were starting to leave. All of a sudden, a Delta rep came out of the gate and said you and you, pointing right to me first, come with me. If there's a seat open, you can take it, otherwise, I will escort you back off.

And, just like that number 22 was boarding the plane and found a seat headed to Honolulu, Hawaii, via Los Angeles. Never give up; anything can change, and, usually in the last minutes when things look completely hopeless.

I took my seat next to a Captain trying to hop a ride home; turns out, out of this entire over-crowded plane, he was friends with the family who had care over my daughter while I was gone—a God-wink, to be sure.

I arrived in the LAX airport too late for any connections to Maui. It was going to be a long night. I had a great dinner of healthy foods, from a fresh Caprese stack to braised Brussels sprouts and the best mascarpone coconut cake ever—good enough to be a wedding cake and make my whole flight worth the trip. Too physically exhausted to carry on, protective of my limited funds, and not feeling a shuttle to a hotel for just five hours, I made my way to what would be my morning gate.

I found a perch on a cold granite slab and bundled up with a coat, a jacket, and a pair of jeans from my pack. "Just keep me safe, Lord." He sent two clean-cut men, Army soldiers, to be centurions on my watch, and I dozed off to sleep. It was cold, hard, and uncomfortable, but I was grateful to be on the West Coast and guarded. "It's okay, He will make it up to me," I thought as I drifted off to sleep.

The next morning found me on the first flight to Maui—first

class. My Daddy was taking care of me! There was a luxurious, wide seat to sleep in, excellent service, and even a pink umbrella in my complimentary celebratory drink. This was more like the Sweet Life I was hoping for!

Arriving at the open airport with no familiar faces and no Hawaiian lei, not so sweet. I managed to arrange a Speedi Shuttle and decided on the resort where my friends were staying. Recall, they made the flight a day earlier, but they already had plans the first night. I had no rental car, was beyond exhausted, and felt sorry for myself, yes, even in Hawaii, it's possible to give in to fear and exhaustion, so, I plopped on the bed and fell asleep, fully clothed, in tears, missing my first Maui sunset.

Thankfully, when I awoke the next day, I repented, pulled myself together, and set out for macadamia pancakes on foot. After blocks and blocks, I saw my first American flag; yes, Hawaii is part of the 50 United States. It was an ice cream shop, but the menu board promised macadamia banana waffles, so I gave in. What a delight. I met owners Cory and Shannon, discovered they left large-size Bibles on their counters for their customers (oftentimes homeless visitors), and enjoyed a fabulous view of the beach and the palms. God is good, and my spirits lifted.

My friends, who had rented a car, invited me along for the day. We enjoyed beach after beach, eating awesome burgers at a fantastic golf resort and walking along the coastline where there were volcanic remnants. My friend and I walked and prayed for Hawaii and the healing of the land. We picked up a rock that looked like a foot; "footprints" came to mind and a heart-shaped pebble too. They now sit on my writing desk, reminding me how God is so amazing and He can do anything.

A special surprise was driving to twin falls, stopping at the side of Hana Road, and hiking through a natural bamboo forest to discover rushing waterfalls. In all my years, I couldn't imagine I would have done that. The drive was amazing, and the hike was empowering. God's terrain and gifts are amazing.

My friends and I said goodbye after just two days. They headed to AzUSA Street Ministries "The Call" event, and I hopped on a flight to Honolulu, but not before we discovered the mistake. It appeared I was only issued a one-way ticket to Hawaii. Yep. Was I moving here? It was probably the only way I would have gotten on the flight, the one-way ticket was just feasible enough; the return ticket was double the price and made my investment to Hawaii all the scarier. But, my friend issued a second pass and a flight from Maui was another overnight seat, saving me yet another hotel cost.

I was called to Honolulu from the very beginning and probably should have flown straight there. I enjoyed Waikiki Beach, Los Olas Boulevard, and Fort Lauderdale on steroids, I thought. I was able to stay at a boutique hotel the first night, eat shaved ice on the beach, and take a trolley around the loop of the island. My first stop was the royal palace, where I was given a semi-private tour with one other guest. It was then I recalled how I read stories of Hawaii and her royal line when I was in middle school. God was preparing me for this journey even then. Every life experience is for a purpose.

After a fabulous tour, I walked around the mall area to the capital building, wondering why I was there. I remembered Franklin Graham had held Decision America right there on the capitol steps, so I prayed into his prayers and a fierce wind came out of nowhere, as if carrying my prayers and his to heaven.

I looked up and saw the Senate and the House and continued

to pray over Hawaii, her people, legislators, and legislation and for a release of God's mighty arm to bless their land. I saw a field of pinwheels bringing awareness to the victims of childhood abuse. It was a spiritual time, for sure.

I was anxious to get home and get a seat on the plane and after a very full day. I headed to the airport. Once there, I learned I would not be going anywhere for quite a while. The Delta attendant said that the Northwest was returning from their spring break, flights were over-sold, and to make matters worse, the carrier had downgraded the size of the aircraft and couldn't accommodate as many guests.

"It looks like Tuesday before you will get out," the Delta representative said.

This was only Friday. "Impossible," I laughed, reflecting on my finances.

So, I hunkered in for the night and prayed. Then, the Holy Spirit hit me.

I couldn't leave. I hadn't been to Pearl Harbor yet. What's the point of coming all this way and missing Pearl Harbor? Both a patriot and a former military spouse, I knew that this patriotic book would not be complete without this stop. And, apparently, that is why I was being detained in the Honolulu airport.

After a night's sleep in a leather massage chair in the main lobby, I sent a text to an acquaintance of my past. I recalled my son's fifth grade teacher, not yet married when we knew her as an educator, had moved to Hawaii; my son is 25-years-old now, having just graduated college; it must have been 12 years since elementary school. When she heard my plight, she drove to the airport and opened up her home for one night. Turns out, she is a mom of five kids and married to a pastor. It was a delightfully entertaining visit of nostalgia and Christ-like hospitality.

After a few board games, a story book, and a shower, she drove me around to a beach and several beautiful stops before dropping me on the doorstep of Pearl Harbor—what an unexpected surprise. Our roots in America run deep.

I put my pack in the mandatory locker room, happy for a reprieve and enjoyed a lovely, reverent day honoring military. It was then, as if sensing the connection and healing the family tree and the next generation, my two daughters called and reached out separately. This National Monument site is a must for all Americans and for the next generation. It was a special day. As a former military spouse, I was especially moved to boat out to the USS Arizona, where soldiers were still entombed, and pray healing over military soldiers and their families and Hawaiians. So much loss and hurt and pain, forgiveness and healing and love are so deeply needed.

Then, to my surprise, I walked into an author's book signing event and the bookstore and right up to the book buyer of the retail center. I handed her the only copy of the *Military Family* book I had brought, and she offered to send it up the retail buying chain for consideration. I do hope they hope to carry the book at this very important military site. Please ask for it by name when you visit, *The Military Family: A Casualty of War* by Jacqueline Arnold.

And, with that, I took a bus back to the airport (plenty of angels along the way helped me with a bus number, transfer points, and directions to the airport terminal). I was hoping now I would get to leave, but, no, God had additional prayer opportunities and divine appointments for me. I met single mothers with kids, prayed for a mother with kids who acknowledged a shaky point in her marriage, and offered my testimony and books for help and healing. Each encounter was a blessing, and they left encouraged, with hope restored and faith renewed after hearing my testimony. I wasn't stuck in the Honolulu Airport; I was positioned.

Day 3 came; I was complaining a tad to God that I was spending a lot of senseless money eating at the airport when I could be home writing the book. So, I set up shop at the terminal Starbucks and in any gate that had an electrical outlet for a charge and continued writing. No time was wasted, except on eating.

I fell asleep on the fourth morning in a hard terminal chair and popped up suddenly when I thought I heard my name, only to discover I was mistaken. I stumbled to another aisle of seats to find a group of three Hawaiian Americans huddled nearby. I saw her cap AzUSA, and I was not able to hold back, running to her like an old friend.

"I was supposed to be at that event!" I exclaimed. "Plus, I don't want to miss any of the blessings. But, God had me detained in Hawaii, praying healing and love and forgiveness over the land, almost as the human bridge from the AzUSA event to the Hawaiian Islands (the ends of America, so to speak)."

I didn't miss a thing as my new friends and I witnessed and prayed aloud in Holy Spirit voice right there in the lobby of the international airport. We were bold as lions, and the Lion of Judah released His roar. It was awe-inspiring. Having exchanged stories and testimonies and contact information, we parted with hugs and joy.

About a full 10 minutes later, one of my new friends came back and said, "The Holy Spirit told me to give this to you."

It was $100 bill folded up and placed firmly into my hand. Grace. The money I had just murmured to God that I was "wasting" on airport food and near the end of my means. And using a total stranger, He replaced it. From Georgia to Hawaii, we are one American heartbeat, souls connected by God and our country.

So, now was I released? I was chasing flights from one gate to another, but I would have one more night in the terminal—five in all. I was achy from lack of a bed, but grateful for the leather massage chairs and my backpack full of supplies (yes, my makeup and hairbrush were in there!).

As I went to wait in the terminal with a direct flight to Atlanta, I sat next to a husband, wife, and young adult daughter. We chatted freely and soon discovered they were from Georgia. I had only met one other Georgian; that was interesting. As soon as the wife and daughter were called, I knew the father would not make the plane and God would have an assignment. Sure enough, it happened. I would soon learn he was pastor of GO Church ("GO" stands for "Gospel Outreach"), in Ball Ground, Georgia—the Ball Ground, Georgia, near Jasper, Georgia, of the north Georgia mountains. God had a plan, all right. We were able to spend a couple hours waiting on the next flight witnessing, sharing, and encouraging. He told of the trials he encountered as a pastor trying to start a church and his walk of fire and faith in finances, and he shared the story of success and how the church is growing and blessed. It was a testimony God used to water and encourage me. And, it would be another month before I would learn it would become my "sending church" with a message of revival and rediscovery across America. God had planted that seed.

Finally, I knew, as I felt in my spirit, I had finally completed every assignment I was sent to Hawaii to fulfill and with boldness, sat at the gates no longer for flights headed to LAX, but the direct flights to Atlanta, Georgia. Finally, after five days stranded in Honolulu, Hawaii, I was sent home. This was no easy trek, and I do hope should I ever return, it's a five star, Ritz-Carlton, luxury kind of experience. In this journey, I also had to balance my 15-year-old daughter returning from a visit with her sister in Orlando, potentially returning to Georgia with no parent home, no ride to school, and no shuttle home from the airport. I was digging my claws in the armrest of my chair and sending prayers up, calling about 15 friends until I finally identified a high school senior who could pick my daughter up from the airport, spend the night at our home, and get her safely to school. This faith-walk took nerves of steel and steely determination to make things work and faith that God would not drop my girl or me in the process. He is faithful.

Aloha, Hawaii! Until we meet again. Which could be soon, for a book signing at the Pearl Harbor National Memorial, I hope. On the plane, I sat between two more appointments, a gal whose family was in need of an outpouring of heaven and a book buyer for the National Parks. The National Parks, really? Yes, this book, *God & Country*, belongs in the bookstores of every National Park bookstore, don't you agree? God asks a lot of us, but He never leaves us without reward. Another passenger gave me tips on how she was on The Today Show. Yes, another outlet for my message. Hello, Today Show, when you need a military family advocate or someone who can Ignite America. I have my buddy pass in hand.

This Southern girl was over the moon happy to be back in her Sweet Life of Georgia. It had been quite an adventure. And, with that, 49 states done and only one to go. *Without even a ticket* and now, *without even a dime*, only God could deliver my dreams for the 50th state, only God.

## CHAPTER TWENTY NINE

# HISTORY MADE, HISTORY IN THE MAKING

There are 30 National Memorials, administered by the National Park Services and other branches funded in part by the NPS, including such memorable ones as the Jefferson Memorial, the Washington Memorial, and the World War I Memorial. You will find them in 14 states, with most of them in Washington, D.C. Mount Rushmore and even the Wright Brothers Memorial in North Carolina also make the list. These are perfect destination points to add to your list of discovery on your travels across America.

While planning your adventure, be sure to research the most visited monuments, memorials and National Parks. You will find a detailed list of the most popular destination points and rediscover American history in the process.

# History Made, History In The Making

There are hundreds upon hundreds of military monuments and memorials in the United States. Be sure to stop when you stumble upon these gems. They help us learn, remember, and they give us opportunity to show honor to those who sacrificed for our great country. There are confederate memorials, a trail of the Civil War, and of course, the Trail of Tears that hold the markers of remembrance of tears and bloodshed for us to enjoy our country and our freedoms. America, it's time to rediscover our roots, to remember our history, to return to the foundation our Founding Fathers laid, and to remember the one who created it all. We are so truly blessed. Bring your children to their heritage, fill your senses with the depths of God's love and the majesty of our great country, and receive your birthright with new accord. Be filled.

Look for Civil War reenactments and Heritage Days. World War II days are events to honor veterans and our American history; they are held annually in my small town.

This year's theme was A Tribute to Pearl Harbor, how fitting since I had just returned from Pearl Harbor. The Freedom Belles were singing their pretty hearts out, just as they did at camp shows on foreign soil decades before during WWII, fans were taking rides in war birds overhead, and America was remembering her heritage.

There was a spirit in the air, *The Spirit of America*—long forgotten, but planted deep in our souls from events of the past, from the blood of our forefathers. Events such as these help us to reconnect, remember, and stir up the good citizenship in us so that we yearn to be a better person, a better people, a better community; the number of attendees and volunteers is a testimony to that. America wants to do the right thing. It's time to get our hearts right again; America and these events are a good starting point.

These events allow us to trace our family history. My own family has deep roots. Every family member up and down both sides of the family tree has military service in their history and blood that runs red, white, and blue. My uncle died in the London Blitz in England, and another served in the United States Navy. My father was a medic in the United States Navy, my oldest brother was in the Navy, and my next brother was in the United States Air Force. I married a United States Coast Guardsmen who transferred to become an officer in the United States Army, making it a career for 23 years, serving in Operation Desert Storm, Operation Enduring Freedom, and more. His father was in the United States Navy during the Korean War; his brothers made military careers their life's work, two in the Coast Guard, two in the Army. My mother was widowed from her husband, a US Marine (Retired) who served in Inchon in the Korean War. Military proud is all we know.

It translated into heavy volunteering ethics and my platform as Mrs. Virginia International and Top Ten in the Mrs. International, 2003—a system focused on volunteerism and a national patriotic observance for patriotism and volunteerism, *The Spirit of America Days*, which garnered congressional endorsements and is still being circulated today. I was a Girl Scout through the rank of Senior and went on to many years and multiple roles of leadership for Boy Scouts and Girl Scouts of America. My three boys all earned the prestigious rank of Eagle Scout in the Boy Scouts of America, and my daughters, from Brownies to Senior Girl Scouts, have learned the rich heritage of America, her leadership, good citizenship, and service.

Talk about your family history with your children. Remind them of the roots that run deep. Military service is noble. There are also reserve opportunities and the guard; there is volunteerism, scouting, and politics that can change communities and impact our heritage. Decide for yourself and discuss with your families what your contribution will be. There is an opportunity for each of us to make an impact. There is a cost to our citizenship. Decide for yourselves today what your contribution will be. Remember the past and then make a plan for today for our future tomorrow. Every contribution has a meaningful impact and leaves a lasting mark.

## CHAPTER THIRTY

# 30 YEARS OF CLEANING THE FAMILY TREE —DEEP ROOTS

And with that, I just know that May will be a month of *more* miracles, money miracles, making dreams come true and doors that open in quick succession. Why? It's all because God is a "Good, Good Father" (as the song by Chris Tomlin goes). I am trusting Him to heal 30 years of pain and grief and clean my family tree once and for all to bless us anew for 1,000 generations.

It is May 1st, May Day. May Day comes to mind. It is my nephew's 30th birthday. 30 years ago, he was on an operating table having just been born with a critical health issue, but God showed our family mercy. But, as is with much of life, there is good and there is bad; the pendulum of life swings. And, at the end of the month, my brother Patrick Michael drowned in a lake while boating. It was just two weeks before his 19ᵗʰ birthday. A muscular, strapping fellow, two boats collided, he was hit on the head and drowned on the lake where he was enjoying a day of boating with friends.

30 years of both grace and pain passed by. These were 30 years of grief, for sure. I, the sixth child of seven, was sandwiched by grief. Born after my older brother drowned in a local canal at the young age of four, likely to bring joy to my grieving family, that was not to be the case. My family again encountered death's grip when my baby brother was killed in the boating accident. We were especially close, close in age, close in relationship. My heart would encounter much grief in life. I was ready for God to now heal the 30 years of family grief and my soul which had been repeatedly fractured along the way.

There has been a lot of life, history, and spiritual events in those years, a lot of Sweet Life to celebrate and a lot of pain to mourn. It is the same for our country, 240 years of history—both tears of joy and cries of victory and deep pain and pleas for God's mercy. We must remember our history and our heritage and hold out our hope for our maker's hand. He is a God of miracles. "Those who sew in tears will reap with songs of joy, according to His promises." (Psalm 126:5).

I was ready for His promise for songs of joy. I was ready to close the door on 30 years of grief, a year of travels and adventures which were also a test of faith and emotional endurance, decades of financial struggles, two months of homelessness, and deep, deep heart breaks that only He could heal. I was holding out hope for May, the month of my graduation. This graduation marked the end of many things: the completion of my fiftieth jubilee, the finality of my fifty state dream tour of America, the graduation of two of my children from college, and what would have been my brother Patrick's jubilee year in June. Let the joy pour down from heaven, let the healing rain cleanse my family tree, let deep, deep roots grow into a firm foundation, and let God's favor fall for 1,000 generations anew.

But, before May, I still had to endure and prepare to be positioned for promotion.

When I got back from April, physically exhausted and financially spent, I clung to the fact that all I had left was one month to the finish line and my fiftieth state of Maine. God had already set it up and shown me His promise that I would make it to the finish line. I was barely recuperating from the physically and emotionally strenuous travels of Hawaii when it hit me—another unexpected travel opportunity.

A friend who is also a Delta employee, the one who planted the thought with a promise a month ago, had reached out to me to make good on his offer to give me a "Golden Ticket," a guaranteed round trip seat to anywhere Delta flies. The ticket was valid for only 13 days more. I knew in an instant I would be going to Israel. It was after all, Passover on the Jewish calendar, and I knew it was an important time. I always thought my first book—*Eat, Love, Praise Him!* would end in Jerusalem, the Christian Mecca, kind of like *Eat, Pray, Love* ended in Bali, a spiritual Mecca, but of a different following. The call of Jerusalem made sense, but it turns out it was for a purpose, but not for me to travel.

When the logistics got too complicated, I realized the Golden Ticket was to serve two symbolic purposes—to get me thinking about Israel and Passover and to include it in this book to symbolize how God could replace my birthday ticket to *anywhere in the world* in the blink of an eye—the one I cashed in to fulfill this mission was being replaced before me. Perhaps, had we pressed and all the details worked out, I would have been able to get to Bora Bora, after all. It was just another example to me that God can do anything. Thankfully, neither trip was meant to be. I, a traveling machine, was glad. I had a book to finish and two graduations to celebrate and, for once in a very long year, I was weary from traveling—very weary.

Who was I kidding? I needed a financial miracle of *thousands* of dollars. I had to ask, with all this dangling opportunity and evidence of financial need, what kind of God would bring me to Hawaii and not deliver me from the mountain of debt in front of me?

> "I will never desert you or forsake you. The Lord is my helper, I will not be afraid"
>
> —Hebrews 13:5–6

God is faithful. I need to just trust Him. I knew this in my spirit, but in my flesh, I was tired of the struggle, confused from what appeared to be facts, and waning in tenacity.

God *is* faithful. Yes, He is, with my sweet life and this jubilee celebration of a lifetime, with relationship and response, with miracles, provision and grace. I need to let go and trust Him.

He has delivered me a "Golden Ticket." Having sacrificed my dream to Bora Bora and walked with Him in faith across America, now, in the 11th hour, He has delivered me a Golden Ticket—to anywhere in the world—right back into my lap! That is how big our God is. That is how much God loves me. That is how much God wants us to trust Him. He will always make it better. He will never return our prayers to us void.

He will not just answer prayers for the ticket to anywhere in the world, but to every dream, even the deepest desires of your heart, no matter how extravagant—He answered with a "ticket to anywhere in the world," after all. Our God is amazing. And, He offers us a sweet, sweet life tethered to His heart. Wake up and grab onto His mighty, righteous hand for the ride of your life. Life is Sweet with Jesus.

But with the sweet, also comes the storms. And, God knew the few weeks ahead would be stressful, with financial darkness and storms aplenty, and I would need His promises to hold onto, so he sent a messenger with a little hope for me to hold onto.

A full two and a half weeks prior to my trip to Maine, I was contemplating my young adult children's college graduations and getting to my fiftieth state. Maybe they would be able to join me on my final trip as a graduation present, and perhaps, I should bring my special bottle of Veuve Clicquot that had been chilling for three or four years now, too special to open. I went back and forth but wondered if it would be too difficult to transport champagne on the flight. And, here's the story I promised to tell you.

That night, late at night, Dr. Dave called and said, "I wanted to get you motivated about your trip in May, so I'm going to send you a few photos to get you excited. And, oh, by the way, I bought a bottle of champagne to celebrate my uncle's birthday, but at 90, thought better of opening it and decided, instead, to leave it for you when you come."

I giggled aloud. My Father sees me, even in the smallest details. Champagne! He had champagne chilling for me. It meant I would be celebrating by May! The champagne was chilling, and I had His promise to hold onto through the next two weeks of storms. This was all the more important as May approached—a historically important month of sadness, loss, death, and change for my family tree.

This May, 30 years of storms and life later, I was believing for more because, while I have my history, I also have the history of God's word full of His promises. And, there was champagne waiting for me, the promise of the victory and deliverance ahead.

It is odd how healing my family tree and holding onto God's promises is so parallel to what I see for my country. America is in the same position; after years, even centuries of history and broken covenants, God's promise to restore remains on the horizon.

We have an outlook of brokenness, waywardness, grief and loss, deep wounds, waywardness, and good intentions gone wrong, open rebellion and unintended sin and yet, the promise of His healing hand. Just as I traveled 50 states on a wing and a prayer and a promise from God to discover all things are possible, in spite of the storms, the circumstances and my position and strength, all things, I believe, are possible for America. God is a God of restoration, provision, mercy and grace, love and healing, and hope. With God all things are possible for America, as well. And, I believe when America wakes up and souls begin to stir and agree with our maker, the world will see what happens when a faithful God returns to reconcile, redeem, and bless anew contrite hearts and repentant souls. His mercy never fails. His grace and love and mercies are new every day. All things are possible; America must believe—the world needs to see. Jesus Christ is our healer and our hope.

America must remember our history, review our lives and family trees, pray for cleansing and clearing of the land and the roots, fight for the freedoms so many fought for, and run into the rewards of God's promises and to the arms of our Father in heaven. Drop our shame, our pride, and our judgment, our hurt, our loss, and our disappointment and fear. He has blessed America for His good purpose. It is not just for us, not just for our children, or their children, but for seeds of global awakening; the world is watching to see what America, the favored child, the one set apart, will do in this moment in history. We must never forget, America. Join me to Ignite *The Spirit of America*. Agree with heaven this day for the land we love, for heaven's sake.

We must never forget the sacrifices made for our freedoms; they are many. We enjoy many freedoms and privileges without giving them a second thought, including even an 8-hour workday. As I near the end of this book on May Day, I stop to research a common day of observation and learn that it has many facets. Which ones will I accept and recognize and which ones might be dishonoring to God? This is a good reflection for all traditions and practices and beliefs we accept in our homes, our lives, and our country. Challenges all your beliefs and traditions this day and discern for yourselves what is right. Don't follow the masses, but do what is pleasing and honoring to God.

One May Day observance started in the 1860s, according to Industrial Workers of the World at www.iww.org/history. May Day was dedicated to the workers of America when organized labor was able to rally for the 8-hour workday and end slave labor working conditions in America.

> Truly, history has a lot to teach us about the roots of our radicalism. When we remember that people were shot so we could have the 8-hour day; if we acknowledge that homes with families in them were burned to the ground so we could have Saturday as part of the weekend; when we recall 8-year old victims of industrial accidents who marched in the streets protesting working conditions and child labor only to be beat down by the police and company thugs, we understand that our current condition cannot be taken for granted—people fought for the rights and dignities we enjoy today, and there is still a lot more to fight for. The sacrifices of so many people cannot be forgotten or we'll end up fighting for those same gains all over again. This is why we celebrate May Day.[1]

It is most important to remember the roots of our traditions as they feed into the land of America and all that she is responsible for. Our first commitment is for God and then to our country, fought for by the blood of many. For these values and principals, we stand firm; for all else, we repent and honor the one true God.

# CHAPTER THIRTY ONE

## TACO TUESDAYS BRING MAY BLESSINGS

May has arrived and with it, God has heralded in favor and a change of season for my family and me. Two of my older children graduated college and got career jobs in the same week. In spite of the storms, they have come through; they have found their way, and God has answered the many, many prayers of this momma's heart.

May also came in full swing, with it a bucket of bills to boot, not to overlook my May rent, third month in a row, which implies a lesson of faith. It was May 1st, and there was less than $45 in my checking account, my rent still not paid. But during worship Sunday at church, God had given me an image of a taco. I remember thinking, "*Taco?*" I was immediately compelled to recall the restaurant slogan "Taco Tuesday." "*Taco Tuesday?*" I laughed aloud while surrounded by others in worship.

## Taco Tuesdays Bring May Blessings

"Oh! Tuesday. There will be a blessing on Tuesday," I discerned. "Thank you, Lord." I knew to hang on and trust Him because Tuesday would hold a special heavenly blessing.

Three days later, it was Taco Tuesday; I didn't even recognize it at first—until all the blessings started pouring in. After a full year of searching for speaking engagements, I had three inquiries on the same day. The first came from the pastor's wife I met in the Honolulu airport to speak at their ladies luncheon in June—to be held in the mountains of Jasper, Georgia. Well, isn't that just sweet vindication, speaking just outside the gates (where my second book is set, offering salve for the wounds of my heart). Our meeting in the airport was divine, just as we both had suspected.

I took the call on speakerphone as I drove my 15-year-old to school. We said all the niceties, exchanged southern sweetness, and then she filled me in on the details of the event. I knew in an instant, I would speak, and though I knew the need for financial increase was great, and, suspected in June, financial opportunities would begin to come my way, something in my spirit spontaneously offered to waive my $1,000 speaker's fee. I knew our meeting had been divinely appointed and this speaking engagement was more than just an invitation. It was my opportunity to speak at a church group in the mountains, as I once had intended to do, and an opportunity to touch GO Church. It was, after all, a meeting God had set up.

I loved that we were planting on these seeds into my daughter's spirit. Two church ladies, busy at God's work even at 8:00 a.m. She was moved nearly to tears that I had responded as such and gushed with gratitude. I was deeply touched to know it was so meaningful to her. My daughter was blessed for her day at school, I was sure.

There I was, giving away the farm when I didn't even have a cow to milk! But, it felt right in my spirit. And her response confirmed it.

I headed to Starbucks and fiddled with emails, organizing and reorganizing my May budget and bills I had been dragging along. It was over the $10,000 mark—seriously, I had been carrying some of these large burdens for many months, some more than a year, and I just kept throwing them into my backpack, on top of the mountain of problems and dragging them along month after month. The Lord kept helping me address the important and urgent ones just in the nick of time, but the others lingered. Some of these couldn't wait beyond this month. I was praying really hard this was the month the burdens would all be addressed and fall off the list. What a relief that would be. Even though these big and important items were carried for so many months, the critical living bills were always taken care of month after month after month, in spite of my employment status. It was God's provision that sustained me.

I was agitated from looking at the numbers again. I just wanted to give it to God, so He would make them all disappear. That wasn't happening, so this must be part of His purpose for me, the thorn in my flesh that I must constantly contend with.

So, I closed up my computer and considered driving to the Voter's Registration Office to follow up on a change of address form and then decide what to do about my rent check and my lack of funds for it. I got in my car and saw the near-empty gas indicator and quickly ditched the desire to go to the Voter's Registration Office, more than 10 miles away, and just drove away, with the intent to head to my landlord's house and write that check—still waiting on my Provider to provide the funds needed to pay my rent or show me how.

While I drove, I said aloud, "Lord, I know you know my need. Thank you for being my provider. Thank you that I can trust you. There would be no point to bring me to Hawaii on funds you froze for an entire month and then let my current rent go unpaid, leaving me without any money for May's rent. What kind of miracle would that be? What kind of story would that make? No, you have a plan; I just have to wait. I trust you to provide or to show me what to do."

And, then, immediately, my phone rang. "Can you meet me in five minutes," came the voice of a friend I know from the church community.

"I'm on my way." Something in me knew the Holy Spirit was up to something. I couldn't go very far as my gas tank had 20 miles until empty. I didn't even ask my friend why, but the excitement in me bubbled up as I felt I was participating with God in something.

I pulled in and this church friend had me roll my window down. Without getting out of my car, my friend leaned in with a tiny envelope and said, "You know, Jesus' ministry started with a woman. It was a woman He first appeared to. I wanted to bless you as a woman in ministry."

"That's so very nice," I said, believing it was a financial blessing and likely enough for gas money. As a solo entrepreneur, writing books for God was a lonesome endeavor; it was nice to have encouragement, especially at this very juncture.

I pulled out, headed home and thanked God for His recognition and the blessing. And, then, my spirit stirred, and I didn't want to wait until I got home. I pulled over to open the envelope, discovering crisp $100 bills—twelve of them—enough to nearly pay my rent! I was wrecked and burst out into a stream of tears. What a large blessing!

"You see me, Lord," I said humbly. "You are my El Roi (see Genesis 16:13–14) and my provider. Thank you, Father." That someone would obediently give that much money astounded me. That they had no idea I was without financial means to even pay my rent this month completely baffled me. That Father would provide enough to pay my rent due at that very moment was so surreal and overwhelming. It made Him all the more real and tangible.

But, the number didn't quite make sense. It fell short of my rent amount. I reflected on all that I had been talking over with God. I recalled that tomorrow would be the day to head to college graduations for my children, and that I would need money for the trip to Florida. I had just been reviewing those expense needs prior to my drive. Surely, my Father would not let me miss my children's college graduations! And, not after all He had brought me through.

I prayed as I walked into the bank, and I fleeced God. "I'm not really sure what this amount is," I'm praying and thinking as I'm smiling and greeting the familiar bank tellers. "If you don't want me to deposit the cash and it's to be used for something besides my rent check, like my trip to Florida for graduations, let me receive a phone call, even if it's at the last minute."

I begin the transaction, and just as the teller pushed to make the transaction, my phone rang; it was my book publisher, needing a $50 installment payment. I was shocked. It had been six months since my publisher had contacted me.

I knew then, Father planned to delay the May rent check, just as He had the April rent check, and that money blessing would now, in part, go toward my trip and the publisher. I prayed in

Thanksgiving, but worried in my flesh how this rent check would be delayed a second month in a row, the last month for 28 days. This delay was well out of character for my landlord's behavior with prompt deposits.

I scurried over to the landlord's house as quick as a wink and left a rent check, believing, with all my being that I had heard God's prompting and was not acting recklessly. And, sure enough, He delayed it a second month! Left under the mat for the landlord to retrieve, it got wet. He placed it on his counter to dry and seeing it as debris, the housekeeper threw it in the trash! He texted me on my drive home from graduation, a full two weeks later, that he needed a replacement check—not a day sooner did he plan to cash it. When I arrived home, a check I was expecting was waiting for me in the mail to be deposited and all the needs were met—from rent to graduation travel, as well.

God is God of the universe; He can do anything. Just make absolutely certain you are hearing from Him and follow His prompting. Guessing with finances is no light matter—I had multiple and clear indications that Father had done this before with smaller incidents and would do it again this time. I have seen the Holy Spirit elongate time, heal my ribs instantaneously, make cash appear in my wallet, move people's spirits to share their tithes, and then prompt me in this bigger walk of faith. This is not man's way; this is God's way. I'm simply sharing my supernatural experiences to give you insights to how God does the impossible. It was, after all, the point of this 50 X 50 trip—that *all* things are possible with God, from the trip to the provision of it.

My Tuesday blessings continued, as if to reassure me; I got a second inquiry to speak, by email. Would I speak at a civic meeting in June? The meeting coordinator had found me while searching online. Nobody, in three years of having my website had found me while doing a Google search.

A third June opportunity was posted through Thumbtack, an online gig search I belong to. It was on the topic of "Perseverance." And, after this entire walk, I am well qualified on that topic; I applied.

Wow! What a shower I was getting! I loved Taco Tuesday!

The month of May could only get better from here. I began labeling it "#MayMoneyMiracles." Though not all the rewards were financial, I was being optimistic.

May graduation was a mother's reward. How touching, that after so many storms, there was joy on the horizon now. Through all the circumstances of life, God had shown favor and blessed each of my children with college degrees, and in the same week, they both would have careers. Now, just five days later, my reward and "graduation" to complete all 50 states would follow. Not only was I going to Maine, my 50th state, champagne was waiting for me to celebrate.

That weekend was a large, victorious celebration of my children's accomplishments, but also shared family time, a special Mother's Day with my 86-year-old-mother and my five children all gathered around the table for brunch, all celebrating me with cards and love and hugs.

And then came another nuance of vindication: my daughter, the first to graduate that weekend, graduated with her BSN in Nursing on National Nurse Appreciation Day, coincidentally, on May 6, which is also recognized as Military Spouse Appreciation Day. I don't recall ever receiving recognition or reward in years prior—during my 23 years as a former Army spouse. Some things are long in coming. It was a beautiful reward. My son graduated the next day with a BA in business and rounded out our beautiful celebration—a testimony to moving toward your goals and never giving up. The favor of God and all my answered prayers were so evident. God was healing my family tree, and I could see 1,000 generations being blessed before my very eyes.

# CHAPTER THIRTY TWO

# MAINE MIRACLES

## 50 X 50

All Things Are Possible. Period. End of Story. Believe.

I had barely two days to recover, regroup, and get my household in order for my absence of the long week ahead for Maine. My mother had returned to stay for an extended visit, though the closer it got to my departure, the less comfortable she got, adding pressure. My daughter had already announced she would be the mother of the house, but not without a golf cart for transportation. (Recall, we live in a golf cart community. Residents take golf carts to school and work and grocery shopping).

She was right, I couldn't leave for five days without a mode of transportation; they would feel abandoned and stranded. She had only a learner's permit, and my mother wasn't comfortable driving in a new town. I would have to address a rental for the weekend.

I also had to squeeze in lunch with my senior and tend to his temporary needs, as he was less than thrilled I would be away for yet another four days. Gheesh. I was caregiver to so many. Calgon, take me away! The pressure was mounting.

"God, you already told me I was going to Maine. You handed me the keys to the cottage. You told me there would be champagne waiting and I'd be celebrating!" I exclaimed through the chaos.

My finances? Other than the rent check, which I absolutely refused to play with yet again, there was only $300 in my account not yet written out. How does one go to Maine for five days on $300? It was going to be a challenge, but I was leaving that to God to arrange my schedule and my expenses. I was already considering that Fly Fishing and a Hot Air Balloon Ride would have to be dropped from my bucket list of things I wanted to do for my Jubilee year on this final trip. They weren't crucial, of course. The purpose of this book wasn't to get and do everything I desired, but to serve God, testify for Him, gather information for this book, and enjoy our God of possibilities and impossibilities.

Everything was in order and everyone attended to, except that I still needed to arrange the airline ticket, my buddy pass. With two and a half hours to go, I figured that I still had enough time. I coordinated the pass by phone en route to the airport. It was coordinated and emailed with a "*Praise God!*" of exclamation. But, I couldn't make my way to the airport efficiently. It seemed there were unique bumps in the typical traffic patterns, a construction project which blocked the interstate for 20 minutes, and more. I kept saying all things were possible and, in spite of the mountains in front of me, proclaimed them moved and continued driving, but I seemed to be blocked and stalled at every turn.

Then the airport parking lots and garages were all marked

"FULL" upon arrival, and the summer travelers filled up the security gates to extend the delay. I knew it wasn't meant to be; I just didn't understand the delays. I forged ahead to the gate, all the way to the gate in case it was delayed in departure, yet, arriving 15 minutes after my flight departed. Exhausted, I stopped at The Blue Moon Brewery for a great angus burger, to marvel at God's plans and accept that I wasn't going to Maine on this day.

Not today. I knew Maine was still on my calendar, but not on God's today.

Heading home, I stopped at the golf cart supplier and rented a golf cart for the following few days. Kellie would be satisfied. Later that night, the steam came out of this tea pot. We all ended in tears of frustration and exhaustion and then in hugs, kisses, and mutual forgiveness. There's nothing like a run to the Bees Knees Freeze snow cone shop in neighboring Senoia and some simple time together to reconnect, repair, and begin anew.

Why do we let things build up to the point of boiling over? Take time for family. Take time to connect. It's the simple things in life, like snow cones in the summer.

Thank you, God, for forgiveness and restoration.

The next morning, I was about to head to the airport when I got an urgent text from a friend. "Don't go yet. I have to see you. I'm on my way." Again, I knew it was Holy Spirit driven, and I laughed as I drove home to greet my friend at my house.

She came to the door, laden with gifts—*graduation gifts*—for me! I was so delighted! God sees my accomplishment, and so does she! I had been feeling disappointed that after all the adventures. This last one, the achievement of my fiftieth state and reaching my decade-long goal, was anti-climactic and unrecognized. It turns out, God was aligning the calendar for historical purposes and preparing a graduation celebration for me before I departed.

Her gifts were so thoughtful, each symbolic, from the gold heart-shaped basket that held an assortment of perfect fruit— to symbolize the fruit of the Spirit—a banana, a golden apple, a heart-shaped peach, and a tomato full of seeds (that I have been planting and will reproduce and yield an abundant harvest).

She brought a silver photo album with a crystal heart to record photos from my journey, two postcards from Hawaii, one with a rainbow, of course; there was a fresh floral red rose in full bloom and a tiny pink sneaker keychain with the beautiful saying, "Blessed is the Woman Who Walks With God." With every gift, she praised and encouraged me. With every gift, I cried tears of joy of Father's recognition. It was a beautiful graduation party just for me, and my mother got to be there to witness my accomplishment!

For Mother's Day, with so little to offer, I simply gave my momma a meaningful card and my One Sheet of all my books, thanking her for encouraging me and the result of mothering me was that I became an author, a Christian broadcaster, a mother of five, and a woman of faith. It brought tears to her eyes; she loved it. Now, she could see the fruit of my faith, too, and yet another graduation and achievement. She was witnessing the fruit of her love, too. Redemption. Vindication. Celebration. God is good.

Now, my friend took our photo together, me on the arm of the chair my mother rested in, and she said to her, "You have a beautiful daughter; you must be so proud of her."

This was a mother's reward for us both. Had I made yesterday's flight, I would have missed this beautiful graduation celebration and today's date. The date is important to the second book, so I won't recant, but let's say when God closes one door, He opens another, and today, that door was opening.

The aligning of coincidences continued to unfold as I celebrated this special journey. And, with that celebration and all hearts full, I headed to the airport with ease, not a traffic delay in sight, easy extended parking and walked right to the gate. When it's God's way, it's easy.

And, with that, God makes a way for Maine, the 50th state of my journey, the last of this big American journey. The final point of this journey was to prove that, yes, all things really are possible with God. Don't ever look at your circumstances, look at our awesome God and trust Him with your whole heart.

While it wasn't 50 X 50, more like 50 X 51 plus 6 months and 19 days, I had once extended it until the end of my fiftieth year due to divorce and disasters and military moves and life; that seemed perfectly reasonable, a celebration of my jubilee the entire 50th birthday year. So, now in essence, it was 6 months and 19 days, plus 1, delayed. Then when you consider I moved again in that next year, moved a child off to college, started my Christian broadcasting gig, and saved a 95-year-old man's life, well, what's another six months? And, the 19 days? I did have two kids' college graduations to celebrate and a Mother's Day to mark before completing my journey—hey, life happens. The point is: it still happens! And, it could have happened 50 X 50, if I got out of the way and pushed it to conclusion then.

In spite of the obstacles, in spite of the storms, in spite of life's circumstances, and in spite of the mountains that had to move, I made it. God is faithful. He saw me through, every step of my journey—50 X 51.5, which will always be 50 X 50 to me—the mark of a monumental 50-year goal in my heart. And, with that, I am satisfied. Trusting in the Holy Spirit, it happened with great flourish and in its perfect timing in spite of life's storms.

The Holy Spirit continued to lead this journey as I got in my rental car and intended to head to the Port of Portland and catch a sunset lobster cruise; I had one block after another from traffic to cobblestone streets that dead-ended, that told me, I was due to head straight to the coastal cottage awaiting me in Saco and not take the cruise. And, boy, am I glad I listened to the Holy Spirit's prompting! I would hate to have driven through Seaside and into this three-story home in the dark of night. When I turned left onto King Avenue, I knew Father had another King's feast and retreat set aside just for me. I was giddy with anticipation of the weekend ahead.

There in the fridge was a cold bottle of champagne waiting for me with a note that said, "Welcome to Maine and congratulations on making it to your 50 states."

Another graduation card—I was delighted, but more overcome when I pulled out the long neck of the bottle to discover the gold Veuve Clicquot label, the same label as the bottle of champagne I had contemplated bringing on this journey back home.

God not only ensured I had champagne, but this very special bottle of champagne—special to me. There was that bottle and a tiny jar of Maine blueberry preserves. After that, I knew it was going to be a great weekend.

I explored the coastal cottage and took pictures of the ocean view, squealing with delight as I identified my favorite spot for tea, a row of chairs lined up in front of a picture window. I flicked a few lights on for my return and flipped through the activities binder by the guest book. I eyed a restaurant menu from Josephs by the Sea and headed straight there. Arriving at 8:00 p.m., I was their last guest of the night to be seated. They made room for me at a table by the window, with an ocean view, just as dusk had set and it was turning dark. The glow of the table candlelight and the outside night lights provided a beautiful ambience and stirred my spirit.

The night revealed a beautiful graduation dinner planned just for me. I was grateful to have come straight to town for this beautiful banquet from mussels to seared lobster stack pancake, there was even a beautiful dessert of bananas and vanilla ice cream rolled into a crepe, drizzled in hot butterscotch sauce and pralines. God was good to me. It was worth waiting a day to travel. This was a marvelous celebration.

And, another reason not to drive to your new accommodations late, late at night? Your phone, with the house code that was texted to you, might suddenly lose battery charge, while you are standing at the door, in the pitch black of night, trying to get in. Yep. That happened.

But when you are under the covering of your Daddy's wings (Psalm 91), He sends a lovely couple to walk their dog, Brody, to your dead-end street at exactly the same moment in the dark of night. Immediately, they offered to wait with me and show hospitality to me and invited me to their house to charge my phone so I can retrieve the door code. They were strangers, yes, but heaven-sent strangers who become friends. We enjoyed a nice neighborly chat while we waited. God is amazing. He protects me. He entertains me. He looks out for me with every step.

Day two in Maine began with long texts from my prayer friend who brought my graduation basket. "Do you know what all you will pray for in Maine?" she asked.

I laughed, as I was just contemplating that. Why was I here again? This was the 50th state, and, obviously, my graduation, so it seemed, but surely there was more, another purpose.

She began a litany of texts: "9 is divine completeness and I felt compelled to share that with you." My 50 states were complete. It was divine. She listed the 12 that had come to her this morning: "Prayer, Praise, Presence, Pause, Petition, Pleased, Power, Promotion and Positioned." I liked these P's, and many were resonating strongly with me. I believed this conclusion; I was being positioned for promotion, too.

After David's writings, he reflected. Yes, I was nearly done with the book and I needed time to reflect, as well. What was next? What did God want to do with this book? How would I bear the cost to publish it? The questions kept coming. It's timely that after a monumental goal is reached, we ask, "What's next," right? I thought about that. After graduation usually comes a job, a promotion, or marriage. Maybe I'm up for one of these. After graduation, the j-o-b starts, meaning time for hard work. Gheesh. This part had been hard enough. I didn't know if I was up for the j-o-b, even after all that training. I was surely hoping it was more like the book of *Job* and it was time for me to walk into my "fully restored" promise in the next part of my journey. Restoration sounded really good.

We agreed it was my Jubilee trip, celebrating 50 years. And, then she came upon a nugget that divine completeness also means, "lifted from a burden," and I agreed wholeheartedly. I had long thought when the book was done, I would receive the spiritual keys to the kingdom, and when it was written and released my vow "to be used by God" would be honored. Then, when May came to its completion, especially with the 30th anniversary of my brother's tragic and sudden death marked this May, a burden would be lifted, the burden and healing and cleansing of my family tree. So, yes, I was in agreement with her statement, "lifted from a burden."

She encouraged me saying I had generational prayers and promotions coming, and I agreed. I shared with her my line of thinking. My prayer, since I was a little girl has been, "Lord, change the generational patterns of my family. Heal my family tree. I see the patterns. You have given us the answers in your word. Help me to unlock them." And, in this part of my walk, I asked for a cleansing of the family tree and blessings, according to the promises of His word, for 1,000 generations. I was in total agreement.

With that, we both started our day. I heated a cup of tea and headed to the rockers to pray with God, but as soon as I sat down, my foot got stuck on the glider's stool and hot tea flew upon my lap, soaking my dress and stinging my leg. I jumped right up to repair the situation and immediately decided the Holy Spirit had put me in the hot seat to get me going, and the morning texts were to be my morning contemplation and devotion. It was time to take a journey across the coast of Maine.

## Archer's Point

Was I to cross Maine and attempt my original itinerary to explore Millinocket and canoe to Bible Point? That would take substantial additional funds because I would have to pay for lodging there, and it included a four hour drive I wasn't really up for, so I started up Coastal Highway 1, toward Rockland to see where the day would lead and waited to make my decision.

As I drove, I kept wanting to find a stop for hot tea, but had missed the opportunity before getting on the highway. These Maine drivers were serious, and there was little opportunity to leisurely find a turnoff. There were a ton of cars driving at a rapid pace, no Sunday drivers here, and all I could focus on was hands gripped on the wheel and steady driving.

After an hour, I was admittedly getting agitated; tea would have distracted me and calmed me down. A car pulled by with the license tag "PCH" on it. I smiled—*peach*. "Oh, yes, the peach!" I realized with quick discernment I had one with me. "Thank you, Holy Spirit." And, with that, I pulled the peach out from my fruit of the spirit basket, part of my graduation bounty, which I had packed along for my trip. It was the shape of a perfect heart!

The peach was surprisingly bittersweet, rather like my trip to Maine. It was sweet to finish the race with victory, but bittersweet because the intimate walk of the last two years with Father might soon be taking a different turn. It was nice to eat a Georgia peach in Maine as I drove to Rockland.

In the course of the next hour, I drove through a coastal town or two, finally just determining to veer off one of the exit streets. I saw lots of artisan shops, political signs aplenty, and many, many American flags. I do believe, that after 50 states, it's not even the heartland, but Maine that has displayed the most American flags prominently from business to business, in yard after yard. I especially liked seeing the flags tying 5 or 6 community mailboxes together and the porch bench painted red, white and, blue. There was plenty of patriotic spirit in Maine.

I loved how God had me pray from "corner to corner" of the North American continent back-to-back from Hawaii to Maine. Wherever I traveled, from Coast to Coast, I prayed for Him to release His Holy Spirit and to Ignite *The Spirit of America*. There was something very unifying about that as the tail end of my journey.

When I finally arrived in Rockland, I knew it was time for lunch and Maine lobster, but I didn't know where that would be until I took a wrong turn and Holy Spirit guided me. I turned onto Scott Avenue—like my nephew's name. Okay, I'll bite (thinking about healing more of my family tree). Upon my left turn onto the street, I looked up to see a large wooden sign for a restaurant, not Bible Point, but Archer's Point, and I knew I had hit the target with the arrow, the archer's arrow. So I parked and took in the beautiful bay view. This would be a perfect spot for lunch; I couldn't have planned it better. The Holy Spirit did.

"In that day I will also make a covenant for them with the beasts of the field, The birds of the sky And the creeping things of the ground And I will abolish the bow, the sword and war from the land, And will make them lie down in safety" (Hosea 2:18). The day for lifting of burdens had come. The day of deliverance and days of safety now lie ahead. Hallelujah!

The lunch spot got me thinking about the arrows of the Almighty. The child of God must be continually mindful that his heavenly Father programs everything that happens to him.

> "Though He slay me, yet I will trust Him"
>
> —Job 13:15

Though it looks as if the world and our lives are spinning out of control, God is in control. He is not dumbfounded. He has only given us over to our free will and the depravity of our minds, waiting for our hearts to return to Him. Just trust Him. Do not walk in fear, walk in faith. Do not walk by trusting your own wisdom, knowledge, or confidence. Walk in His might and wisdom and power. He is in control. He's got you in the palm of His hand. He is a merciful, loving Father and will hold you until you do.

I was shown to a window seat near three other seated tables, ordered water, and asked the server for directions to the restroom and if she would mind charging my cell phone while I ate.

"I'm sorry, I'm so needy today," I said with a laugh, but she didn't seem to mind at all.

As I got up from the table, the linen tablecloth clung to my brushed denim jeans and twirled around my leg as I simultaneously twisted to the left to head to the ladies room. And, you guessed it, in a first-time-ever, horrifying, slow motion move, my entire table setup, salt, pepper, table flower, and ice-filled water goblet came crashing to the floor amidst everyone's upscale afternoon lunch. I was mortified and immediately apologized to the first table about how sorry I was to disturb their lunch. They were laughing.

The lovely server, Kali, immediately came up and dismissed it saying, "Things happen in Maine, no worries." She set out to clean it up, brushing me off to the restroom. I was near in tears, with my face covered. Once inside the bathroom, I recalled the hot tea from my morning meditation and now the table service and loudly rebuked any spirits playing mayhem with my day. I asked God to show me grace. And, when I returned to my table, He did just that. It seems I had changed the atmosphere and was soon everyone's friend.

A sweet lady, Barbara Forrest, "with two R's," she informed me, said not to worry as she had a similar spill of ice water at the same restaurant, but another location. I shared that I was an author, finishing my fifty states and was coming to enjoy a lobster to celebrate. Well, she was delighted, and so was the Holy Spirit, as we both broke out in goose bumps and talked about it openly. She was happy to hear about my book and share that she was both a Christian and a conservative. I was delighted Father had sent her. Be that person; show grace and encouragement where grace is needed. Don't judge or stare or glare or show offense. Love wins every time.

The solo man at the corner table, it turns out, was an author, too—a lyricist, actually. Charles Packard, whose book, of all titles, is *Folly on Folly*. And, as he had just observed my folly, he presented me his book and I exchanged it with a promise of one of mine in the near future. We talked about Bible Point and Millinocket, and he assured me there were miles of trees and state park I would driving toward; Bible Point was unknown to him. I decided then that I had done my job as an American Revolutionist, albeit at Archer's Point, not Bible Point, but that my work in Maine was finished.

And, funny, another oddity, out of 75 diners, multiple states away, one diner wore a sweatshirt with Georgia Southern emblazoned on it. That is the alma mater of my oldest, firstborn son. There were an awful lot of coincidences here at Archer's Point indicating the healing of the family tree through the next generation.

And, with that, at risk of having the spotlight even more for my green thumb with a crustacean, I ordered a full, steamed lobster, at the waitress' urging. The sea critter and I had quite a time, but it was a fun adventure, for sure.

With that memorable lunch, I felt as though my journey was complete, though half the state was yet to be seen; I felt peace that I hit my mission on the mark, as the archer's arrow hits the target—bullseye—and headed back to Saco, Maine through mist and fog and heavy traffic.

I looked with spiritual eyes and there before me was a white horse, signifying victory (Revelation 6:2). Its rider held a bow, and he was given a crown, and he rode out as a conqueror bent on conquest. I had just taken the land for Christ; I had just claimed America for God and His victory. With each of the final 16 states, I was bent on victory for Christ, releasing His Holy Spirit wherever I traveled and crying out for Him to save America. I am bent on God to swoop down on America and save us and restore us and release our birthright for blessing and freedom. Archer's Point was symbolic that I, the warrior for Christ, would draw back my bow one final time and release the archer's arrows to mark the target for him: Bullseye! The flaming arrows of revival have been released in Rockland, Maine this day! Jacqueline, in partnership with Jesus, ignited the wick of revival from Maine to Hawaii and with it, *The Spirit of America Days* (Revelation 6:2).

I was glad for the short two-hour drive home as it was beginning to mist and the fog was setting in. Since it was only late afternoon, I ventured downtown to Portland, Maine, to see about that sunset cruise, but again, lots of blocks, one way streets, cobblestone alleys made me realize, it's a "no, not this trip" excursion. Instead, I passed a Whole Food Market on the way back and decided to put together a spontaneous champagne smorgasbord for my new Maine friends and myself. What fun would a bottle of champagne be for one?

As soon as I arrived back to the house, I knocked on their door, but, no answer. So, I headed home, only to pass them walking the dog, again. I made the invitation and it was a quick and resounding

"Yes." What fun, God has planned company and a party for me, even here in Maine. He has thought of everything.

Cheese and crackers, mango salsa, and caramelized pecans, it's a perfect celebration shared with my new friends Wendy and Doug. We sat in the rockers with the best view and sipped my favorite champagne as we each recount world travel adventures and God-moments we have each experienced. It is a sweet life, for sure.

The next morning, Father gave me more insight and wisdom about the clamoring of tableware at Archer's Point. I'm still unraveling the meaning, but in my research, I found that Archer's Point means: the arrow of God's deliverance has gone forth; it has already found its mark and done its work. You have now, if you will but believe. They are already at your feet. (see 2 Kings 13:15–19).

Deliverance sure did sound good. Deliverance did fit with what I had been thinking regarding divine completion, the fiftieth state, my faith mission, and the Month of May after my long journey.

Also, the second part of the verse refers to "the smiting on the ground with arrows, providing a test of the character and of the faith of the King of Israel."

The breaking of my glass symbolized the smiting that was necessary, otherwise, the glass may have fallen, but not broken. I think the breaking to the ground was hugely symbolic.

And then there were the many family connections, Scott Avenue and the Georgia Southern sweatshirt, to name two. Then there was the "graduation" lobster; it was all quite symbolic to me of passing it on to the next generation. The deliverance was symbolic of my deliverance, having carried out my mission for my children and the next generation(s) and for all of America, as well. Wouldn't you agree?

> "Behold, children are a gift of the Lord, the fruit of the womb is a reward. Like arrows [Archer's Point], in the hand of a warrior [this momma is a prayer warrior for her children!], so are the children of one's youth. How blessed is the man whose quiver is full of them [with five children, I am abundantly blessed!]"
> —Psalm 127:3–5

And, now God had shown me how He was blessing them. Using a Georgia Southern sweatshirt to represent the first fruit, whom the blessings flow through.

It's amazing what God is up to when we open our eyes to Him.


## Old Orchard Beach Brings New Blessings

Day 3 was an unseasonably sunny day, prescribed just for me. I had just dressed, had tea, fluffed the cottage, and grabbed my purse to go for a walk when my new Maine friends rang the doorbell for me to join them on a walk; how perfectly timed. We enjoyed a long walk on the beach, more than a half-mile hike on the long-loop of the state park trail where we discovered fiddleheads, just like I had seen at the Whole Foods Market, and combed for shells and rocks on another long walk in the reverse direction. It was a great outdoor adventure that was so nice to have company and conversation, plus I had the added bonus of having a photo taken.

Afterward, I set out to find a lighthouse and drove through Biddeford, where I picked up an artist's rendering of a lighthouse, gummie lobsters for my daughter, and a Maine postcard. I passed

Atkinson's Florist (my maiden name) and enjoyed one coastal town after another, including Old Orchard Beach and the boardwalk of amazing vendors and their foods. It was a fun beach town and a nice drive through the intricacies of Maine's coastal area.

By afternoon, I was happy to stumble upon The Lobster Claw and enjoy a typical Maine Lobster Roll, drenched in drawn butter, while sitting on the patio under the sun. It was sweet. I followed the day with a nap and some pecking away on my computer. I was refreshed just in time for my final farewell dinner at Joseph's By The Sea.

Yes, I broke my once-only, don't go to the same restaurant twice rule because the food, ambiance, and experience were so awesome, and they did not disappoint a second time. With a 7:30 p.m. reservation, I got a tablecloth seat in the dining room and a server who recognized me from the night before. I took care with this tablecloth setting.

Dinner was lighter because I was still slightly satisfied from my late lunch of a lobster roll and a milkshake, which was more like an upscale version of a hot dog and a root beer float. It wasn't really much, but I was still "floating."

I texted my daughter as I waited, "Yesterday was 12 years since we moved from Virginia." It was 12 years since I started this supernatural walk. One touch of the master's robes and the woman was healed from 12 years of bleeding (Luke 8:43–48). I believed yesterday was deliverance for me from all the storms I had been through, and indeed, today, I was *freed*. I passed Freed Street today; maybe that was symbolic, too.

Then, ironically, there were only two choices of Pinot Noir by the glass, and my selection was from the bottle of Stephen Vincent Pinot Noir. My brother, Stephen, had taken my entire family to

Brios Italian Restaurant on May 14, 2004 as our official "Welcome to Florida" dinner. Due to multiple hurricanes, we were never able to make the move and instead, moved to Georgia in September 2004, after a summer without a home, evading hurricanes. Vincent is my former husband's name. What an unusual name combination for an unusual celebration on this unusual anniversary date 12 years later. Another milestone met, another door closed, another release, and this time there would be a toast.

I toasted to heaven and marveled at God, recognizing the Meritage of life. The start of a storm (hurricanes, to be exact), to today, the graduation of a journey and deliverance from broken dreams to dreams come true—50 X 50; the whole experience was so very interesting—so very God.

My dinner tonight was mushroom crepe napoleon with a demi-glace and a fresh seafood cioppino appetizer. I had absolutely no room left for their world famous crème brûlée with lavender shortbread. None. The entire meal, my dining experience, was marvelous yet again. Oh, how I will miss Joseph's By The Sea.

My Maine finale the next morning was a drive to Cape Elizabeth, Maine, to see the Two Lights State Park before I drove to the airport. It was a windy drive through small towns. I enjoyed the abundance of waving flags and the steepled churches, and just as I arrived to park, the misty rain came. I snapped a few quick pictures since I had earned them after that long drive, but knew the red picnic tables waiting on the top of the hill would not be my lunch spot.

Instead, I drove back toward town and chose Rudy's. It was the most delightful brunch I believe I have had on my long journey. The atmosphere was cute, the table had a steel teapot, milk jug, water bottle, a blue mason jar for a cup, and every dish was inventive and eye-appealing. I had caramelized pink grapefruit with blackberry garnish and crisp wheat toast with avocado mash, scrambled egg, fresh feta, and finely diced tomato and dill. It was a delightful finish. And with that last memory of Maine, I was ready to head to the airport.

# CHAPTER THIRTY THREE

# PAUL REVERE'S RIDE, JACQUELINE ARNOLD'S JUBILEE

## AMERICA'S CALL TO ACTION

With all the schlepping, leaps of faith, and walks of blind risk, you would think I would have earned a first class seat home after 50 states, but, instead, every flight was shy just a seat or two, and there was no room for me on the outbound planes.

I had lobster quesadilla for dinner with lobster bisque in the terminal and stayed up in the airport, through the night, writing the ending of the book. Just like Paul Revere who rode through the night to tell of the British who were coming and Samuel Chase, the signer of the Declaration of Independence, who rode through the night to bring news for the deciding signature, every moment, every ride, every effort, to the very last minute—every vote—counts. And, so with the last few brushstrokes of my pen (or keystrokes on my computer) I am calling my fellow Americans to rally boldly, to take action, and with that, I am prepared for God's full deliverance as He ushers me into the next season of this journey and America into a season of turmoil and mercy. But prayerfully, I believe this is a time for deliverance and healing for 1,000 generations, as well.

I pray, fellow neighbors, that you will remember the supernatural walk God provided me and remember who He is. I pray you will yearn to reconnect with America and remember our land, our covenant with God, those who have sacrificed and served for us, and every historic event and day in our history. History repeats itself until we learn the lesson. Make wisdom your friend. Read the book of Proverbs. Make Jesus your friend. Read the book of Second John. Make friends with your neighbors again. Love one another. Read the book of Revelation. Know that there is a time soon that God will return for His Bride. Be prepared. We are all but one breath away. Don't wait to make things right. Reach out to God now right where you are. Continually pray for those you love who are still lacking the light. Never give up; God won't either.

Join together and Ignite *The Spirit of America*. Bring America back to life.

It's a Sweet Life, America; it's a Sweet Life USA. Return, Repent, Reconnect, Reconcile, Refresh, Remember, Rediscover, and Re-engage; this is the day, America. This is the time. God is calling. Can you hear His voice?

Reconnect with your families and your children. Reconnect with America. Remember the dates of our history. Remember those who fought for our freedoms.

Refresh your spirit again to believe in a God who can.

Re-engage this day while opportunity still awaits us.

Rise up, America; together, we can be America strong.

With our prayers and our voices released in unity, God will answer our prayers.

America will be saved and blessed when first we choose to step out on faith.

I have lived out my dream to see America. I have witnessed, prayed, walked, talked, and eaten my way across America, releasing the Holy Spirit and praying for revival fires everywhere I have stepped foot, claiming territory for the Holy Spirit and the American flag. I am not more than the spark; I am part of the flame; I am a tiny ember waiting for the flame to ignite across America, and praying God will continue to bless America and that my next book might be: *America Prayed and God Answered: Seeds of Global Awakening.*

It all depends on you. It depends on *every* American.

For we will all stand before God's judgment seat. It is written,

"As surely as I live says the Lord, every knee will bow before me; every tongue will confess. So then, each of us will give an account of himself to God"

—Romans 14:10–12

# CHAPTER THIRTY FOUR

# AMERICA'S CALL
# TO ACTION!

I wrap up this year having moved a household without a home to go to, as a single mother, stayed afloat for 64 days, opened the eyes and healed the heart of an angry 18-year-old, moved him into college and relocated him to another, moved into a new home, downsized again, cleared three of four storage units, nursed a 95-year-old man back to life and helped him celebrate 96 years of life, celebrated the victories of another school year, attended evangelical events from coast to coast, wrote another book, and realized my 30-year dream to be in broadcasting—all in one calendar year. It really is a Sweet Life God has given me.

It's been an eventful year as I celebrated two more college graduations (now, I have three graduates) and toasted my travels to 50 states by 51.6 months, my own graduation. In spite of the storms of my life, I did it, and I shall always say 50 X 50 and know that through the God of the impossible, all things are possible and dreams really do come true. It's time for America to call to arms, to come to action and take her charge, to hold onto her dreams and her birthright. It's time to hold up the lamp of Lady Liberty's light and shine bright for all to see.

It's time to respond to the revival that is here. It is time for an American revolution. Let's join together in unity; let's be of one accord. Let everyone show up for the privilege of voting. Let everyone pray for our President and leaders. The conversation is not about politics, but about our identity as America. Take a stand for what honors God; take a stand for what upholds our founding documents and our freedoms. Don't fuel the wrong fires with slick rhetoric or anger boiling over. Let us all show kindness and love to one another. Reach out to family and friends and neighbors and make a difference in our communities and our country. Let us do whatever it takes to serve and make a difference in the lives of others; let's all leave a legacy instead of a lie.

Whatever lies have been told, bring them to light. Walk in integrity and truth. Heal past hurts; forgive and be forgiven. The price has already been paid. Walk in grace. Walk in redemption. Walk in the boldness of a loving and forgiving God.

Know that God is a trustworthy God. In spite of Wall Street, the stocks and the markets and in spite of the news and the turmoil and the grief that we see, let us trust a God who can and does care for us, in spite of what we see. Let us walk in faith and not in our flesh, knowing that the God who created us will see us through. Let us not be defined by our circumstances, but by our hearts and our actions and our strength as Americans to love and to serve and to give and to pray. God will keep us under the covering of His wings. Are you ready to trust Him? It's one easy step at a time. May God of all the earth, bless America, and may the world see what's possible with a God worth trusting.

The Christian faith is the only faith where God shows us how much He loves us by first loving us and sending His only Son as a sacrifice while we were still sinners to show us how far and how wide and how deep is His love. Return to God, America, and let the world see how God shows up to bless and to heal. Let us leave a legacy that is an inspiration to the world.

It is time, America, to *rise up* and be the *United* States of America. As Jesus said,

> "If a house is divided against itself, that house cannot stand"
> —Mark 3:25 NIV

Another version put it this way:

> "Similarly, a family splintered by feuding will fall apart"
> —Mark 3:25 NLT

It's time to roll up our sleeves, like Rosie the Riveter, America. It is time to do the hard work. It is time to heal our hearts, heal our families, and unite with our neighbors; let us come together to be united as one. Let us come together to agree with heaven. Let us Ignite **The Spirit of America** from coast to coast, from Georgia to Hawaii to Maine. Let us celebrate the Sweet Life that God has blessed us with.

Let us invite God in to Bless America and 1,000 generations to come.

**www.sweetlifeusa.com**

America's Call to Action!

## THE LORD'S PRAYER

Let Heaven Reign with the Words our Father gave us.

I'm blown away by the majesty of the King. I have seen with my own eyes the masterpiece of America. I have heard the whisper of my Father's voice. And, with these words from Matthew 6:9–13, I begin with a contrite and humble heart.

### The Lord's Prayer

This, then, is how you should pray:

> Our Father in heaven,
> hallowed be your name,
> your kingdom come,
> your will be done,
>     on earth as it is in heaven.
> Give us today our daily bread.
> And forgive us our debts,
>     as we also have forgiven our debtors.
> And lead us not into temptation,
>     but deliver us from the evil one.
>                         —Matthew 6:9–13 NIV

Though I say it more like this:

> Our Father, who art in heaven,
> Hallowed be your name
> Your kingdom come,
> Your will be done,

On earth as it is in heaven.
Give us today, our daily bread
And forgive us our trespasses as
We forgive those who trespass against us.
Lead us not into temptation, but deliver us from evil.
For thine is the kingdom, the power and the glory.
Forever and ever. Amen.

—Matthew 6:9–13 KJV

I recite this prayer a gazillion times in a day. I can never surrender to God's will enough or repent and return from my wayward thinking and ways. This prayer grounds me. This prayer is the first thing I often say when I get in my car, when I drop my daughter off to school, and 100 times along this journey. When I was lost, fearful, overwhelmed, unsure, and extraordinarily grateful, I found comfort here. It is a great, go-to prayer. I love the strength I gain from saying it. I love reflecting on different words and being reminded of its many facets. I loved saying it with my children every night at bed and reminding them still to "say their prayers." It is the one rote prayer indicated in the Bible and knowing it was prescribed by my Father, gives me comfort. I invite you to it. Get caught up in His majesty. In fact, I invite you to Him. If you don't know Him. If it's been a while since you've said this prayer, read it again, from your heart.

## CALL TO SALVATION

And, while you are in the quiet of your heart, I invite you to renew your commitment to follow Him as your Lord and Savior. Revive the seeds of childhood. Reap the harvest of seeds planted in your yesterdays or discover anew a life of grace and His goodness and salvation.

## GOD'S EXPECTATIONS ARE SIMPLE

What is it God expects from us?

Simple Love. Love Him above all else. Love Him more than yourself, your spouse, your children, your home, your job, your car, your wealth, your goals, your dreams, your education, your career, your free time, and your ideas. Above all else, love.

Love one another. To forgive is to love. To choose God is the highest form of love.

My baby grand piano? My golf cart? My career? My household goods? My financial security? My life? My way? These are all His. They're all meaningless, just as the word says.

To honor God and follow His decrees and commands is my highest calling, with the greater satisfaction.

## THE TEN COMMANDMENTS, HIS DECREES AND COMMANDS

And God spoke all these words:

"I am the Lord your God, who brought you out of Egypt, out of the land of slavery.

You shall have no other gods before me.

You shall not make for yourself an image in the form of anything in heaven above or on the earth beneath or in the waters below. You shall not bow down to them or worship them; for I, the Lord your God, am a jealous God, punishing the children for the sin of the parents to the third and fourth generation of those who hate me, but showing love to a thousand generations of those who love me and keep my commandments.

You shall not misuse the name of the Lord your God, for the Lord will not hold anyone guiltless who misuses his name.

Remember the Sabbath day by keeping it holy. Six days you shall labor and do all your work, but the seventh day is a Sabbath to the Lord your God. On it you shall not do any work, neither you, nor your son or daughter, nor your male or female servant, nor your animals, nor any foreigner residing in your towns. For in six days the Lord made the heavens and the earth, the sea, and all that is in them, but he rested on the seventh day. Therefore the Lord blessed the Sabbath day and made it holy.

Honor your father and your mother, so that you may live long in the land the Lord your God is giving you.

You shall not murder.

You shall not commit adultery.

You shall not steal.

You shall not give false testimony against your neighbor.

You shall not covet your neighbor's house. You shall not covet your neighbor's wife, or his male or female servant, his ox or donkey, or anything that belongs to your neighbor."

—Exodus 20:1–17

They seem simple enough. They're ten commands—ten ideas. But, they are so much more. Every command has multiple levels of meaning.

What is the Sabbath? Rest? Going to church? Playing golf? What if you have to work? Or what if you work and have to plan for your week?

What does it mean to not steal? Bankruptcy? Borrowing without returning?

You shall not murder. What of the millions of abortions in the United States every day? Are we not part of one body? Are we not also guilty for the bloodshed?

They are simple, yet complex. They are not meant to be followed legalistically, but out of love for the one true God. The Ten Commandments are more than a list of rules or a guideline of right and wrong, they are a framework for society, for developing souls to create a moral compass—something that affects all of society and all of America. The Ten Commandments are relevant today and need to be posted in every home as a gentle reminder as we wake up and go about our day's work, as we raise our kids and live our lives.

America is fractured and so are our souls. Returning to this framework, returning to God and His decrees, is the mortar that can restore the foundation of our homes and our country. They need to be posted in the doorways of our homes and on the walls of our schools and in the foyers of our government buildings. These commandments aren't placed to offend others who practice other faiths, but to remind every person who walks on American soil of the principles this country was founded on and the principles we live our lives by in America, how to behave in our Father's house, on His soil, every day, in every way.

The Ten Commandments help us to live right, alongside one another, regardless of race or religion. Wouldn't you agree, a country without murder, adultery and theft or coveting a neighbor's property or wife, would be a safer country for all, a country of peace and joy and love? Love one another as I have loved you. Here are working guidelines, His decrees and commands, to help us get there.

It's getting a little preachy here, but patriotic revival is akin to spiritual revival because it affects not only the foundation of our souls but the foundation of this country, and it is the essence of why and how this country was founded. And it's all in need of repair. Why would we turn our backs on these principles, the very ones our founding fathers fought so vigorously for? Today, we Americans ought to take note and begin to fight vigorously for America, what's left of her, before we are relegated to ships and sent away from our homeland, before the country we know is left in cinders, before passports are needed to travel state to state and privileges dry up and mandates are made and freedoms are lost.

Perhaps, in reading my story, your heart has become tender to the possibility of a merciful God, the hope of a country restored and the calling to return to God in a mighty way.

God desperately wants His children to turn back to Him. He is giving us a time of mercy to gather together, repent and reconcile. I am one lone Paul Revere who braved the ride across America to challenge you to rethink your love for your Father.

Turn to Him that He might yet relent and heal our land.

I love America, I love my God, and I would love nothing more than for my fellow Americans to be restored to Him, singing "God Bless America" and praising His holy name for our blessings, our freedoms, and our America.

## RECONCILED TO GOD

### Tools for Recovery and Healing

If this resonates with your heart and spirit, here's a good starting point in prayer:

"Oh, Lord, forgive us our wicked ways. Forgive my family and my forefathers for their sinfulness. Forgive us, O Lord, and restore us to you. I repent. I stand in the gap for my family. Open my eyes to your ways. Remind me and restore me to you. I accept you as Lord and Savior. I accept you as Lord over my life and our land.

Ask for God's help. The words aren't nearly as important as a humble and contrite heart. Tell God how truly sorry you are. Remember that true repentance means to acknowledge the sin and walk away from it, determined not to sin again.

Review your life on the Ten Commandments, but go deeper than the surface of the words; they are multi-layered.

Maybe it wasn't adultery, but perhaps lust. Maybe it wasn't theft, but perhaps irresponsibility with finances, even bankruptcy. Maybe it wasn't murder, but stifling a spirit from being all they were destined to be. We are all sinners, so let go of the judgment and shame. Jesus is the just judge; we are only called to bring our sin to His altar, humbly. By the blood of the Lamb we are washed clean, white as snow. We are each forgiven and have each sin forgotten by His blood and His grace. He only asks us to acknowledge Him and our need to be forgiven.

> "Every knee shall bow"—Romans 14:11

Release all sin to God by simply speaking it, telling Him, acknowledging it, and allowing Him to forgive you—completely, once and for all, and stopping the flow of it into your family tree. Once you have confessed your sin, God's word says you are forgiven. It is blotted out—completely and forever. Forgive yourself. Thank God for His mercy, compassion and grace. Bless your heart and soul and your family tree, too.

> "Purify me from my sins, and I will be clean, wash me and I will be whiter than snow"
>
> —Psalm 51:7

There is nothing more freeing than repentance and reconciliation. We are washed clean. No more shame or pain or guilt or darkness. He lifts the burden and the yoke from off our shoulders and takes it to the cross for us. He shed His blood for us to live *free*. He shed His blood for America to be free. We don't have to do the struggle anymore. We merely need to return to the Father and repent and let Him free us of the struggle and the burdens and the oppression. He is longing for us to live *free*.

## PRAISE HIM ABOVE, THE KING OF KINGS

When cleansing and freedom come, there's nothing more satisfying than spontaneous worship to fill that empty space with the fullness of a God who yearns to love you to your soul. A litany of praise confirming who God is will fill you with a new joy.

> "Praise the LORD. Praise God in his sanctuary; praise him in his mighty heavens"
>
> —Psalm 150:1

## Who do you say Jesus is? Praise Him for that.

- Praise You, the King of Kings.
- Praise You, my Lord and Savior
- Praise You, my Protector
- Praise You, my Father in heaven
- Praise You, the Christ, the Son of the living God
- Praise You, my Redeemer
- Praise You, my Great Counselor
- Praise You, the Worthy Lamb
- Praise You, God and Creator
- Praise You, my Protector
- Praise You, Provider of all things
- Praise You, The Great I Am

Then, be bold. Ask God to lead you on your new journey. And watch Him show up in a big way.

## AMERICA'S ROOTS

## PATRIOTISM AND THE PLEDGE OF ALLEGIANCE

Now that you are restored to Christ, let us remember the roots of America and the foundation our Founding Fathers poured for us to live in Freedom at home.

Merriam Webster gives us these definitions:

## PATRIOTIC

"Having or expressing devotion to and vigorous support for one's country."

*Synonyms:* Patriot, nationalist, loyalist, loyal.

## PATRIOTISM

"Devoted love, support and defense of one's country; national loyalty."

In the United States of America, "patriotic" is defined as standing up for one's country with fierce allegiance, pride, and support. Patriotism is displayed by posting the American flag, wearing red, white, and blue, and signing up for service where needed, whether in expression of love and compassion for one another, in volunteerism, or military service.

# America's Call to Action!

## The Pledge of Allegiance

(Thanks to President Eisenhower, who in 1954 encouraged Congress to add "one nation under God).

"I pledge allegiance to the flag of the United States of America, and to the republic for which it stands, one nation under God, indivisible, with liberty and justice for all."

## Remembering What We Stand For

Teddy Roosevelt laid the foundation for the pledge in 1907. He said:

"There can be no divided allegiance here."
"We have room for but one flag, the American flag."
"We have room for but one sole loyalty and that is to the American people."

This is the type of Americana that I support. These are the roots I implore America to return to, America—the red, white and blue. Remember all that we stand for.

Start the conversation with yourself, your family, your neighbors, your co-workers, and your community.

Who do you say Jesus is? Who is America? What is your vision for America's future?

Ask yourself this question: "Where is your allegiance?"

I pray, fellow Americans, it is solely to God and country!

## I SALUTE OUR VETERANS, OUR MILITARY AND THEIR SACRIFICES.

As a former military spouse of 23 years and the mother of five children, born over a 23 year military career, my heart is for military families and that each one would be recognized for their service and sacrifice and loved through their healing.

Military service impacts the whole family from soldier to spouse, from child to original and extended family and friends; military service is a true sacrifice that impacts many, many lives. America can play a role in supporting, healing, and helping military families. Learn more in my book, *The Military Family: A Casualty of War.*

Military service is noble, worthy, and admirable. It is an honor to serve and takes a true American to sign up for service at the hour of our country's need.

### Recognition of Military by Branch and the birth dates of their institution:

- Army, June 14, 1775
- Navy, October 13, 1775
- Air Force, September 18, 1947
- Marines, November 10, 1775
- Coast Guard, August 4, 1790

### Famous Military Mottos:

- Army: "This We'll Defend"
- Coast Guard: "Semper Paratus" (Always Prepared)
- Navy: "Non sibi sed patriae" (Not Self, but Country)
- Marine Corps: "Semper Fidelis" (Always Faithful)
- Air Force: "Aim High. Fly, Fight, Win"

- Navy Seals: "The only easy day was yesterday"
- Coast Guard Rescue Swimmers: "So Others May Live"
- National Guard: "Always Ready, Always There"
- Army Rangers: "Rangers lead the way!"

Learn more interesting facts about our military at www.military.com.

## How to support soldiers.

Healing Programs, Retreat Centers and Programs are available. Search online for more information.

Organizations dedicated to helping and healing soldiers are listed below. I found these organizations while searching on the internet. Please do your own due diligence before performing. I have no connection to any, although I will reach out in the future to offer copies of *The Military Family* book and to organize speaking opportunities where appropriate.

I have no knowledge of their operations; please do your own research as to their effectiveness. Please note, due to the ever-changing dynamics of the web environment, these addresses can frequently change. I offer this information to help you get started on your search to help soldiers and their families.

www.supportourtroops.org
www.soldiersangels.org
www.adoptaussoldier.org
www.operationgratitude.com
www.woundedwarriorproject.org
www.anysoldier.com
www.troopssupport.com
www.healing4heroes.org

Organizations that help and serve with retreat centers and other support:

www.akmissions.com- based in Alaska

www.operationhealourpatriots.com

www.samaritanpurse.org

www.operationwearehere.org

www.militaryfamily.org

www.bouldercrestretreat.org

www.healourheroes.org

The best way to support a military soldier or family is to identify those in your neighborhoods, churches, or communities. Please offer a copy of *The Military Family* to any soldier to show your support.

As a former military spouse, I share my true, transparent story here in my award-winning book *The Military Family: A Casualty of War As Told By a Former Military Spouse.* I share my story, not to point to the pain, but to reveal the impact of war and military life on the whole family and to provide the solution of what America can do to heal the hurt and support the military family.

Every American should read this story. It's compelling—as said by an Army Brigadier General, Retired, "Share this book with military soldiers, spouses and families both active duty and retired and also with every American who has a heart for the military or America."

Read to Learn. Learn to Love.

Books offer healing, encouragement, transformation and hope.

America's Call to Action!

A 19-year-old Marine read this book and said "This author rocks at life. This book changed my life and helped me decide the kind of husband and US Marine I'm going to be."

## HISTORY DATES TO REMEMBER

- World War I, 1917–1918
- World War II, 1941–1945
- Korean War, 1950–1953
- Vietnam War, 1965–1973, 1975
- Gulf War, 1990–1991
- Bosnian War, 1994–1995
- Afghanistan War, 2001–2014
- Iraq War, 2003–2011
- War in North-West Pakistan, 2004–Present
- War on ISIL, 2014–Present
- War in Afghanistan, 2015–Present

When asked, most Americans list the first four or five wars as our United States history. An internet search of just 20th century wars will open your eyes to many more conflicts. I have listed significant ones here, including the current war campaigns. Yes, America is currently at war. Do your research. It is eye opening.

We must remember, America. We seem to have short-term grief and memory loss. After the tragic events of 9/11, our country came together, and then, we forgot. We walk in slumber, comfortable in our complacency, having let our daily living numb us to the pains of these events we consider isolated. We must remember; we must reconnect and recommit. Remember, history always repeats itself.

Even in the last year, terror events on United States soil have been on the increase. We have been invaded on our own home turf from San Bernardino, California, to Orlando, Florida. Wake up and stand up, America! Protect the freedom of our lifestyles; protect our homeland. Write your politicians, vote, run for office, engage in your community, get to know every single neighbor on your block and in your neighborhood or apartment community. Determine to teach your kids. Fight to protect our rights and our founding documents; pledge allegiance to our flag and our country. Unite together. Post your flags. Take a stand that is visible from the street, on camera, and around the world. Ignite *The Spirit of America* and take the 52 action-steps as a bold step forward for America. America is worth fighting for. It is our duty as Americans. We owe it to each other, to our founding fathers, and to our God.

## IT'S A PATRIOTIC MOVEMENT

Learn more about *Spirit of America Days* and the proposed National Observance of Patriotism and Volunteerism, Memorial Day–Fourth of July, including an annual SAMJAM on the anniversary of the events of 9/11 at our website (www.sweetlifeusa.com).

## PATRIOTS TO WATCH, LEADING THE CHARGE:

- Author Jacqueline Arnold, God & Country, Spirit of America Days
- Taya Kaya, Team Never Quit, The Patriot Tour
- Dutch Sheets, Appeal to Heaven
- Franklin Graham, Decision America

## America's Call to Action!

I was always very patriotic. My mother was quite patriotic, a child of the depression era and World War II, she had a special love for our country. I learned to have faith and trust in God from my mother who raised seven of us on a waitresses' salary and trusted God for His daily provision. I always loved God and felt shame and sadness if I stumbled, but it wasn't until my adulthood that I started seeing the parallels in life between patriotic themes and spiritual themes. I began to realize God could speak to us in supernatural ways and truly interact with us. It wasn't until I began my walk of preparation for Mrs. Virginia International that I started praying The Prayer of Jabez and truly prayed into God's intervention into my life and His plans for my future. He prepared me for my adventure across America for some time before I actually departed. It was when He called me to start writing books that I experienced Him in new ways. The doors of heaven opened for me. In my search for more, I came across each of these Christian leaders through books, events or their online presence. Sure, there have always been evangelists like Charles Swindoll and Norman Vincent Peale, but in this new season, the messages of the leaders are overlapping and prophecy is being showered down from heaven in a new way. There is an energy and a silent momentum that is resounding throughout the Christian community. It is different. I encourage you to listen to some of these leaders and these messages and determine for yourself if God isn't calling all of us to wake up to His leading. I'm not a fanatic. I'm just a typical American woman with a heart for God. I'm just a mom of five kids trying to juggle cheerleading and college applications with time for Starbucks or a seat at my antique wooden desk at my favorite local tea shop, Beautiful Earth Organics. I am just a gal who was raised to be a good citizen, fell in love with a career military soldier, and had a patriotic passion to make her country better and lead the charge so America would wake up and see the blessings and beauty of our country. I want people to dare to believe in their dreams and experience God in a new way, for themselves, for my children's sake, for their children's sake, for America's sake. I'm not weird or "out there." I just went all in for Jesus and one day, and He showed up in a bigger-than-life kind of way and called me across America to take notes for Him so His children could dare to believe He was real and relevant and available to them, too. I'm not the only one. These leaders have prominent positions and followings, and we're all saying the same thing. They just have had the opportunity to share their message with hundreds of thousands of people. I am just stepping up to share my message now, with anyone who will listen. My story is real. It happened to me. God is real. It could happen to you.

## CHRISTIAN LEADERS ARE ON THE MOVE

Are you following spiritual Christian leaders for this time? Here are a few I follow:

Dutch Sheets—Appeal to Heaven
Tim Sheets—Angel Armies
Reinhard Bonnke—America Will Be Saved
Daniel Kolenda—Christ for All Nations
Franklin Graham—Decision America
AzUSA Ministries—The Call
Johnny Enlow—Seven Mountain Prophesy
Anne Graham Lotz—Angel Ministries and Fasting Prayer for
    America

There are so many more. This is only a partial list! Do your research; be inspired.

## Apps for Android and Apple Smart Phones:

"Give Him 15: An appeal to Heaven"—a downloadable app for National Daily Prayer, sponsored by Dutch Sheets. Let America join in prayer together for our nation.

"Pray40days"—Available from PursueGod.org. Pray 40 Days for our Neighborhoods.

## Prodigal Sons

Wherever you are, run in to the arms of a Father who loves you.

We are all Prodigal sons. He is waiting to celebrate our return.

Find your *relationship* with Him in every moment of your day. Let your life honor Him and bring Him glory. May your life and your soul and your family and our country be blessed.

## Live Out Loud. Be the Church. Go to a Church for Corporate Worship and Accountability, not Rules or Religion.

Forget the spirit of religion, the rules, and the man-made mistakes, run into your Father's arms by pursuing relationship with Jesus Christ and getting caught up in His word. Take a pause and reflect on our great country and the One who created it. Pursue Christ. Receive His love and forgiveness. Love one another. Live a Christ-like life. Forget the past, and run into your future and a restored future for your life and America, our country.

***Spirit of America Days***
America's Call to Action
**52 Action Steps to Ignite *The Spirit of America* NOW!**

**Live *The Spirit of America* Daily.**
**Love America. Celebrate America!**
**This is *The Spirit of America Days* Program:**

1. Fly a Flag at your home. 24/7. Observe proper etiquette and care.

2. Observe Flag Day, June 14. Ask your family and neighbors to join you.

3. Wear a Flag Pin often. Wear it on the left lapel, close to the heart.

4. Ask your representative to endorse and proclaim *Spirit of America Days*.

5. Sign the petition and get your neighbors to also observe *Spirit of America Days*.

6. Observe *Spirit of America Days*, Memorial Day through Fourth of July.

7. Organize a neighborhood event during *Spirit of America Days*.

8. Organize a neighborhood parade on or near Fourth of July.

9. Volunteer Once per Month in your neighborhood and/or community.

10. Organize a volunteer day in your neighborhood from Memorial Day through Fourth of July. Clean up and spruce up your neighborhood. Help a neighbor, a senior, a military family, or a single mom.

11. For fitness, faith, family, and community, eat dinner as a family once a week and walk, bike, or jog as a family afterwards. Target 4-7 p.m., and meet your neighbors. #FamilyFridays, #SundayFundays.

12. Register to vote. Vote. Early Voting is best. Encourage your family members and neighbors. Keep your address current and your voting card handy. Help your neighbors stay eligible to vote by distributing voter's registration applications or hosting a voter's information table at your events.

13. Ask your town to fly flags every day, not just patriotic holidays. If expense is an issue, request them displayed for *The Spirit of America Days*, Memorial Day through Fourth of July. Approach a City Hall meeting or a civic group to help.

14. Encourage your town to apply for All-America City designation.

15. Ask your VFW to install a Wall of Honor for all veterans and current service members in your town in a central location.

16. Ask your church to install a display of active and retired soldiers and family members. Encourage a military committee to support these families monthly.

17. Pray for America every day. Pray for America's leaders every day. Research the names of the current administration. Make a list of their offices. Download the "Give Him 15" app on your phone. Join in unified prayer daily.

18. Support Military Families. Change lives. One way is to buy two copies and give one of *The Military Family: A Casualty of War*, an award-winning, true story as told by a former military spouse (www.sweetlifeusa.com).

19. Thank a service member. Buy a book or write a letter. Buy them coffee. Lend a hand. Send a package to any soldier overseas. Choose to serve or support!

20. Offer service or organize support for military families in your neighborhood or community. Read *The Military Family: A Casualty of War* for more ideas.

21. Read aloud the names of all Presidents, Vice Presidents, and First Ladies with your children. Discuss the impact of their leadership on our country.

22. Learn and share the meaning of important dates such as: D-Day, Patriot's Day, Flag Day, etc.

23. Look up your elected local and state officials. Teach your children their names. Write a letter of thanks, petition, or encouragement. Take part. Know when the elections are and who is on the ballot. Should your name be on the next one? Prayerfully consider putting your life skills to use. Make America great!

24. Go to city council meetings—monthly. Be aware of

current issues. Pray for your community leaders. Know their names. Thank them. Love where you live. It's a Sweet Life in the town you live in. Be grateful. Be connected.

25. Support your local library and our freedom of speech by visiting regularly. Read to a child. Support a local author. Make a list of your 10 favorite books. Buy them. Share them with the next generation.

26. Teach a kid to do their taxes. Explain why we pay taxes. Remember. Be sure to research the Tea Party and talk about it. Point out one thing in your community you are thankful for and how taxes provide for it.

27. Support freedom of religion. Visit a new church. Thank the pastor. Join a church and connect. Fellowship. Invite a friend to go. Start the conversation.

28. Write a letter to the editor sharing your heart and actions for America. Encourage others to take a stand with flags and patriotism.

29. Trace your family heritage. Share it with your kids. Frame it. Remember. Highlight your family trail in America and discuss the events that brought you to live where you do. Where do you consider home? Claim your state.

30. Research the signers of the Declaration of Independence. Learn the biography of one you did not know. My favorite is Samuel Chase. He rode through the night to offer the deciding signature. Against all odds, he rode and it made the deciding vote; *every single* vote counts. Every

American voter counts. Every effort makes a difference for our country. Our number one responsibility is to *vote*. Bring a friend, and bring your neighbors. Make a commitment to vote. Do your research about every candidate before voting day. Know the issues of your community and country. Be informed; be active.

31. Make a goal to visit Freedom Hall in South Dakota, Mount Rushmore, and America's National Monuments. Make a list. Be inspired. You will want to catch them all. Our country's foundation is solidified with incredible history. Rediscover, remember, reconnect. Be utterly amazed.

32. Read the Preamble to the Constitution aloud at your family dinner table.

33. Google the citizenship test and review or take the test and see if you can pass.

34. Memorize "America the Beautiful." Belt it out. Play it while you recite the 50 United States and their capitals aloud. Be grateful. Teach the next generation.

35. Get a map of the United States. Put a star or pushpin on every state you have traveled. Recall the memories. Remember. Connect with your feelings, your memories, your family, God's amazing gift of His beautiful landscape to us. Make a goal to see the other states. Determine to experience all 50 blessings in your lifetime and show your kids how all things are possible, how blessed America is, and how amazing our creator is. Enjoy the uniqueness of

each state, the population, the culture and yet, the unity under the umbrella of one strong America, thanks to pioneers who took a chance, soldiers who fought for our freedoms, and a great God who first blessed us with an awesome foundation. Reconnect with America. Every American should commit to 50 X 50, or make a travel plan to catch up. Give the gift of travel to every child, teen or college kid you can. And, if you can't see the possibility, do a study on each state. Rent videos from the library. View some color pictures. Be inspired.

36. Memorize the Star Spangled Banner. Go to a baseball game with your family or someone special. Talk about the game, the National Anthem, and America's pastimes with your kids and your families. Support a food vendor, and talk about entrepreneurism in America.

37. Buy Lee Greenwood's "Stand Up" and Alan Jackson's "Where Were You When the World Stopped Turning?" Play it often. Ask your organizations to play it at meetings. Remember 9/11. Never forget. America depends on it. History repeats itself. We must do our part to stop it from recurring. Take action.

38. Research soldiers who have served or serve from your town. Identify those who were killed or currently serve by name. Ask your community newspaper to run a feature article to thank them.

39. Visit a military recruiter's office. Know the differences of the military branches. Stay informed. Support those considering military careers.

40. Visit your local fire station. Thank them. Organize a community potluck to thank them. Thank your local police officers; create a community that respects law enforcement officers and public servants. Create safe neighborhoods. Teach all youth respect and reverence for public servants.

41. Thank a teacher in your community. Write a note to the principals of your community schools. Thank them for their hard work and impact on your community, whether you have kids or not; children are our future.

42. Host a community event to thank VFW, Kiwanis, Rotary members, or other community volunteers for all they do, or simply send the president a thank you note to read to the group for the support they give to your community.

43. Join the Kiwanis or Rotary Club or another civic organization or attend a meeting in your town to support great causes, volunteerism, and programs that keep our communities going. You will be amazed at how much they do.

44. Feed the homeless once per month, consistently. Be more thankful. Be more generous, sharing out of your abundance. Share meals with your neighbors. Give grocery cards to families in life transitions. Feed the needy; lend a hand.

45. Buy extra grocery or gas gift cards and add to the church basket for needy parishioners, new moms, widows, or the homeless, or leave them in the mailbox of someone in need in your very own neighborhood—anonymously.

46. Thank a farmer. Buy/donate local as often as possible. Increase public awareness to support farmers in your town. Send them cards of thanks and support. Offer to be hands in the garden for seasonal relief.

47. Support small businesses in your community. Check the Chamber of Commerce before hiring or making large purchases. Buy USA, American-made products. Remember Small Business Saturday following Black Friday.

48. Visit and support our National Parks before they are gone. Identify the National Parks in America. Send a donation. I don't want to live in a country where a passport is required to visit from state to state. Visit now and keep our states sovereign and accessible. Your donation helps sustain them.

49. Wear red, white, and blue more often and talk boldly about your patriotism!

50. Do a random act of kindness for a family of another culture. Invite them to a neighborhood or community event. Give them an American flag.

51. Volunteer for the Kingdom by doing a spiritual act. Worship. Volunteer at church. Invite someone to church. Stock the food pantry. Share a Bible. Be a heavenly volunteer! Do an act of mercy or random act of kindness. Volunteer for someone who can't give you any recognition or payment in return. Be the hands and feet

of Christ. America was founded on helping one another up, one helping hand after another. #TeamAmerica

52. Visit www.sweetlifeusa.com and follow my journey. Sign up for my blog, www.itsasweetlifeblogspot.com and visit http://www.sweetlifeusa.com to follow Jackie and my conversation on other social media.

**Support and Share our Sweet Life!**
**It's a Sweet Life USA! It's a Sweet Life, America!**
**Share the Sweet Message**
**For**
**God & Country**

Invite Jacqueline Arnold to speak, educate, inspire, and Ignite *The Spirit of America* in your town. Ask your Congressman to support and endorse a proclamation for a National Patriotic Observance in America, *The Spirit of America Days*. It is important to have a season to reflect on our God–given gifts, blessings, and freedoms of this great country through a National show of patriotism and volunteerism. May we never forget. May we always remember, for *God & Country*.

There is no "I" in team. Let's team up, let's unite, and let's take action and Ignite *The Spirit of America* together for today and tomorrow, for God & Country. Be thankful. Be grateful. Give thanks and praise aloud and often. And, at day's end, remember to thank the creator of this magnificent, beautiful land, the maker of heaven and earth and all its inhabitants, the one true God (2 Chronicles 7:14). Our Father who art in heaven.

***May God continue to Bless America!***
**For God & Country!**

## AMERICA'S PLEDGE

### America's Call to Action

I Pledge to:

- Fly an American flag 365 days a year and employ proper flag etiquette. Encourage my neighbors to do the same, until my entire neighborhood has American flags posted.

- Wear a flag Pin on all Federal holidays and more often.

- Observe *Spirit of America Days*, Memorial Day through Fourth of July annually. Share the Spirit with your families and all generations.

- Write my representative to make *SAM* an official National Observance.

- For fitness, faith, family, and community, eat dinner as a family once a week and walk, bike, or jog as a family afterwards. Target 4-7 p.m. and meet your neighbors with all of America reconnecting together. #FamilyFridays, #SundayFundays, or choose whichever day works best for your family.

- Organize a neighborhood or community event, knocking on doors to include many.

- Organize volunteer efforts in your neighborhood on a specific day and report it to your local newspaper.

- Contact the election office. Register to vote. Update your contact information. Find your voter's card. Vote in *every* election—local, state and federal.

- Identify leaders in your community, including yourself! And encourage them to run for office. Help them campaign. Share with other neighbors.

- Ask your town to:
  - Fly flags in town year round
  - Host a patriotic parade or event, May–July
  - Submit for All America City designation
  - Create a Wall of Honor with Veterans' names
  - Support the Pledge of Allegiance in classrooms

- Ask your church to host a display of servicemen and families.

- Honor military soldiers and family members with gift cards in your church and your neighborhoods.

- Follow us at www.itsasweetlife.blogspot.com

- Buy/Give/Sponsor books for military families www.itsasweetlfiegeorgia.com

- Share this book for *God & Country* to spread the Spirit of America!


## Sign The Pledge!

**I support *Spirit of America Days*, Memorial Day through Fourth of July, as a National Observance of Patriotism and Volunteerism in America and encourage a National Proclamation to Ignite *The Spirit of America* from Coast to Coast.**

## FLAG ETIQUETTE

There are plenty of online sources for purchasing a National Flag of the United States of America. They can also be found at local grocers, hardware stores and often, card stores. YouTube videos can guide you on the detailed installation of flags in your yard.

### How to fly and retire the Flag:

"No disrespect should be shown to the flag of the United States of America." *Section 8*

"The flag represents a living country and is itself considered a living thing." *Section 8j*

Treat her with respect. Perhaps, then, respect will return when reverence is shown.

The American Legion is a great resource for the caretaking, flying and disposal of flags.

The Flag Code states it is the universal custom to display the flag only from sunrise to sunset on buildings and on stationary flagstaffs in the open. However, when a patriotic effect is desired, the flag may be displayed 24 hours a day if properly illuminated during the hours of darkness.

Torn and ragged flags should be removed from service.

The US Flag code states that, "the flag, when it is in such condition that it is no longer a fitting emblem for display, should be destroyed in a dignified way, preferably by burning." Thus, when a flag is torn and tattered beyond repair, it's time for it to be retired.

Contact the Veteran's of Foreign War or The American Legion

lodge in your community. Boy Scouts of America often will host retirement ceremonies, as well.

## THE TRUE EDUCATION OF TRAVEL

My heart is for every American to honor the privilege we have been given with America and determine to travel and explore her entire territory. Often, we are so eager to have passport, will travel, we forget we must honor our first family first.

How can we travel the world without first knowing about our own backyard? How can we be ambassadors for America, let alone for Christ, if we don't first explore, learn, and know our own country, what we have, who and what we stand for? Not enjoying the gift from our creator is a form of ingratitude for the treasure we have been given. We can no longer take America, all her benefits, and our creator for granted. "Praise the Lord, my soul and, forget not all His benefits"(Psalm 103:2).

We can no longer take our faith or our flag for granted!

Traveling reconnects us and reminds us and fills our heart with gratitude for all that we have to enjoy. When we do travel and are ready to explore outside of our borders, we can bring the treasure of America to others, as well. Spiritually, we are one body, and so traveling to other countries, praying for other people and other countries, is a biblical truth. Explore, enjoy, unite—it opens our awareness to humanity. Be open to the people within our borders. Share what's within our borders with the nations, God's people of the world. We are ambassadors for Christ everywhere we go and ambassadors for our great country when we travel. Hold this honor and privilege in high regard and pass this gift on to the next generation, as well.

When we fine-tune our thinking and open our eyes in a new way, we might discover that traveling across America stirs our souls and opens our spiritual eyes. With new perspective comes new thinking and then we can think outside of ourselves and realize how intertwined God's people are the world over. Traveling is an education that cannot be bought in a classroom. It brings us outside of ourselves, and we gain new perspective on how massive, yet small, how different, yet similar our world and God's people are. Understanding, acceptance, unity, and love may follow. Peace. Shalom.

# CHAPTER THIRTY FIVE

# JERUSALEM—FIRST TO THE JEWS

One truth we cannot over look is that USA must remain united with Jerusalem. We may have questions about this—why should we care? I never understood this, though I see it often on bumper stickers. I know the Jews are God's chosen people. Jesus was King of the Jews. Israel is God's chosen land, a land that has always been set apart. They fight for their freedom daily. They struggle to hold on to their birthright. How can we simply ignore this? I am not on a soapbox here. I am not an expert. But, I do believe the time for us to begin asking questions, to educate ourselves, is now.

Jerusalem Day, the day of victory and celebration that ended the tragic Six Day War, was just celebrated on its anniversary, June 5th. Their sovereignty is still under attack daily.

So, Why? Why do we pray for Israel? Do you know they pray for us!

Gideon's prayer room was established by John and Amanda Van der Walt in Israel because Jerusalem and USA are united—it is a biblical truth. Because God made a holy covenant with Israel and us, we are bonded together. Because God placed it on their heart to pray for America, shouldn't we then remain in prayer for them? And, if ministers from other countries can pray for America, can't America stop and pray for America, too? And, then reciprocate and pray for the rest of the world, beginning with the Jews and Israel.

Should you want to visit the Gideon's room and tour Israel, be baptized in the Jordan, or pray for America from Israel, you will be richly blessed. You will be invited to become a Gideon and pray for America from Israel. Perhaps then you will discover your own truths. It is to the Jews first and from the Jews the blessings flow. It (their blessing and the fulfillment of Scriptures) is the communion and the completion of the written word. To visit or for more information, contact John and Amanda Van der Walt, Gideon's Room. There are many other such ministries around the world praying for America, I am sure, from Australia to Africa. This is one example from Israel. I encourage you to do your own research and unlock the biblical mysteries of Israel to determine how this is relevant to us today. It is imperative for America that we do so.

## Be Bold and Active in Your Faith

"I will declare your name to my people; in the assembly I will praise you"—Psalm 22:22

"Feed my sheep"—John 21:15

Feed my lambs is our mandate. I carry out that command through my daily witness at Starbucks, through writing books regarding my true testimonies, through my regular blogs, and most recently, as a co-host of The Christian View, a weekly broadcast where five co-hosts, including myself, discuss today's hot topics against God's lasting view. It is spreading like wildfire from WATC-57 to Sky Angel's "Angel Two" Network, now in five states and on Dish Network, satellite—look for it to grow and build momentum, and don't be surprised if God's View makes its broadcast debut on national television networks. God has a view, but it's up to you to watch it, request it, and share it, too. Do your part to call your local cable company and request it. We need God's view and His word broadcast on the media more than popular television shows currently supporting liberal views that are damaging to our children, family, faith, and country. Television ratings and movie ticket sales carry great power; let your voice be heard. Make it part of your mission work to support all faith-based movies. It is a fun, easy way to share the message of truth with others. It is our responsibility as the Body of Christ. This is part of America's call.

This *Spirit of America Days* is for our country. This call is for our people to rally. But, I also hear God saying this is the seed for global awakening. The world no longer sees us as an eagle, but a wayward child, broken, forlorn and lost, but through prayer and repentance and unification, we can return to the Father as a nation healed, forgiven and restored, like a phoenix rising from the ashes—for the world to see and the media to report what happens when His people return to Him. *Spirit of America Days* is a vehicle for this unification that will lead to seeds of global awakening for a future harvest globally.

> "Look, you scoffers, wonder and perish, for I am going to do something in your days that you would never believe, even if someone told you"
>
> —Acts 13:41

This is God's promise to me. This is God's covenant with me. This is His promise to each of us, to America. God has prepared me since I wore the crown of Mrs. Virginia and placed Top Ten in the Mrs. International Pageant, where I first introduced this message as my national platform, to carry the torch to ignite *The Spirit of America* all across America. Since that time, I have been through the journey, to the Garden of Gethsemane and experienced exile for over a decade preparing for this very season. God is good, and since 2013 when He broke my heart to bring me back to the throne of grace, He has primed me with frankincense and myrrh to prepare me, Jacqueline Marie, to intercede for my fellow Americans, the very same way He called Esther to intercede for the Jews.

I am nobody. I am fallen and broken, just like each of us. But, my heart is on fire.

You are my people. I am pleading and praying and crying out to the King for His saving grace for the good of my people and my country. He has prepared me to share my message so that you may know there is hope; hope, not like Obi-Wan Kanobi, but hope like Jesus the Christ, the Savior of the world—the King who can and will.

I pray you will overlook my heartfelt passion to go out on a limb and be empowered by the Holy Spirit in my disposition. I have lived it, sacrificed, and fasted for this message and experienced Father's calling. It is real, and it is worth it. I only pray you will open your eyes, your ears, and your heart to receive the message. I am but a scribe, a messenger of God. I pray you allow me the grace to share my extraordinary experiences.

> Then He said to me, "Son of man, eat this scroll I am giving you and fill your stomach with it." So I ate it and it tasted as sweet as honey in my mouth. He then said to me, "Son of man, go now to the people of Israel and speak my words to them."
>
> —Ezekiel 3:3–4

> But the people of Israel are not willing to listen to you because they are not willing to listen to me, for all the Israelites are hardened and obstinate. But I will make you as unyielding and hardened as they are. I will make your forehead like the hardest stone, harder than flint. Do not be afraid of them or terrified by them, though they are a rebellious people.
>
> And he said to me, "Son of man, listen carefully and take to heart all the words I speak to you. Go now to your people in exile and speak to them. Say to them, 'This is what the Sovereign Lord says,' whether they listen or fail to listen."
>
> —Ezekiel 3:7–11

I am like Ezekiel proclaiming to Israel that an end is coming upon "the four corners of their land" (Ezekiel 7:2). I, too, have been compelled to go to the "four corners" of America and spread the news and stir The Spirit of America. Ezekiel asks the unrepentant to repent or else four judgments will come. They are the sword, famine, wild beasts, and pestilence (Ezekiel 14:21). The only ask of our creator is to acknowledge Jesus Christ as the one and only begotten Son of God. Spare us the rod and the sword and famine and destruction, pestilence and peril that our land is headed into. Return to Him. Repent and be blessed, America.

My prayer is that after reading my true, first-hand experiences as my witness (Hebrews 2:4), where I saw miracles, works, wonders and His spiritual gifts, you will dare to believe and receive them for yourself and choose this day "to listen" (Ezekiel 3:11).

Don't walk away or disregard it as Pixie Dust, my friends. It is real and I have months and years of testimony to testify to the possibilities of a very real God. Don't even take my word for it; ask God for your very own experiences. Turn to your own Bible and read for yourselves and uncover your own relationship with Him. Acknowledge Him. Repent. Reconnect. Reconcile. And, then ask Him to lead you. He will not fail you.

I am like the Paul Revere of today. I am spending every bit of midnight oil to rally my fellow Americans, to release this book with my heart's message, and to stir the troops for revival and to take action for America. This is America's call to action. This is America's call for the American revolution. This is the revival of our times, America.

Don't despair. I am only one; you are only one. There are plenty of examples of one person making a difference. And, where two are gathered in His name, so, too is He. Maybe your role is simply reading this book and reconnecting. Maybe it's you giving this one book to others to inspire them to act. Maybe it's the biblical figures who were only one person like David in the story of David and Goliath that inspire you. Trust me when I tell you, even one voice can make a difference and change the atmosphere. One vote, one effort, one heartbeat, or one prayer can truly make an impact; don't let the devil or the majority let you think differently.

Our most important mandates right now are to pray for America, register to vote, and, then, to go and *vote*! Don't talk about it. Do it. Votes make the difference! Votes are America's voice. This election is a defining moment for our country. Bring friends; rally your neighbors. Your vote counts. Let America's voice be heard, and let it honor the King of Kings, His decrees and His commands! But, more importantly, this is a defining moment in your life. Whatever you do next has the potential to define you, your life, your family, and our country. You have the potential to leave a legacy for your family, for God & Country. What action will you take today?

# AMERICA'S DATES TO REMEMBER

How much do you really know about America, her laws, her holidays and history?

We have Federal Holidays when businesses are closed and special days are observed, but there are many more days that are important. These are great days to research, remember, and to share. Encourage others to wear a flag pin or flag tie on these days. The flag is a symbol that draws us together and reminds us of our roots. Determine to observe the day for more than a day off of work. Determine to talk about them and their meaning to teach the next generation. It is by these observances and determined actions we will wake one another out of our complacency. We must observe. We must remember. We must appreciate and applaud our freedoms so that they may endure for our lifetime.

## American Dates to Remember

Inauguration Day, January 20$^{th}$

Martin Luther King, Jr. Day, Third Monday in January

George Washington's Birthday, Third Monday in February

President Abraham Assassinated, April 15, 1865

Military Spouse Day, Friday before Mother's Day

Military Family Appreciation Month, May

Armed Forces Day, May 21

Memorial Day, Last Monday in May

D-Day, WWII, June 6, 1944

Flag Day, June 14

Army Birthday, June 14, 1775

Korea War, June 25, 1950–July 27, 1953

America's Birthday, Independence Day, July 4

Declaration of Independence Ratified, July 4, 1776

Apollo 11, Lunar Landing, July 20, 1969

Coast Guard Birthday, August 4, 1790

Gulf War, August 2, 1990–February 28, 1991

Labor Day, First Monday in September

WWII, September 1, 1939–September 2, 1945

America under Terrorist Attack, September 11, 2001

Constitution Day, September 17, 1787

Air Force Birthday, September 18, 1947

Patriot's Day, September 20

POW/MIA Day, Third Friday of September

Native American Day, Various, September–October

Navy's Birthday, October 13, 1775

Columbus Day, Second Monday in October

Vietnam War, November 1, 1955–April 30, 1975

Election Day, The Tuesday, Following the First Monday
of November

Marine Birthday, November 10, 1775

Veteran's Day, November 11

WWI Ended, November 11, 1918

John F. Kennedy Assassinated, November 22, 1963

Thanksgiving, 4th Thursday in November

Pearl Harbor, December 7, 1941

Bill of Rights Day, December 15, 1791

Christmas Day, December 25

**Proposed:** *Spirit of America Days,* Memorial Day through
Fourth of July

Help me get a proclamation signed for The National Patriotic
Observance.

Ask your local representative, senator or governor to sign it into
action!

Look for ways to support the effort online through my website.

Participate in your neighborhood; get the momentum going.

To contact your elected officials, visit: www.usa.gov and contact
your elected officials online, or by phone or fax. They are very
accessible and have staff standing by to field your communications,
facilitate, and return the appropriate response. Elected
officials work for you; be sure they know your opinions. Your vote
counts.

## PRESIDENTIAL LEGACY

Know your leaders and those who support them!

| YEAR | PRESIDENT | FIRST LADY | VICE PRESIDENT |
|------|-----------|------------|----------------|
| 1789-1797 | George Washington | Martha Washington | John Adams |
| 1797-1801 | John Adams | Abigail Adams | Thomas Jefferson |
| 1801-1805 | Thomas Jefferson | Martha Wayles Skelton Jefferson (no image) | Aaron Burr |
| 1805-1809 | Thomas Jefferson | Martha Wayles Skelton Jefferson (no image) | George Clinton |
| 1809-1812 | James Madison | Dolley Madison | George Clinton |
| 1812-1813 | James Madison | Dolley Madison | office vacant |
| 1813-1814 | James Madison | Dolley Madison | Elbridge Gerry |
| 1814-1817 | James Madison | Dolley Madison | office vacant |
| 1817-1825 | James Monroe | Elizabeth Kortright Monroe (no image) | Daniel D. Tompkins |

| YEAR | PRESIDENT | FIRST LADY | VICE PRESIDENT |
|---|---|---|---|
| 1825-1829 | John Quincy Adams | Louisa Catherine Adams | John C. Calhoun |
| 1829-1832 | Andrew Jackson | Rachel Jackson | John C. Calhoun |
| 1833-1837 | Andrew Jackson | Rachel Jackson | Martin Van Buren |
| 1837-1841 | Martin Van Buren | Hannah Hoes Van Buren | Richard M. Johnson |
| 1841 | William Henry Harrison | Anna Tuthill Symmes Harrison | John Tyler |
| 1841-1845 | John Tyler | Letitia Christian Tyler and Julia Gardiner Tyler (no images) | office vacant |
| 1845-1849 | James K. Polk | Sarah Childress Polk | George M. Dallas |
| 1849-1850 | Zachary Taylor | Margaret Mackall Smith Taylor (no image) | Millard Fillmore |
| 1850-1853 | Millard Fillmore | Abigail Powers Fillmore | office vacant |
| 1853 | Franklin Pierce | Jane M. Pierce | William R. King |

| YEAR | PRESIDENT | FIRST LADY | VICE PRESIDENT |
|------|-----------|------------|----------------|
| 1853-1857 | Franklin Pierce | Jane M. Pierce | office vacant |
| 1857-1861 | James Buchanan | (never married) | John C. Breckinridge |
| 1861-1865 | Abraham Lincoln | Mary Todd Lincoln | Hannibal Hamlin |
| 1865 | Abraham Lincoln | Mary Todd Lincoln | Andrew Johnson |
| 1865-1869 | Andrew Johnson | Eliza McCardle Johnson | office vacant |
| 1869-1873 | Ulysses S. Grant | Julia Dent Grant | Schuyler Colfax |
| 1873-1875 | Ulysses S. Grant | Julia Dent Grant | Henry Wilson |
| 1875-1877 | Ulysses S. Grant | Julia Dent Grant | office vacant |
| 1877-1881 | Rutherford Birchard Hayes | Lucy Webb Hayes | William A. Wheeler |
| 1881 | James A. Garfield | Lucretia Rudolph Garfield | Chester A. Arthur |
| 1881-1885 | Chester A. Arthur | Ellen Lewis Herndon Arthur | office vacant |
| 1885 | Grover Cleveland | Frances Folsom Cleveland | Thomas A. Hendricks |
| 1885-1889 | Grover Cleveland | Frances Folsom Cleveland | office vacant |

| YEAR | PRESIDENT | FIRST LADY | VICE PRESIDENT |
|---|---|---|---|
| 1889-1893 | Benjamin Harrison | Caroline Lavinia Scott Harrison Mary Lord Harrison [Harrison's second wife, but never a first lady] | Levi P. Morton |
| 1893-1897 | Grover Cleveland | Frances Folsom Cleveland | Adlai E. Stevenson |
| 1897-1899 | William McKinley | Ida Saxton McKinley | Garret A. Hobart |
| 1899-1901 | William McKinley | Ida Saxton McKinley | office vacant |
| 1901 | William McKinley | Ida Saxton McKinley | Theodore Roosevelt |
| 1901-1905 | Theodore Roosevelt | Edith Kermit Carow Roosevelt | office vacant |
| 1905-1909 | Theodore Roosevelt | Edith Kermit Carow Roosevelt | Charles W. Fairbanks |
| 1909-1912 | William H. Taft | Helen Herron Taft | James S. Sherman |
| 1912-1913 | William H. Taft | Helen Herron Taft | office vacant |

| YEAR | PRESIDENT | FIRST LADY | VICE PRESIDENT |
|---|---|---|---|
| 1913-1921 | Woodrow Wilson | Ellen Axson Wilson and Edith Bolling Galt Wilson | Thomas R. Marshall |
| 1921-1923 | Warren G. Harding | Florence Kling Harding | Calvin Coolidge |
| 1923-1925 | Calvin Coolidge | Grace Goodhue Coolidge | office vacant |
| 1925-1929 | Calvin Coolidge | Grace Goodhue Coolidge | Charles G. Dawes |
| 1929-1933 | Herbert Hoover | Lou Henry Hoover | Charles Curtis |
| 1933-1941 | Franklin D. Roosevelt | Eleanor Roosevelt | John N. Garner |
| 1941-1945 | Franklin D. Roosevelt | Eleanor Roosevelt | Henry A. Wallace |
| 1945 | Franklin D. Roosevelt | Eleanor Roosevelt | Harry S. Truman |
| 1945-1949 | Harry S. Truman | Bess Wallace Truman | office vacant |
| 1949-1953 | Harry S. Truman | Bess Wallace Truman | Barkley, Alben W. |
| 1953-1961 | Dwight D. Eisenhower | Mamie Doud Eisenhower | Richard M. Nixon |
| 1961-1963 | John F. Kennedy | Jacqueline Kennedy Onassis | Lyndon B. Johnson |

| YEAR | PRESIDENT | FIRST LADY | VICE PRESIDENT |
|---|---|---|---|
| 1963-1965 | Lyndon B. Johnson | Lady Bird Johnson | office vacant |
| 1965-1969 | Lyndon B. Johnson | Lady Bird Johnson | Hubert H. Humphrey |
| 1969-1973 | Richard M. Nixon | Pat Nixon | Spiro T. Agnew |
| 1973-1974 | Richard M. Nixon | Pat Nixon | Gerald R. Ford |
| 1974-1977 | Gerald R. Ford | Betty Ford | Nelson Rockefeller |
| 1977-1981 | Jimmy Carter | Rosalynn Carter | Walter F. Mondale |
| 1981-1989 | Ronald Reagan | Nancy Reagan | George Bush |
| 1989-1993 | George Bush | Barbara Bush | Dan Quayle |
| 1993-2001 | Bill Clinton | Hillary Rodham Clinton | Albert Gore |
| 2001-2009 | George W. Bush | Laura Bush | Richard Cheney |
| 2009- | Barack Obama | Michelle Obama | Joseph R. Biden |

The Library of Congress, Prints and Photographs Reading Room

Online Resource: https://www.loc.gov/rr/print/list/057_chron.html

## WHICH STATES HAVE YOU BEEN TO?

- Place a check in the first box if you have been to the state.

- In the second box, number the states you still have to visit, based on your interest and travel priorities!

| | | | | | | |
|---|---|---|---|---|---|---|
| 1. Alabama | ❏ | ❏ | 26. Montana | ❏ | ❏ |
| 2. Alaska | ❏ | ❏ | 27. Nebraska | ❏ | ❏ |
| 3. Arizona | ❏ | ❏ | 28. Nevada | ❏ | ❏ |
| 4. Arkansas | ❏ | ❏ | 29. New Hampshire | ❏ | ❏ |
| 5. California | ❏ | ❏ | 30. New Jersey | ❏ | ❏ |
| 6. Colorado | ❏ | ❏ | 31. New Mexico | ❏ | ❏ |
| 7. Connecticut | ❏ | ❏ | 32. New York | ❏ | ❏ |
| 8. Delaware | ❏ | ❏ | 33. North Carolina | ❏ | ❏ |
| 9. Florida | ❏ | ❏ | 34. North Dakota | ❏ | ❏ |
| 10. Georgia | ❏ | ❏ | 35. Ohio | ❏ | ❏ |
| 11. Hawaii | ❏ | ❏ | 36. Oklahoma | ❏ | ❏ |
| 12. Idaho | ❏ | ❏ | 37. Oregon | ❏ | ❏ |
| 13. Illinois | ❏ | ❏ | 38. Pennsylvania | ❏ | ❏ |
| 14. Indiana | ❏ | ❏ | 39. Rhode Island | ❏ | ❏ |
| 15. Iowa | ❏ | ❏ | 40. South Carolina | ❏ | ❏ |
| 16. Kansas | ❏ | ❏ | 41. South Dakota | ❏ | ❏ |
| 17. Kentucky | ❏ | ❏ | 42. Tennessee | ❏ | ❏ |
| 18. Louisiana | ❏ | ❏ | 43. Texas | ❏ | ❏ |
| 19. Maine | ❏ | ❏ | 44. Utah | ❏ | ❏ |
| 20. Maryland | ❏ | ❏ | 45. Vermont | ❏ | ❏ |
| 21. Massachusetts | ❏ | ❏ | 46. Virginia | ❏ | ❏ |
| 22. Michigan | ❏ | ❏ | 47. Washington | ❏ | ❏ |
| 23. Minnesota | ❏ | ❏ | 48. West Virginia | ❏ | ❏ |
| 24. Mississippi | ❏ | ❏ | 49. Wisconsin | ❏ | ❏ |
| 25. Missouri | ❏ | ❏ | 50. Wyoming | ❏ | ❏ |

## CAN YOU MATCH THE CAPITAL TO THE STATE?

1. Alabama: Montgomery
2. Alaska: Juneau
3. Arizona: Phoenix
4. Arkansas: Little Rock
5. California: Sacramento
6. Colorado: Denver
7. Connecticut: Hartford
8. Delaware: Dover
9. Florida: Tallahassee
10. Georgia: Atlanta
11. Hawaii: Honolulu
12. Idaho: Boise
13. Illinois: Springfield
14. Indiana: Indianapolis
15. Iowa: Des Moines
16. Kansas: Topeka
17. Kentucky: Frankfort
18. Louisiana: Baton Rouge
19. Maine: Augusta
20. Maryland: Annapolis
21. Massachusetts: Boston
22. Michigan: Lansing
23. Minnesota: St. Paul
24. Mississippi: Jackson
25. Missouri: Jefferson City
26. Montana: Helena
27. Nebraska: Lincoln
28. Nevada: Carson City
29. New Hampshire: Concord
30. New Jersey: Trenton
31. New Mexico: Santa Fe
32. New York: Albany
33. North Carolina: Raleigh
34. North Dakota: Bismarck
35. Ohio: Columbus
36. Oklahoma: Oklahoma City
37. Oregon: Salem
38. Pennsylvania: Harrisburg
39. Rhode Island: Providence
40. South Carolina: Columbia
41. South Dakota: Pierre
42. Tennessee: Nashville
43. Texas: Austin
44. Utah: Salt Lake City
45. Vermont: Montpelier
46. Virginia: Richmond
47. Washington: Olympia
48. West Virginia: Charleston
49. Wisconsin: Madison
50. Wyoming: Cheyenne

Make flashcards using index cards and increase your knowledge by using these every time you are in the car or taking a family trip exploring America.

## NATIONAL PARKS CELEBRATE 100TH ANNIVERSARY

In this, the 100th anniversary celebration of our National Parks, what a great time to set out on your very own adventure of America to see America's crowning glory and God's majesty in our United States.

I was selected to volunteer for a week at Theodore Roosevelt National Park in Medora, North Dakota. It was such an honor to be selected and was going to be the grand finale of my tour to be brought back full circle to serve what I had celebrated and enjoyed the summer of 2015. Again, I made a higher choice. The senior, having celebrated his 96th birthday, was now on the decline and had become gravely ill. I rushed him to the hospital just days before my scheduled departure where he spent five days before returning to his care facility. It was necessary to move him from independent living to assisted living, and I led the charge of the physical move and his adjustment. I hope that there would be a future opportunity for such service at The National Park.

But, this 100th celebration, this time in our country's history, is an ideal time to for each of us to adventure across America and enjoy the many National Parks along the way. I hope the Theodore Roosevelt National Park is a priority on your travel list.

In fact, I know a retired military family with a heart for America who just spent 48 days on the road and this is what they wrote on their timeline upon their return, May 26:

Arrived home today: 48 days, 10,306 miles, 23 sates, 21 National Parks, 10 National Monuments later. Enjoyed boats, rafts, balloon flights, jeep rides and trains. We hiked, took hot spring baths, saw Elvis, visited Area 51, tried our luck in Vegas, stood in Al Capone's Alcatraz, went glamping in Wyoming, enjoyed the fruits of Napa Valley, drove the Pacific Coast Highway, were chased by snow storms, 8 inch hail stones, tornadoes in Oklahoma and Kansas, but managed to avoid all the bad weather these brought. We saw mountains, canyons, caves, wide open spaces and big skies. It is great to be an American. —A Retired Military Family who loves America and adventure in the USA.

This. This is America. This is a perfect example of an adventure across America. Having traveled extensively to other parts of the world, they decided it was time to explore their own backyard and support small business along the way.

I hope my journey (and theirs), inspires you to plan yours today. And, to your children, give the gift of adventures and memories across America. There's so much to explore. Make memories to pass down through the ages and preserve our American heritage along the way.

**May God Bless America and This Beautiful Land of Ours!**

## NATIONAL PARKS OF THE UNITED STATES

There are 30 National Memorials and Monuments administered by the National Park Service. Here's a list of 59 protected areas identified as National Parks and administered by the National Park Service. Map your adventure using these landmarks as stopping points. Yellowstone National Park was the first protected area.

1.  Acadia, Maine
2.  American Samoa
3.  Arches, Utah
4.  Badlands, South Dakota
5.  Big Bend, Texas
6.  Biscayne, Florida
7.  Black Canyon, Colorado
8.  Bryce Canyon, Utah
9.  Canyonlands, Utah
10. Capitol Reef, Utah
11. Carlsbad Canyon, New Mexico
12. Channel Islands, California
13. Congaree, South Carolina
14. Crater Lake, Oregon
15. Cuyahoga Valley, Ohio
16. Death Valley, California
17. Denali, Alaska
18. Dry Tortugas, Florida
19. Everglades, Florida
20. Gates of the Arctic, Alaska

21. Glacier, Montana

22. Glacier Bay, Alaska

23. Grand Canyon, Arizona

24. Grand Teton, Wyoming

25. Great Basin, Nevada

26. Great Sand Dunes, Colorado

27. Great Smoky Mountains, Tennessee

28. Guadalupe Mountains, Texas

29. Haleakala, Hawaii

30. Hawaii Volcanoes, Hawaii

31. Hot Springs, Arkansas

32. Isle Royale, Michigan

33. Joshua Tree, California

34. Katmai, Alaska

35. Kenai Fjords, Alaska

36. Kings Canyon, California

37. Kobuk Valley, Alaska

38. Lake Clark, Alaska

39. Lassen Volcanic, California

40. Mammoth Cave, Kentucky

41. Mesa Verde, Colorado

42. Mount Ranier, Washington

43. North Cascades, Washington

44. Olympic, Washington

45. Petrified Forest, Arizona

46. Pinnacles, California

47. Red Woods, California

48. Rocky Mountain, Colorado

49. Saguaro, Arizona

50. Sequoia, California

51. Shenandoah Valley, Virginia

52. Theodore Roosevelt, North Dakota

53. Voyageurs, Minnesota

54. Wind Cave, South Dakota

55. Wrangell St. Elias, Alaska

56. Yellowstone, Wyoming, Montana, Idaho

57. Yosemite, California

58. Zion, Utah

Blue Star Memorial Highways make good stopping points too. Learn more here: www.gardenclub.org, sponsored by National Garden Clubs

# WISDOM FOR FAITH WITH FINANCES

So many places, so many dreams. How will I become
prosperous enough to travel America?

## A WIDOW'S MITE

My journey took a significant turn in 2003, with The Prayer of
Jabez. A spiritual journey of faith through CHRP and the living
Word touched by the Holy Spirit led me to walk in such strong
faith as a testimony to His faithfulness. But, it wasn't until I walked
into the Jordan, into the most uncomfortable leap of faith that the
Holy Spirit showed up, and even then, it was another two years of
one long journey until I saw a hint of the destiny I was meant to
walk into. I gave everything I had—my heart, my home, my career,
my dreams, my finances, my stability as I knew it and just trusted.

And, when there was but a few dollars, I gave fifty cents, $20 of
$100 and so on, as dollars trickled in. Being generous feels good,
especially when I get to sow into the work of someone local who

is pursuing God and His calling with their whole heart; what a blessing to sow into those ministries. And, when I sow into a healthy church, it's good soil, and I almost always experience a harvest immediately.

The Word holds the promise:

"Honor the Lord from your wealth and from the first of all your produce so your barns will be filled with plenty and your vats will overflow with new wine"

—Proverbs 3:9–10

And, I've tasted the fruit—blessings and favor like never before.

I once went on a beach trip with just $50, a tank of gas, and the gift of accommodations. I called it my honeymoon with Jesus because He delighted me with one surprise after another and seated me with new friends at restaurants along the way who bought dinner and He provided a beautiful, refreshing holiday to rest in Him.

"Command those who are rich in this present world not to be arrogant nor to put their hope in wealth, which is so uncertain, but to put their hope in God, who richly provides us with everything for our enjoyment"

—1 Timothy 6:17

Sure, I sold treasures from my home and in my garage to fund things along the way, but God made a way, and He provided exactly when I needed it, even for the purpose of my sheer enjoyment.

When I was weary, He would intervene and give me relief. For example, one night I was at a low point and craved a nice night out and social interaction. I went to the local Longhorns and sat at the counter where I met new friends, the Britt family, visiting from Athens, Georgia, who enjoyed hearing about my journey and walk of faith and showered me with a nice meal. I wasn't expectant; I was prepared to pay, even if my account balance was just at $30 that night—yet, they insisted that it was their good pleasure—they, too, were serving God as they were called in their spirit. They didn't know my financial circumstance; they listened to my stories, heard my heart, and in turn, extended the love of Christ that night. That grace fueled me on many a dry day of my journey, and now, we are friends on Facebook and I enjoy seeing their beautiful family and how they live out a Christ-like life.

Six years earlier, I learned to walk away from man's ways and trust in God's ways while still operating in this world. Best decision ever? To walk away from credit card dependency and walk in to dependency on God is a long, hard walk with life-long lessons and a rich future. I share this so that everyone can walk in faith and freedom and learn to trust God for every provision.

> "The rich rule over the poor, and the borrower is slave to the lender"
>
> —Proverbs 22:7

It requires trust and patience and denial, yes, but blessings and favor and peace abound. Delight in a faithful God who provides in unique and powerful ways. He is faithful, *every time.* I have countless stories of walking with no finances, but trusting the prompting of the Holy Spirit. I went to the airport with no ticket and made it to Maui, Hawaii, with a first class seat. God is good. Faith in finances is very, very challenging. And, I am still not financially free or unburdened, but learning lessons and reaping manna and financial miracles every day because He is faithful and worth every dime given and worth every drop of faith and trust. He wants to give us the desires of our hearts, but, first, He wants our hearts. He is a good, good Father.

## Understanding Giving to God

Tithing? Test me in this. Malachi 3:9–10 says this: "You are cursed with a curse for you are robbing Me—the whole nation of you! Bring the whole tithe into the store house so that there may be food in My house. See if I will not open for you of heaven and pour out for you a blessing until it overflows."

Tithing is for God's purpose. Tithing helps churches operate and ministries get planted. Tithing brings blessings upon the giver. It is said about 5% of the church tithes, which means *95% doesn't!* This creates operational challenges for churches and ministries. Pastors consider quitting every day; about 75% of pastors battle with depression, and many rarely retire in the profession of pastor because they have walked away due to discouragement. Financial struggles heavily impact this. I know; I almost walked away from my walk of faith and my ministry of writing and witnessing many times, but God would show up with a unique provision every time to encourage me to continue in my walk of faith to get these God-inspired messages written.

It breaks my heart to see sweet servants of God struggling so much to do the good work that needs to be done when their own modest needs are not met. God has given ample supply, if only we would open our clenched fists to be generous to give. It's not ours anyway; it all belongs to God. For this reason, we need to pray for our pastors, pray for our churches, pray for our ministry leaders and our missionaries, and sow seeds where we are fed and led. Every penny shared is His message spread.

In spite of your circumstances, even if it means starting where you are and determining to give some percentage of your income consistently week to week, whether it's $5 or $50 or $500, give until you can hit your breakthrough of 10% or 90%. That's right. I heard Pastor Rick Warren (author of *The Purpose Driven Life*), lives on only 10% of his income and God keeps dumping it back in his lap because of his faithfulness to give 90%. You can't out-give God, so I hear, over and over again. All the resources of the earth belong to Him, come from Him, and should rightly be used to honor Him.

## WHAT'S HOLDING YOU BACK?

*All things are possible.* Not kids or finances or storms of life can hold you back because God has given you the authority to say to that mountain to move into the sea and it will. You have His word on it. And, God is not a man that He should lie.

Don't let finances, of all things, be the block to your dreams or your relationship with your heavenly Father. Give and give generously, in both time and talent and heart and treasure; it all adds up to a beautiful, bountiful return, with Him as your r eward.

> "If my people, who are called by my name, will humble themselves and pray and seek my face and turn from their wicked ways, then I will hear from heaven and I will forgive their sin and will heal their land"
>
> —2 Chronicles 7:14

Hold out your arms and give America a great big hug; she's waiting for you. She's waiting for you to remember and reconnect. And, there's someone else waiting for you to return, too—the creator of the moon and the stars, the universe, you, me and the America we love. Run into your Daddy's loving arms again; He's waiting for you. He knows you by name. Come back, like the Prodigal son, come back. Heaven will rejoice! And, America will be restored.

I'm not suggesting for a minute that tithing buys you financial success or your ticket across America. I am certain I was highly favored primarily for the purpose of this book and to share how awesome God's grace is. I'm suggesting that you reflect on God's word and uncover for yourself the correlation of tithing and finances and prosperity, according to His word. Stand on His promises. Determine for yourself to not let finances be an obstacle when all things are possible. Be an overcomer; let God move your mountains.

Yes, we are all in this together, bound by the borders of every state and enveloped within the borders of our native land. Seeking God and aligning with His word is the avenue to healing our land!

Faith in finances, showing generosity to others, helping one another through life, it's what a Christ-like life is about. One season you are on top with plenty to give, another, you may be in the desert, the one in need. Helping one another, not with handouts, but with sincere charity of heart, expecting nothing in return, but knowing you have done your part to make this world a better place and to honor God, the one whom all things belong to, anyway, is good citizenship. We are all in this together.

While in Hawaii, I met a couple from Australia who shared that their heart was heavy due to the heavy homeless issue in Hawaii and America in general. My heart tendered that these lovely international visitors had more of a heart for our citizens than we do. What if we helped one another: the single mother down the street, the lonely and forgotten senior who tends his yard alone day after day, the unemployed Dad with three kids and a stay at one mom? I'm not suggesting you go broke doing it; I'm suggesting you think of others with generosity, whether it's with a gas gift card, a potluck meal, or money for utility bills for a month; imagine the boost to the spirit and the healing of their hearts that could soon infiltrate your neighborhood, community and our country? It can be given anonymously, so there are no awkward feelings or strings of obligation attached. It can be given personally, with a sense of neighborly love.

And, at the very least, we can begin with prayer over every home and family in our neighborhood and along the routes we drive in our communities.

In the Bible, it took only one stone—one act—to take down Goliath and only seven days of a persistent, faithful prayer walk to take down the walls of Jericho.

The Word says if only one would stand up. If only a remnant of one stood in the gap, God would hear the appeal. Appeal to heaven, my friends. Appeal to heaven that marriages and families and finances and communities and America will be healed, restored and accepted unto Him.

Heaven hears your prayers and renders an answer even before you pray. God already knows how far off we are from a walk of purity with Him, but He is longing to hear our cries and answer our prayers. God honors the prayers of our heart, especially when prayed aloud! So, be bold as Lions. Do not demure to "they" or "them." Be the one to take a stand with the only one worth standing for.

Be open-minded; there is no longer time for doubt, unbelief, reluctance or awkwardness. We were born for a time such as this to stand up for America! Let our actions and our prayers go down in history that America prayed and God Answered!

## MAY OUR AMAZING GOD BLESS OUR BEAUTIFUL AMERICA!

And may our barns all be overflowing from the storehouse of heaven!

May our prayers be heard and our land be healed!

> "If my people, who are called by my name, will humble themselves and pray and seek my face and turn from their wicked ways, then I will hear from heaven, and I will forgive their sin and will heal their land"
> —2 Chronicles 7:14

www.sweetlifeusa.com

## THE SWEET LIFE STORY

**It's a Sweet Life Georgia** celebrates our tremendous quality of life in the heart of the south. Unable to find a traditional job, I looked for creative ways to connect with my community. Attempting to create a partnership with birthday retail merchandise at a local bakery to no avail, I left, carrying my wares, swinging the glass door and muttering how sweet it was! Immediately, I heard "Yes, it is sweet, in fact—It's a Sweet Life." And, so, I started this business with gratitude for the sweet things we do have, the things we get to enjoy in our own backyard—especially, a terrific quality of life and abundant blessings. In spite of fluctuations in the economic environment, we have great opportunity in America and a beautiful place to live. It truly is a Sweet Life in Georgia, in the South, and in America. God has blessed us mightily!

An entrepreneur at heart, I love to see other small businesses grow from just a seed of an idea, on a wing and a prayer and a mustard seed of faith. Imagine how far we could go with neighbor helping neighbor, focusing on supporting small businesses in our community, buying and hiring locally whenever possible.

Small businesses I frequent, in turn, support me by displaying my unique car magnets and books about my true stories of life experiences. My business grows from support of friends, families, neighbors, and small businesses. Your purchase is bigger than a magnet or a book or two, your purchase is making a difference to my family and having a ripple effect in our community—supporting small businesses I support.

Sweet Life proudly supports small business, Georgia enterprises, and made in the USA vendors. We dream big, but support small. We hope you do, too.

**Available at www.sweetlifeusa.com or on Amazon.**

Jacqueline writes God-inspired, true stories of Heartbreak, Hope, Healing and His Amazing Grace. She is leading the charge for Patriotic and Spiritual Revival across America!

## Inspiring Books With a Christian Message

Book 1: *Eat, Love, Praise Him: Unpacking Your Suitcase on a Journey of Faith*

Book 2: *eLph: A Love Worth Fighting For*

Book 3: *Eat, Love, Praise Him: Finding Boaz and the Keys to His Kingdom.* (Pending Release).

Book 4: *Love, Praise Him: Travel Journals of a Dream Believer.* (Pending Release).

## Patriotic Books, supporting military soldiers and their families and America

*The Military Family: A Casualty of War As Told By a Former Military Spouse*

*God & Country: America's Call to Action for Spiritual & Patriotic Revival*

Please consider purchasing two each of these patriotic books, one to read, one to give. Let's support military families and do our part to impact our America. In return, I'll send you a *free* Sweet Life USA magnet for your car!

A stronger America starts at home.
Make it a Sweet Life wherever you live!

www.sweetlifeusa.com

## Books by Jacqueline Arnold

Books by **Jacqueline Arnold** are available on
www.sweetlifeusa.com

## IT'S A SWEET LIFE America

*But,* **NOW** *is the time for an* **AMERICAN REVOLUTION!**

Do you feel Helpless and wonder "What Can I do?"

Travel with me, Jacqueline Arnold, as I embark on an epic, Spirit-led journey across America! I reveal my incredible journey across 14 states in 18 days, finishing with prayer in Hawaii and a special reward in Maine, to travel and pray across our 50 states, in my upcoming book.

### Ignite *The Spirit of America*

Wisdom For Faith With Finances

**For**
**God & Country**
*One Woman's Journey across America for Patriotic and Spiritual Revival*
## BY JACQUELINE ARNOLD

 **Post Your Flags! Ignite *The Spirit of America*!**
**This is *America's Call to Action!***

*Cost $20, plus shipping. Order in Bulk to Give Away. Quantities of 25 or more, discounted 20%.

**Corporate Sponsorship is welcome to get this timely story into the hands of every American. Invite Jacqueline to speak at your next event or to your church to share her story across America!**

Follow my Journey on www.sweetlifeusa.blogspot.com

Do You Have a Heart for America?
Do You Love Our Soldiers, Veterans and Their Families?
Are You American Proud?
*The Military Family: A Casualty of War:*
*As Told By a Former Military Spouse*
**by Jacqueline Arnold**

An **Award- Winning, True Story** And **A Must-Read**
for You and Everyone You Know!

**An Army General said,** *"It's a compelling story. Every American needs to read this book."*

**The Problem**: Deployments, Wars, Multiple Moves, Wars, Loss of Careers, Gaps in School, Anger, Grief, and Loss. **The Solution: A 52 Action Step Program**: *The Spirit of America Days,* outlining how you can do your part to support military families, offer thanks and give back for their sacrifices.

**Every campaign is America's campaign. Take action today to make *The Spirit of America* your campaign to be American Proud!**

**Read, share, and do your part.**

*"The author rocks at life. Inspiring. This book helped me make a decision about the type of husband and soldier I will be."*
**—A 19 year old Marine**

Autographed Books are $20, plus shipping.
Bulk Orders of 25 or more, discounted 20% each.
Corporate sponsorship is welcome to get this eye-opening story
into the hands of military soldiers and their families through
retreat centers, soldier benefits, and speaking events.

## LET'S GET SOCIAL

## FOLLOW ME
## AUTHOR JACQUELINE ARNOLD

**WEB:** www.sweetlifeusa.com

**BLOG:** www.sweetlifeusa.blogspot.com
Sign up to follow my travels and the miracles, works, and wonder
God is doing in my Sweet Life.

**FACEBOOK:** @sweetlifegeorgia
Post your comments on Facebook and blog; start the chatter. Let's
encourage others to have opened eyes to the Sweet Life we
enjoy in America.

**TWITTER: It's A Sweet Life @Eatlovepraisehim**

**AMAZON: www.amazon.com/jacquelinearnold.**
Please leave a review for every book you read! I appreciate your valuable insight and so do my other readers!

**TV: The Christian View on WATC-57.** Check the following web address for listings: thechristianview.tv.

THE
*Christian*
VIEW

**Facebook:** Ignite *The Spirit of America* online. Post your Facebook picture with: **#FlameStarter. Don't forget to join the #MiracleMondays Facebook Group and post Every Monday!**

**Miracles and Manna are Real Still Today. Do You Believe?**
**Do You have a Testimony to share?**
**#MiracleMonday Facebook group**
**@Sweet Life Georgia**
**Join the Facebook group #MiracleMonday**

Let God invade America with more of His miracles and let's get the conversation started on Facebook! Boldy share these miracles as a testimony to Him!

## NEXT ADVENTURES

God willing: I'll be Livin' the Sweet Life! Speaking across America to spread this

Message and Ignite *The Spirit of America!* I'll be sure to create a

"60 X 60" and save Alaska for my 60th birthday celebration because God can use us at every age!

**"He said to them, 'Go into all the world and preach the gospel to all creation'" (Mark 16:15).**

## NEXT BOOK PROJECTS

**Courage for Cinderella**—Healing retreats to give women hope and a fresh start to write a new happily ever after ending when their life isn't the fairytale they dreamed.

**Youth on a Mission**—Highlighting youth on mission trips and their miraculous testimonies.

**50 X 50 National Parks, a Senior Adventure,** *True Stories of Adventure.*

**Livin' the Sweet Life—Life Out Loud.** Highlighting non-traditional ways to do life and featuring people who actually live life this way. Featuring others who are bold in their faith and their life.

*And, the one I'm most looking forward to writing:*

**America Prayed, God Answered, Seeds for Global Awakening.**

God inspired me with this title April 21, 2016. I'm holding Him to His promise—which I plan to take to the nations.

I believe God has given this book to me. Franklin Graham of Decision America has laid the foundation and our prayers are tilling the soil in preparation. I have prayed into it with my journey across America as have many, many others. His children cry out and our Father is listening. He will answer. Trust God. Wait patiently. Keep praying.

"Though an Army besiege me, my heart will not fear; though war break out against me, even then I will be confident" (Psalm 27:3).

Keep an eye out for an online magazine publication featuring real stories of real people, real adventures, and miracle experiences across America. *Coming soon.*

Please, continue to follow It's A Sweet Life. Pray and support the ministry and the mission that has been placed on my heart for America and for His glory! Thank You.

—Jacqueline Arnold

## NOTES PAGE

Let this book, inspired by God and my patriotic heart, inspire you to make today and all of our country's tomorrows different, better.

Let the words and dreams and visions and travels and adventures and inspirations in this book take root in you. Let them not be read and put away on a bookshelf, but read and saturated into the fabric of your spirit, running over into your family and the roots of their families.

Let this book inspire you to leave a legacy, with your fingerprint on it, for your dreams, your family, and your America.

At the end of your days, may you hear your creator say: "Well done good and faithful servant" (Matthew 25:21).

## MY LEGACY:

_____

_____

_____

_____

_____

_____

_____

_____

_____

_____

_____

_____

_____

_____

_____

_____

_____

_____

## TRACK YOUR COMMITMENT HERE:

Make a fresh start today: renew your commitment. A call to salvation follows.

52 Action Steps. Flags Posted. Pledge signed.

States I've Been To:

_____

_____

States I'm Going To:

_____

_____

My prayer for America:

_____

_____

Topics I'm passionate about for America:

_____

_____

List of people, politicians, and purposes you are praying for:

_____

_____

Congressman I want to write:

_____

_____

My dreams for my children:

_____

_____

My dreams for my grandchildren:

_____

_____

The one thing I want to be remembered for/my legacy:

_____

_____

The one thing I want to say to my Father in heaven:

_____

_____

What I am willing to give up or do for God:

_____

_____

Pledge my commitment to my church—financial, spiritual, volunteerism:

_____

_____

My contribution to my community and neighborhood:

_____

_____

My pledge to my country:

_____

_____

The one thing I regret I didn't do or haven't done:

_____

_____

The one thing I want to do (my 50 X 50 type dream):

_____

_____

The one thing I want to do starting today:

_____

_____

## TIME IS RUNNING OUT. THE TIME IS NOW.

John 3:36 reminds us best: Jesus sets before us the gift of life and our most important decision. We are responsible for the consequences of the choices we make—whom we will follow and if we choose to ignore Him. God is yearning for us to choose Him freely.

Reject God and God will have no choice but to reject you. This consequence is for all of America. America, if we reject God and instead choose to have faith in our finances or our ability to provide, if we strive and stress and worry, instead of choosing faith in God, if we carry on in our unbelief or our idolatry, if we pursue our own desires and not His for our life, if we continue to deny Christ, the creator of all things, we will reap our own harvest and havoc.

Here's the key point to ponder: putting off the decision to choose to follow Christ or to be lukewarm, instead of going "all in" for Him, is a fatal decision. We are all but one breath away from our eternity. Won't you trust Him today and set things straight—for God and country, for self and soul, for family and legacy?

> "People will be lovers of themselves, lovers of money, boastful, proud, abusive, disobedient to their parents, ungrateful, unholy, without love, unforgiving, slanderous, without self-control, brutal, not lovers of the good, treacherous, rash, conceited, lovers of pleasure rather than lovers of God—having a form of godliness but denying its power. Have nothing to do with such people"
>
> —2 Timothy 3:2–5

It is time to return to Him. It is time to return to America and the values that are foundational to our families, our soundness and our future,

> "Put to death, therefore, whatever belongs to your earthly nature: sexual immorality, impurity, lust, evil desires and greed, which is idolatry"
>
> —Colossians 3:5

Remember the America of the 50s? Was life really that bad? Families were whole. Meals were enjoyed together around the table where memories are made. American flags waved from many a flagpole. People strolled the streets in safety, greeting neighbors with a friendly wave, delivering newspapers filled with delightful articles about life and achievements, not news of horror and perversion. Sundays were a day of rest, refreshment and worship. Summers were spent catching lighting bugs, sipping sweet tea on the front porch and exploring the great state you lived in. America was respected because to be respected you must first respect yourself and others and be worthy of respect; respect is earned. Where has our shame and our self-respect gone? Has it disappeared in pursuit of things that fade, of what moths can eat or what will rust and fade away, of things that will tarnish our souls? Return, America. Remember, America. America is now His prodigal child. He is longing for us to run home to Him.

> "For you have spent enough time in the past doing what pagans choose to do—living in debauchery, lust, drunkenness, orgies, carousing and detestable idolatry"
>
> —1 Peter 4:3

## CALL TO SALVATION

**Salvation begins with a prayer in your heart to
the one who can save.**

- Acknowledge in your heart that Jesus is Lord.

- Confess with your mouth that Jesus is Lord.

- Believe that Jesus died on the cross for your sins and was
  raised three days later.

- Repent of your sins and be baptized in the name of Jesus.

**Salvation prayer as an act of faith and commitment to Jesus.**

*"God, I recognize that I have not lived my life for You up until
now. I have been living for myself and that is wrong. I need
You in my life; I want You in my life.*

*I acknowledge the completed work of Your Son Jesus Christ
in giving His life for me on the cross at Calvary, and I long
to receive the forgiveness You have made freely available to
me through this sacrifice. Come into my life now, Lord. Take
up residence in my heart and be my King, my Lord, and my
Savior. From this day forward, I will no longer be controlled
by sin, or the desire to please myself, but I will follow You all the
days of my life. I ask this in Jesus' Holy name. Amen."*

Now, pursue Him with all your heart and all your soul and all
your might and go and tell the world the Good News.

## God Bless America and 1,000 Generations of Your Family Tree!

Thank you, Lord, for hearing my childhood prayer to change the patterns of my family tree. Thank you, Lord, for teaching me your ways. Thank you, Lord, for wiping me clean of my sins. Thank you, Lord, for delivering my dreams come true, for taking me to 50 states and for showing me the land that I love. Thank you, Lord, for being faithful. Thank you, Lord, for favor upon my children. Thank you, Lord, for a full refrigerator and for a place to lay my head and for homes with a view. Thank you, Lord, for the richness of an intimate walk of faith with you. You *are* the great I AM.

Thank you, Lord, for the keys to your kingdom. Thank you, Lord, for healing America and for restoration and for using us as an example for the world to see what can happen when we trust you and love you with our whole heart.

I look forward to writing my next book: *America Prayed, God Answered: Seeds of Global Awakening,* in your perfect timing.

"In the LORD alone are deliverance and strength" (Isaiah 45:24).

You are an amazing God and I live on amazing grace every day because You are faithful.

Come invade America and bless us still, in spite of our waywardness because your grace, mercy, compassion, and love will heal our land. Bless your people, Lord.

Let your light shine for your glory and the good of all your people.

**God Bless America and our Sweet Life USA!**

# JACQUELINE ARNOLD

AUTHOR, SPEAKER, AUTHOR'S COACH

TV CO-HOST, WATC 57

MRS. VIRGINIA, 2003, TOP TEN,

MRS. INTERNATIONAL, 2003

WWW.SWEETLIFEUSA.COM

**Jacqueline Arnold** celebrates life in the heart of the south with her small business **It's a Sweet Life Georgia.** She is a published Christian author, writing faith-based, film-ready books including *Eat, Love, Praise Him! Unpacking your Dreams on a Journey of Faith* and *A Love Worth Fighting For.* Her writing has recently won a Christian Author's Award by Xulon Press for *The Military Family: A Casualty of War As Told By a Former Military Spouse.*

Her newest release is *God & Country: America's Call to Action for Patriotic & Spiritual Revival: One Woman's Journey of Faith Across America.* Based on her True Story.

Jacqueline has learned to dance through the storms of life by holding onto a faithful God and trusting Him for manna, modern day miracles, and one amazing story after another. Her stories will inspire you to trust, believe, and dare to dream in the power of God.

# ENDNOTES

1. Eric Chase, "The Brief Origins of May Day," *Industrial Workers of the World*, 1993, https://www.iww.org/history/library/misc/origins_of_mayday.